THE LAST LAWMAN

Advance Praise for *The Last Lawman*

"*The Last Lawman* provides readers with a trove of compelling, hard-boiled, true crime stories, many of which could serve as a noir movie. This insider's glimpse into Los Angeles' dark side could only be written by someone with Nils Grevillius' experience—as a US Army counterintelligence officer, Pinkerton agent, and decades as a renowned private detective. If you want to know how real-life private detectives work—as opposed to the Hollywood version—this is the book for you."

—Miles Corwin,
veteran *LA Times* reporter and author

"While the old Chinese saying, 'May you live in interesting times,' may have originally been intended as a curse, Nils Grevillius has pretty much used it as his life's roadmap. And most of the 'interesting' parts of it were by choice, leading him through an eclectic array of careers. These included US Army infantryman, military intelligence, and private investigator. And, of course, writer. As such he's chronicled his life here in all its humorous—and hazardous—aspects. His insider knowledge of things military, historical, and legal bring to life cutting observations of how things *really* work in the real world."

—Payton Miller,
editor and writer for *Guns & Ammo*

"*The Last Lawman* will leave you questioning everything you thought you knew related to justice and law in America. With one unforgettable story after another and in a voice of experience that sounds like the godfather detective of Noir crime, Grevillius reveals an uncomfortable truth: Unless you're a deadeye yourself, at some point in your life you'll need a hired gun. *The Last Lawman* is a blast of a book, and Grevillius—the lawman you want on your side when the bullets start flying."

—Don Rearden,
author of *The Raven's Gift*
and *Without a Paddle*

THE LAST LAW MAN

True Stories of a Private Detective

NILS GREVILLIUS

A POST HILL PRESS BOOK
ISBN: 979-8-89565-331-9
ISBN (eBook): 979-8-89565-332-6

The Last Lawman:
True Stories of a Private Detective

Cover design by Jim Villaflores

Post Hill Press
New York • Nashville
posthillpress.com

Published in the United States of America
1 2 3 4 5 6 7 8 9 10

When you go about delving into a Subject's background, first you must know who he actually is. Document and verify every little detail: name or names, date and place of birth, parents, education. Without collecting these, you will not get to the bottom of what motivates him, his loyalty, whether or not he is a traitor, a cut-out for someone else, or a member of a Hostile Intelligence Service (HOIS).

—Instructor Sergeant David C. at the US Army Counterintelligence School

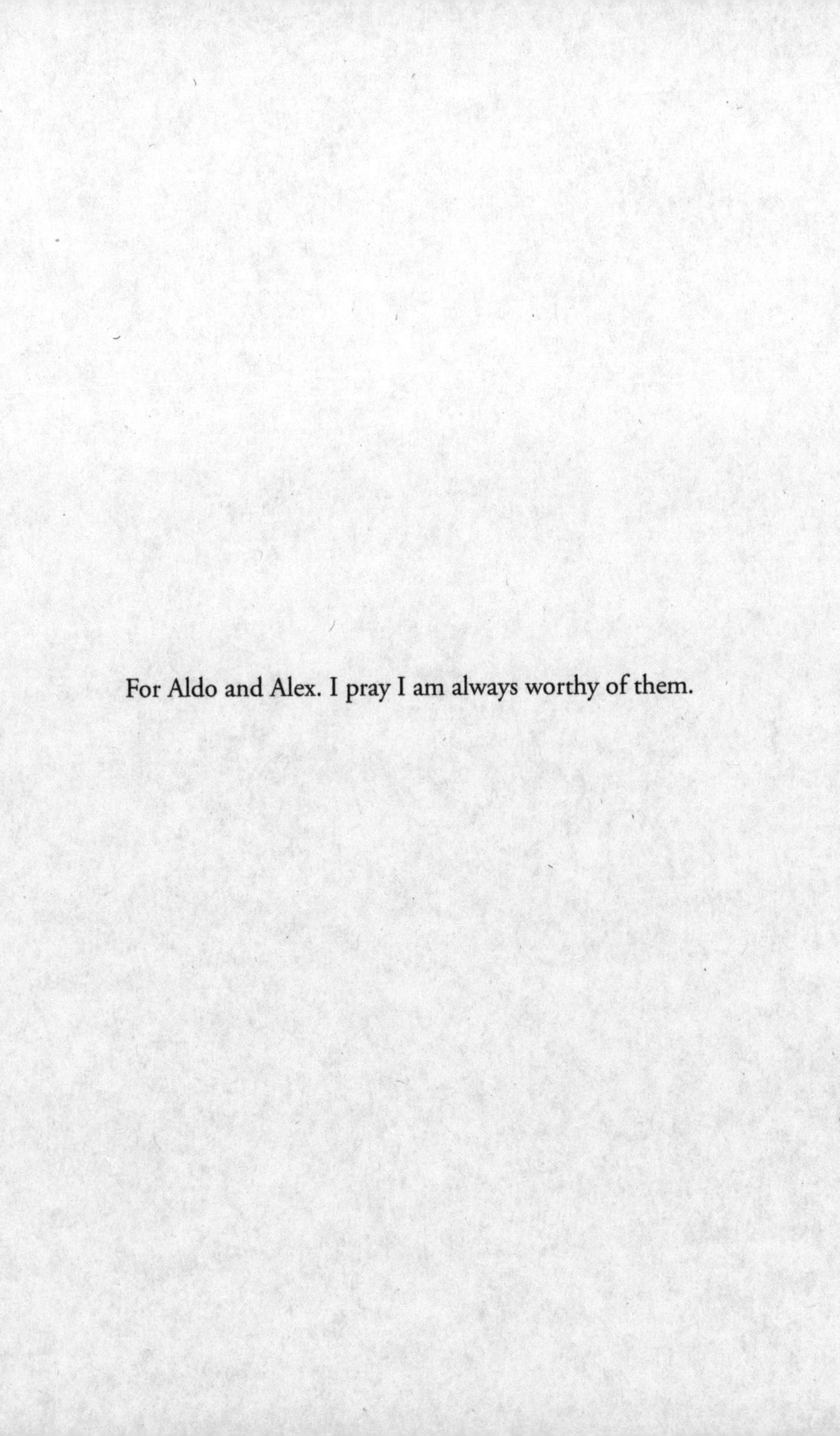

For Aldo and Alex. I pray I am always worthy of them.

TABLE OF CONTENTS

FOREWORD

Look, in this era of soy lattes, safe spaces, and elite libs who think "law enforcement" means politely asking criminals to pretty please stop looting, it's refreshing—no, it's downright essential—to crack open a book like *The Last Lawman* by Detective Nils Grevillius. This isn't some whiny memoir from a coastal trust fund kid navel-gazing about his "trauma" from a mean tweet. Nah, this is the raw, unfiltered story of a guy who stared down the barrel of real evil on the mean streets of LA, and came out swinging. This is the kind of American hero we used to celebrate before the woke brigade decided toughness was "toxic masculinity." And let me tell you, this book hits like a .45 to the gut—in the best way.

We need this kind of hot blast from the furnace of real-life, as opposed to the tepid nonsense banged out by spoiled brats with Ivy League degrees and peanut allergies. Turn on Netflix and behold a hundred shows about a young nonbinary battling the patriarchy; *The Last Lawman* shows why patriarchy is the only thing keeping the wolves at bay. The late great Andrew Breitbart famously observed that politics is downstream from culture; here is where the bodies wash up on the shore.

Nils starts us off right, channeling the wisdom of old-school Army and then cop life, with no body cams and no apologies—just justice served hot and fast. Meet legendary Detective Charles Higbie, the guy who taught young Nils that "men who tell the truth never have to remember anything." Pure gold. In a world where politicians flip-flop faster than a fish on a dock, Nils writes about that unyielding code. He doesn't sugarcoat the grit: the flashes of gunfire, the

DOA lowlifes, the cigar smoke masking the stench of a shootout gone right. Back then, cops knew the score—good versus bad, in contrast to today's "restorative justice" clown show.

But Nils isn't just recounting cop tales; he's baring his soul. It's raw stuff, the kind that reminds you life's not a Hallmark movie. He switches off fear to hunt scumbags—1911 on the hip, .38 under the arm, shotgun in the trunk—but admits it nearly killed his capacity to love. That's the cost of the badge, folks, and Nils pays it without whining. Chapters like "Running and Gunning", "Organized Crime", and "Working Dope" read like a roadmap to why we need hard men in soft times.

This book is a wake-up call for conservatives who know defunding the police is suicide by stupidity. Nils Grevillius is the last lawman in a nation forgetting its backbone, but his story reignites it. Read it, libs—maybe you'll learn why we back the blue. For the rest of us? It's a toast to the warriors who keep the wolves at bay. Grab a cigar, pour a stiff one, and dive in. You won't regret it.

—Kurt Schlichter

PREFACE

It was early morning in Watts, the LA neighborhood with the worst of reputations for crime and gang activity. As a private investigator, I was hired to apprehend a robbery suspect out on bail. A dicey situation made worse by the area and the fact that I was working alone. My assignment had me in the most "ghetto" part of South-Central Los Angeles, in the immediate aftermath of the Rodney King Riots. Much of this part of LA consists of blocks of postwar apartment buildings, interspersed among old houses constructed before the Great Depression. As Mexicans moved in, block by block, the houses they'd bought were denoted, defined, and demarcced by pillared gates, made from construction discards, inexpensive block, and steel gates welded by hand at a hundred different shops.

As I was about to the enter, this is when the adrenalin surged, and everything leveled out. Contact imminent. The door gave way with a single kick, and I was in. Our suspect, Junior, was stretched out on the sofa, in boxers and a T-shirt. I got a minging blanket off of him to make sure he wasn't sleeping with a machete or a Glock. I could smell the blanket as it came off. As I flipped Junior over to cuff him, I saw a youth in a do-rag race out the door. My .45 drawn, I cleared the rest of the apartment. Kids were asleep in a room with an adult woman, who turned out to be Junior's aunt, and his girl stretched out in another bedroom, too drunk to be woken.

His shoes were the biggest pair next to the door, and I got them on him and hauled Junior to his feet, my sidearm holstered.

"The fuck you want?" He stank of cannabis and booze but was ambulatory. Seventy-six steps to the sidewalk and the backseat of my car. These are the situations where I'm not sticking around for a cup of coffee and a reading of the *Jet* magazine.

Why was I working solo that day in Watts? It was a small bond. Not many men worth working with would get up so early for a caper in South Central, upon so skinny a fee. There is also the fact that I'm cheap.

A man with his hands cuffed behind him can be a burden, a weight, and the way to keep him moving in sneakers and boxer shorts is a hold called the *wristlock*. It is an essential arrest-and-control hold, which works just as well when a man is cuffed. Properly applied, I can have a man on his toes, moving forward, or to his knees, begging I not break his arm.

In the courtyard of the building, it was like a canyon. Waiting for me were six or seven of Junior's friends. I drew my sidearm to make my case and cranked pressure on Junior in the hold with my left hand and arm. It helped that he was almost as tall as myself.

"Motha'fukka, you caint shoot all of us!" said the one with the biggest mouth. Two of them were carrying pistols. He had amber eyes, gapped teeth, and his hair tied into cornrows.

Putting my gun on Junior's shoulder, equilateral with his handsome face, I pointed it at the ringleader, who was seven meters in front of me. "I can shoot you. And I'll make sure if anyone gets shot today, it is you," I replied.

Junior chose that moment to attempt dropping to a seated position with all his weight. I flexed my knees, my hips, and matched his drop before Junior could plant his ass, smacking his head, hard, with my 1911 and cranking all my pressure on his captured arm. He winced and stood anew, and I resumed my stance, ready to defend the apprehension as the circle got smaller.

They were all yelling, and two tried to rush me as I backed up against a doorway, certain the security door could only open outward. There was an alley behind the building, but I'd just be in deeper weeds taking that route. Two had pistols out, and Junior was my intervening shield as their volume intensified. I had eight rounds in my pistol and a single reload on my belt, provided I could get to it. Weighing the chances of running the gauntlet, shooting it out with these guys, I needed help, a break—and it came just in time....

CHAPTER

1

MEN WHO TELL THE TRUTH

My father worked doing typography after he gave up on journalism. He did this solely to earn a living, so from him I learned how to do maintenance on Linotype machines and redistribute handset type. At the age of ten, I didn't need a pica pole to measure the pitch of a typeface. The device is just another ruler, one peculiar to the analog printing era. I knew what each font was, could identify Helvetica from Bodoni. I knew every typeface in the book. While now we have the great luxury of several hundred different fonts in Microsoft Word, back then, a good typography shop in Los Angeles possessed around eighty to one hundred typefaces, and this was all mechanical from the good old analog, kinetic world. But I learned more than just typefaces there with my father.

One night while working at the shop with him, we watched an LAPD unit pull over what looked like a gangster car—an older black, General Motors sedan, low to the ground. The car rolled to a stop in front of the Teamsters' Hall at 9th and Union. The paint job glistened beneath the streetlights and the cruiser's flashers behind. I felt as if the two of us were watching a movie scene unfold before my very young eyes.

My father's voice came in a hushed but calm tone, "They've got their sidearms out. Get down." Each officer held his pistol pinned against his leg, and I scrambled to get down beside my father. We squatted behind the low wall beneath the window. Peering out, the only light that was on in the shop was the fluorescent one over the Linotype keyboard. We could observe the situation outside as it unfolded.

The officer on the driver's side started a deliberate approach to the opened car window. Then came what looked like sparks shooting out from the driver's window, with the infinitesimally delayed *pop!* of a gunshot. The officer on the passenger side of the lowrider lunged forward, his pistol extended. An instant volley of flashes and pops followed more flashes as the officer emptied his revolver into the car.

I looked over, and my father was already on the phone with the operator. There was no 9-1-1 back in those days; you had to call the operator. My father said into the phone something along the lines of, "There are officers in trouble at Ninth and Union. You need to get more officers over here right away."

Within minutes, all of Rampart Division arrived—lights and sirens, the business. Neither of the officers involved in the shooting appeared to be hurt in any way. Two in the car were seriously injured, and one DOA—dead on arrival.

That first shot from inside the car came from a sawed-off shotgun. Police didn't wear bulletproof vests back then. The driver's side officer could have had his ticket punched that day with a fist-sized hole in his chest. Sometimes luck is on the side of the good guys.

First, a detective questioned me as a witness to the shooting, then my father. We couldn't leave until the investigation was complete, and with the dead gangster still inside the car, we would be waiting a while.

Sometime after midnight the detective in charge of officer-involved shootings arrived. He took me aside in the shop, separated me from my father, and began to interview me. His demeanor was engaging, but very precise and pointed in questioning me. He wore a neat straw hat, shirtsleeves, and a dark necktie. He said to me, "Kid, I want you to tell me the truth, and if you lie to me, I'll know that you're lying to me." He paused and studied me, then asked, "Can you tell me the truth?"

I nodded and said, "I can tell you the truth," which is what I proceeded to do.

Then he patted me on the back and said, "Okay, good man. Am I going to hear anything different from your father?"

I answered the only way I could: "I don't know, sir."

And then this man, who I would later find out was a legend at the LAPD, a detective named Charles Higbie, told me an essential piece of life wisdom that night. He addressed me squarely, looked me straight in the eyes, and said, "Men who tell the truth never have to remember anything."

Bob Souza, decades later, after he'd retired from LAPD's Robbery-Homicide Division, told me about a time Higbie pulled out a cigar and started smoking the stogie at a crime scene to cover the smell. According to Souza, the LA Metro Division had a rather explosive encounter with a known stickup crew in an armed motel robbery. Confronted by the stakeout unit, the crooks refused to surrender, which ended in an early retirement for them, their body parts scattered all over the office. The issued shotgun in LAPD in that era was the venerable Ithaca Model 37, in 12-gauge. The Ithaca is made for social purposes with no trigger disconnector. The operator can hold the trigger down, and it will discharge with each stroke of the slide.

Detective Higbie stood at the shocking, grisly panoply smoking his cigar, his hands in his pockets as he looked at the scene, rocking back and forth on his heels. One of the harness bulls from Metro Division, the sergeant with the strap over, asked him, "You ever see anything better than that, lieutenant?"

Higbie blew out some smoke from his cigar and turned to the officer to say, "Only if they were on fire. Only if the motherfuckers were on fire."

Back then there were no shades of gray between good and bad. Men were good, or men were bad. Bad men might be made good through the processes of criminal justice, and good men could be made bad when exposed to vice and licentiousness and disorder. They weren't conflicted about this. It was important, and it's something we've lost. Today, society tries to make house pets out of crocodiles.

That night with my father exposed me to the gritty dark side of LA streets at a formative age. Had I wanted to go out and across the street to peer inside the car at the body, my father would have restrained me. He had good tactical sense, and this is what I can tell you with no uncertainty: Norman Edwin Grevillius had no physical fear of any man. As a marine, he had probably stacked up more men than cheap wine and cancer, but my father never wanted me or my sisters exposed to anything the likes of what he saw at war in Korea. His fears were more pedestrian. If the IRS sent him one of those green-edged valentines by certified mail, he'd quail, but if he had to go fight five men in the parking lot, he wouldn't hesitate. Norman never backed down.

I inherited some of this, the good and the bad, from him. It has never bothered me to step on bad men, but it has always bothered me to step on a good man. And even the bad men that I step on—to the extent that I can, when the moment is appropriate—I pick them up and dust them off.

There was a time when I didn't care if I lived or died, and I wasn't afraid of death. I learned how to switch all that off. But the problem with switching off the fear of death is this process can also switch off the ability to love. Maybe you pray to God, and you say, "God, take this feeling away from me." It goes, this fear flees, and takes with it everything else, leaving me with nothing, emotionless. You're a nothing, a machine. Driving around Los Angeles with a 1911 on your hip and a .38 two-inch under your arm with a shotgun in the trunk. On the hunt.

At those times, maybe I wasn't so good a guy. The younger Nils was a landmine, waiting to be stepped on.

In the years that I was in the army, my parents became consumed by a problem, one that each had their own unsuccessful approach to. My younger sister, Louise, fell into drugs. I am unsure, today, as I write this book, where she is, certain she is compromised in ways that only happen with narcotics addiction.

Her debasement started at sixteen or seventeen, and with a few respites, has been continuous and ongoing. This vexed our mother and consumed Norman as a father. When I was forty-one, my then-wife and I took in a baby, born to Louise, adopted, and raised him. In a moment of rare, good judgment, she said to me, "It is better that I am Aunt Louise than trying to be his mother."

With all that I have seen of dope, addiction, booze, and the rest, my belief is that as long as a man, or woman, is alive, they have a chance…they can recover. But this also means that I keep her at arm's length and pray she finds her way. It is beyond whatever powers I might have (none!) and to paraphrase Carl Jung: "This is the exclusive province of God."

CHAPTER

2

A MOTHER, ANGEL, AND A TOY JEEP

Who am I if not a product of eccentric parents, the US Army, and an American education?

You could call my mother a complex character. My father, too, but in a different way. A prep-school girl, classically educated in the Anglican tradition, she went to Sweetbriar, which is a posh finishing school in Virginia. My grandparents were well-connected, staid, and rock-ribbed. But she totally rejected her class. Not her physical class of female graduates, but her social class. Mother scorned that world in her own way, including by marrying the man, ten years her senior, who would become my father. To her, Norman must have cut a heroic figure. He had infiltrated the citizens council's meetings and KKK groups in Arkansas during the forced integration of the Little Rock schools. He possessed a mysterious job at the *New York Times* with no byline and carried a gun. A decorated Korean War veteran, he'd been disinvited from the Marine Corps as a radical for his involvement with the NAACP in 1954.

She could be quite harsh, my mother, but in my earliest years, quite gentle as well. We'd moved from New York City to Terre Haute, Indiana, and lived in a Greek Revival–style house—complete with the classic facade with a low-pitched gable roof and a row of impressive columns—built well before the Civil War. The man who'd owned the place before us made his living pulling teeth as a dentist and corks as a bootlegger. He'd left behind a hoard of homemade wines and corn lightning in bottles in our basement upon his death.

On one of our early Christmases in Terre Haute, lacking other tasks, our dear mother, Enid, summoned my sister and myself, four and three, to help her make a special Christmas decoration entirely of her own design and thought. She had no diagram or example, but on lined paper, she sketched out a kneeling, shrouded angel and used as the corpus of this sculpture an ancient champagne magnum. The glass of this bottle consisted of a rich-yet-uneven purplish blue, and the surface was awash in bumps and ripples, almost as if it was hand-blown. Perhaps it was, and Mother reported, to our amazement, that the bottle appeared to be antique and quite empty. She took a piece of muslin rag and dipped the material in laundry starch, like papier-mâché, and fashioned each element. She allowed me to thread a length of florist wire through the shroud to make it hide where the face of the angel kneeling in devotion should be.

My sister did the same to fashion wings to the back of the angel, and when the piece had dried in a subsequent day, my mother allowed us to carefully paint the angel with a tin of gold leaf, also discovered in our basement. To my astonished eyes, for all the world, the work came to life and looked like an angel. This decoration would be lovingly stored after the Christmas tree came down and last for as long as we lived in Indiana. It was a family treasure, but is now gone, carelessly lost by movers when we quit Indiana for California.

While the angel might be lost, this memory of the angel and the moment with my mother, and sister, shall remain forever perfect—locked in the amber of my heart.

Not long after that Christmas, I enjoyed a near-fatal bout of pneumonia and was in the lung unit of St. Anthony's Hospital, now part of Indiana State University. They told me what a great time I'd have, that I'd get to live in a tent. Little did I know they were talking about an oxygen tent with an IV drip of antibiotics and fluids, emitting an incessant snakelike hiss.

My mother would be there during the day, and my dad by night. The only toy they allowed me to bring along was a Tonka Jeep—the army version. My father irritated me by allowing the only other child in the ward, a blond and ghostly pale three-year-old, to play with *my* prized vehicle. The kid had checked in the same night I did, initially with his mousy mother, clad in a long brown coat, but otherwise he remained by himself, lying in an oxygen tent like my own.

At one point the boy flung the Jeep to the hospital floor. The clatter startled me, and through the film of my own plastic tent, I could see the toy on its side with the tailgate busted. To compound the irritation with my now-broken Jeep, my father spent time at the other boy's bed, reading to *him* when I could not sleep. In my mind, I've a crystal-clear memory of the hospital, the green Jeep, and Dad reading to the strange boy who'd so offended me. The recollection stands in sharp relief against the general memory of nearly dying, of being unable to breathe without great effort. After a day or so, the pale child was gone, and my Jeep sat at my own bedside where I would reside for another five or six days to get past the infection.

Decades later, my father, with no prompting from me, told the real story of the boy. "His mother was a waitress," he began in his voice that could perfectly mimic the stentorian delivery of Orson Welles—deep, an almost woodwind quality. He'd played the trumpet in the Marine Corps band and had overdeveloped his diaphragm. "They lived in a tough part of Taylorville called Saint Mary-of-the-Woods. She never came back, and as the boy had no father, I read to him and may have said a prayer or two. He died the second day, when you were asleep, with no one to claim him, claim his body. I helped the nurse wrap him in his blanket."

Had anyone called the boy or his mother white trash in my father's presence, he'd have said, "No one is trash."

You can be sure I gave my parents too little credit in my youth. I'd not much to compare them to, but now, as a man and a father, I know them to have been extraordinary. My mother might have broken a few hairbrushes over my head, and back then it was my opinion that she was prone to overreaction, but I kept this opinion to myself, lest my father serve up his version.

Once a drill instructor, he had a parade-ground shout that could decalcify my spine as a child. He usually held it in abeyance, unless he was hungover. He wasn't prone to euphemism or slang; each word was enunciated in perfect English. Like any news editor of his generation, he knew *Strunk & White*, spelled perfectly, and could recite and explain any rule of grammar. As a child, my parents were in a constant rhetorical war with each other over Sacco and Vanzetti, Grant at Vicksburg, and even the Gettysburg Address. Was FDR a neo-Marxist, or was FDR a populist, good-government democrat? The two would argue over these things, she as passionately as my father. They were both well-read, well-educated people. But both were alcoholics, ultimately, and flawed. The mark of Cain or the heel of Achilles, this deep-running flaw speaks for itself.

When we had moved to Indiana, my dad was engaged as the city desk editor at the *Terre Haute Tribune Star*, a glorious, shining city newspaper on the banks of the Wabash River. Norman and Enid would entertain, hosting fantastic cocktail parties. All the cognoscenti of Terre Haute, Indiana—from the champion international harvester tractor salesman, the guy from Studebaker Technical Products (STP), to a local emergency-room physician in the public health service whose parents were death camp survivors—were in attendance.

The art history professor from Indiana State University, Harriet Cappello, would be there. And they'd smoke their faces off and play Dean Martin on a Fisher stereo—one of those magnificent cabinet sets—and get drunk and have a fantastic time. I loved those events as a small child and would disappear into the background, absorbing the stories and observing the behaviors of those in attendance. My mother would be in a dress and pearls, as befits a Sweetbriar girl to entertain, but then she would also be part of the action. She always wanted to be in on the action, really.

In her thirties, after they divorced, she would go to law school. Her very first case would be a noteworthy event, and one that's nearly forgotten now. This was an *in pro per* case, meaning she represented herself as a second-year law student. We'd fallen on a bit of hard times. The household didn't have a lot of money. Enid had a full-time job at *The Los Angeles Times*. She worked nights and unfortunately was laid off while attending law school. For the first time ever, she applied for unemployment benefits.

The State of California asked her, "Will you quit law school to take an eight-hour job, a full-time job?"

And she said, "I will take a full-time job that doesn't interfere with law school."

For this unwillingness to quit law school, they denied her unemployment benefits. Not one to back down from a fight, she recognized an injustice. Here is a person willing to work and who had been working—a person who had never filed an unemployment claim. At one of her hearings she said, "I am not someone who just works for the summer and then hopes to collect unemployment benefits through the year. I am the sole supporter of three children. I have successfully worked my way through school carrying a full-time school load, caring for my children. I graduated from Cal State with high honors. I was admitted to UCLA Law School. I think that denial of unemployment benefits places an unfair burden on the student-workers who are making a good faith effort to work their way through school or are trying to better themselves. I see no social utility in penalizing people like me."

Two years into law school, our mother fought the State of California, brought them to a standstill, and *won*. The decision is titled *Glick v. Ballantyne*. My mother was Enid Ballantyne.

After this initial success in the courtroom, people assumed Enid would go on to a career in employment law. Not my mother. She was not one to make assumptions about. Instead, she chose criminal law and family law. And just as crime doesn't pay, the criminals she would represent often escaped paying her. Justice, as it turns out, is not always doled out fairly, and the togs worn by some police, some prosecutors, and some judges cannot camouflage their dark acts. I'd like to think I inherited some of my mother's sixth sense for injustice, or at least bullshit—her sonar for something amiss. One famous instance of this, another case of hers, involved a gangster who in 1995 went up on kidnapping and ransom charges of a La Puente couple in the San Gabriel Valley of Los Angeles County. After freeing the couple, deputies searched the Rowland Heights home and found explosives, weapons, handcuffs, and bootleg computer programs.

The three players involved, Ming Ching Jin, a card sharp suspected to have Asian organized crime ties; Pifen Lo, Jin's wife; and Yu Ching Chu, their housekeeper and my mother's court-appointed client. Strange things started occurring in the trial, where suddenly, the wife had been pled out and was no longer in the case. The judge, one George Trammell, sentenced her to probation over the objections of prosecutors, who requested prison time.

There was a rumor afoot that Lo and George Trammell had their own extrajudicial courting in the works. On several occasions, the judge had Lo brought to chambers. Despite these eyebrow-raising actions, everyone considered Trammel as the hang-'em-high, law-and-order judge in Pomona. And if the guy really was law-and-order in his outlook, God bless him, right?

As it turns out, Judge Trammell was the party that needed to be prosecuted. While popular culture lionizes judges who are bleeding hearts, there is also a need for the law-and-order sort. Occasionally a judge is, ideally, a bleeding heart who also dispenses law and order. A jurist who says, "Fuck this, we are going to follow the letter and spirit of the law." A real judge, a man like Ron George. Ron George was the LA county judge who decided that the district attorney at the time wasn't handling the Hillside Stranglers (Angelo Buono Jr. and Kenneth Bianchi) case wisely and called in the Attorney General's office to prosecute these notorious serial murderers. That was an act of judicial heroism. Ron George went on to become the state supreme court chief justice.

Obviously, George Trammell wasn't cut from the same cloth at Justice George, as he started making threats to the defense counsel to hold them in contempt. To hold defense counsel in contempt is to convict them of a crime. Naturally this concerned my mother. She started taking her files home. Her defense investigator was a private detective named Frank Mackey, and the judge tried threatening

Frank with various things to hide what was going on. In a story with more twists and turns than a tapeworm, George Trammell had been honey-trapped by Lo, the gangster's wife, to the benefit of the gangster, to throw the trial. Lo had found her way beneath the judge's robes, and Trammell fell for this scheme. He fell for her and ultimately fell for his crimes.

When the scandal broke, the sheriff's department served a search warrant on his chambers, his home, his car, everything. George Trammell retired the next day and eventually wound up being convicted and going to prison. This was a process, as there were scarcely hidden hands attempting to dilute the justice Judge Trammell had coming. So, while he might have wanted to hold my mother in contempt, the man in the robes behind the bench was the contemptable one.

In sharing the story of my relationship with my mother, I cannot deny or explain a certain level of what I felt as her contempt for me or what she viewed as my failures in life. Perhaps it began when I was three, and I disobeyed her and went out to play with the older boys. I paid for that crime with four hundred beestings. I used to try to rig my own parachute to jump from our garage roof in Indiana. I did jump off the garage roof several times, but my parachute never opened. It still doesn't.

I once ran away from home on a Schwinn Typhoon bicycle—a red one. I made it all the way to Illinois before I got picked up at sundown by the Illinois troopers and driven home. A young boy heading west, trying to get to California. I was six.

She wanted me to be a lawyer or an academic or something worthy of my pedigree. I don't think she deliberately tried to emasculate me, but she wanted me to be nice. Liberal. And I am a liberal, in the classic sense.

But she would tell you that I wasted my potential becoming a private detective. In 2021, a month or so before her death in a hospital's lung unit, she would tell me, "You are the least accomplished man in either lineage of your family."

Had I brought home for dinner a woman like Caroline Kennedy or Olga Korbut, Mother would have assured any such woman that she could do far better than the likes of Nils Grevillius.

I was supposed to go to Dartmouth or somewhere prestigious, but I couldn't drop out of academia fast enough. If I could have enlisted in the military at thirteen, I would have. And while the Ivy League used to be as meritorious as it is prestigious, it has slowly turned into an asshole factory.

Perhaps I am already an asshole. I don't need to be made into one. But that's how I see it. My mother also…she would come to me sometimes and want my counsel on this and that, and I wouldn't hold back. If disagreements were bullets, we were loaded for bear. My mother did with words and legal briefs what men did with swords: She wielded a verbal claymore that could cut her opposition in half.

Despite our disagreements, my sister insists that I was "Mother's favorite," though I'm hard-pressed, even as an experienced detective, to secure much evidence of this preference, either direct or circumstantial. She was so intensely harsh and demanding that I just can't see it.

At age sixteen, I'd discovered I was a genius and took up tobacco, beer, and women. As this curve went up, high school grades and attendance were in severe retrograde. By pure coincidence, John Muir High School expelled me the same day I quit. In my school years I found jobs cleaning at bars around Pasadena and working for an auctioneer. The latter turned out to be a great education in the value of work, with my boss telling me, "Nils, if you'll do a man's work, I'll pay you a man's wages."

He paid me three dollars an hour for labor to haul things around, get them cleaned up for auction, and store new inventory in the upper floors of an old building. Hard work for a young man, but I was under no illusions. In the same intellectual vein that helped me find my way out of public schools, I'd taken up reading men's magazines and pulp novels. The characters I identified with served in the military. They had great adventures, capers, and intrigues.

Almost seventeen, I took the entry test for the army called the ASVAB and managed to pass it. My mother wasn't keen on much of this, and it harkened back to a conversation she and I had when I was in grade school. She had asked, rhetorically, what I planned to do with myself when I became an adult. The school had mailed her a report card enumerating my serial disinterest.

"I'd like to have a life like a Steve McQueen movie," I answered.

Her father, uncle, brother, and cousins had all attended Dartmouth, and this is what she expected of me. "You're an idiot!" she responded in summation of my ambition. "No one has a life like that. Not even Steve McQueen."

There was a time when an Ivy League education might have unlocked a lot of doors for a young person. A plurality of those at the tables of power and influence arose of the Ivy League. A few of them can even see themselves in a mirror.

To my seasoned, calibrated eye, the Ivies have all the looks of a bilking scheme, whereby the lofty, upper echelons of our middle class enrich the elites, send their dullard youth off to learn which necktie to cinch around an effete neck, what color nail polish is worn to a meaningless protest, and which professor might grease the ways to better grades, an internship with a thieving senator, or graduate-school assistantship in exchange for office sex.

I couldn't finish high school. I was completely disinterested in what school had to offer. Dating adult women and drinking proved much more enlightening. Upon my army enlistment at seventeen, Enid wasn't in any way keen on this career path. A week in, with my one telephone pass, I called home for my sister with an instruction about a gun of mine, and Mother took the phone. I made a flippant remark about the cavalry recruits I was to commence training with the next day, which she took to mean I was going to take the army as seriously as I'd taken scholastic achievement. She bristled and snarled at me, "In ancient Greece when a boy left for military service, his mother would tell him, 'Come home with your shield or upon your shield. Otherwise, not at all.'"

In November of 1982 my mother and my sister came out to see me at Fort Irwin. It was a pretty cold, miserable, and windy fall. Covered in filth from head to toe, I gave them both a big one-armed hug, the other arm at my side in a cast and broken from time afield. I'd been in the scrub desert for three weeks and smelled as bad as I looked, like a grunt only gets in the field. They'd concealed some beer in their car, and there was enough beer for every guy in the platoon to have two cans—just enough. We weren't supposed to have alcohol, but fuck it, we had it, right? They could have court-martialed me then, and I would have smiled. Two cans were reserved for the first sergeant, just in case. My sister told me how dirty I was and how skinny I'd become and everything else, and my mother wept. I knew she didn't want me to be a soldier, and I knew better then, seeing her face awash in tears, not to tell her I had reenlisted the day before.

Joining the military was something I wanted to do, and I'm glad I did it, and I'd do it all over again. In fact, maybe I'd do a little better job on the second go. But we don't get mulligans in life, do we? We can't expect to thrive in the present if we spend our days awash in regret for hasty or even disastrous decisions, especially not the ones that forge the steel of our being.

In vetting the origins, pathos, and ethos of a subject start with the mother—as this is where all our stories begin—much can be revealed about a person's character when you take into consideration whether the love and support of a mother or mother figure played a role in the development of that child. When analyzing my own complicated situation with my mom, I started down a dark road. If I hadn't found my way, I could just as easily have been a bank robber or the guy who tunnels into the vault. If that younger version of me had been forced to sit in a suit in some business tower or real estate company, I'd just be daydreaming, *How do I clean these bastards out tonight?*

Perhaps it was between my choice to enter the army and my mother's innate sense of justice that I didn't become a criminal. My father certainly played a pivotal role in this as well, in toughening me up and preparing me for this line of work.

CHAPTER

3

A *TAEGEUK* CIRCLE, THE GOOD, AND THE BAD

I went into the US Army as a cavalry scout and shipped out for training in Kentucky. Things were heating up with Iran, then, and American Embassy personnel were being held hostage. We didn't know it in that moment, but we had entered the last ten years of the Cold War.

Every enlistee must undergo training of some sort, in all our armed services. We were received by a character at World War I barracks named Sergeant Baltimore, who gave us the basics of military courtesy, appearance and marching. He took us from station to station, first to be shorn of our ridiculous civilian hair, then inoculated numerous times. We were measured for uniforms by bored, slack-jawed civilians, then handed piles of olive drab issue. Every American who enlists goes through this chain of process, slowly being transformed.

I took basic training as a recruit in Third Platoon, A Troop, Fifth Cavalry. Our drill sergeant was Staff Sergeant Jerry Wallace Parrott, an American cavalryman, stem to stern with high standards but also the means, will, ability, and context to enforce them. I didn't know why my father chuckled when he signed off on my enlistment, but the joke soon enough became starkly clear when Parrott yelled at us,

"It ain't but two ways we gonna do things in Third Platoon, shitheads: my way, or the highway. If you can't complete training as a cavalry scout, I'm a do my goddamndest a make sure you serve out your enlistment at Fort Leavenworth, making big rocks into little rocks, little rocks into gravel, and patching the Kansas roads in the hot afternoon sun. And I'm telling you yardbirds that you won't leave here in a single stitch of my proud army green—no, sir. You assholes going to wear convict stripes. *That's* the highway."

I would hear this speech countless times over the subsequent fourteen weeks, time that passed with drab meals, day-long group activities like forced marches, gas chamber, bayonet drills, rifle marksmanship, machine guns, hand grenades, map reading, and something Parrott called "battlefield surveillance," which was the job of a scout platoon. What we were training for back then was the unimaginable conflict of a World War III that could consume and destroy the whole world.

The army that we had in Europe, the Seventh Army, was all about tank-on-tank warfare, mechanized infantry, and masses of aircraft. Our government commissioned the A-10 Thunderbolt II to fight that war. Under Parrott we trained up to do this, including chemical, biological, and nuclear warfare.

And we still had to do small arms. We had to know how to handle machine guns, rifles, pistols, anti-tank missiles—anything you could think of, including demolition. I became a student of weapons *and* destruction, learning all I could of our capabilities and those of the enemy, and there was much to learn.

In that distant era, coal miners and steel workers were being laid off for a fallow economy and changing job market. Many of the men I trained with were a few years older, already experienced in work, some with families to support. Several had a penetrating gaze beyond their years, veterans of the Vietnam War, reenlisted at thirty or older, and having to be trained and evaluated anew. We believed them to be above reproach, and even though they, too, were privates, we showed them the respect an American veteran should modestly enjoy.

The army graduated me and sent me home on leave with orders for Korea. This last bit rankled my father. He'd fought in the ugliest battle of the Korean War, the infamous Chosin Reservoir. There he faced temperatures on the order of thirty degrees below zero. He walked out of North Korea wounded, his feet frozen and body peppered from head to toe with shrapnel. Norman was ambulatory, but he possessed a haunted emotional cast, a condition I later came to understand was PTSD.

My father drank, and he told me it helped him sleep. I imagine the alcohol subdued the ghosts from the reservoir.

The marines and soldiers of X Corps escaped encirclement by several Communist Chinese Armies in the winter of 1950–1951. All units took heavy casualties from Chinese forces, who wiped out the US Army task force fighting the delaying action at the northeastern part of the reservoir.

Later, after I'd been a soldier some years, he told me that he'd been ordered to execute Chinese prisoners—a source of unending nightmares for him. The way my father described this act, I knew those actions weren't anything he wished to do. The Chinese troops overwhelmed X Corps, their ceaseless numbers on the battle lines every night. The captured soldiers had frozen feet and could not be marched. If they'd been set free, they would have found a way to rejoin the attack.

The intelligence troops of the Seventh Marines were ordered, "Take these prisoners to X Corps HQ and be back in twenty minutes." Incapable of being marched to a rear area, and with no rear area to evacuate them to, X Corps had a tactical dilemma: If the Chinese captives were freed, their army would put them right back into the fight. With no other options, marines and soldiers shot their prisoners and left them in the snow. Fighting to survive, this: this is the hell of war.

Despite this, if anyone asked my dad if he had PTSD, he would've equated this condition with shell shock. No man would admit this, as the way things were handled in the field under fire were very different from how they are ideally handled now.

Another time he told me, "I once saw a marine smothered by his squad leader, in a fighting position at night. He couldn't handle himself and endangered the whole platoon." These are but a snapshot of the horrors he faced in Korea, so it's easy to understand the man's disappointment in hearing the news his son would be deployed where his nightmares began.

In Korea, they assigned me to the only fraternity I'd ever pledge: the Thirty-First Infantry Polar Bears, a unit continuously overseas from when it was formed during the Philippine Insurrection, to that point in the early 1980s. Part of the Second Infantry Division, our units took turns patrolling the "demilitarized zone," the acronym being the DMZ. When the 1953 armistice was signed, this line demarcated the disposition of all forces, friendly and enemy. The jagged line bisecting Korea replaced the prewar boundary of the Thirty-Eighth Parallel. The DMZ is a misnomer, however, as it is a heavily armed frontier separating South Korea from North.

They informed us that we would have very little notice if North Korea chose to attack, so our training was demanding and realistic, in harsh winters followed by sodden, hot summers. We trained for movement to contact, disengagement under fire, break from encirclement, movement under direct fire, ambushes, raids, reconnaissance, demolitions, clearing mines with and without antihandling devices, and nuclear, biological, and chemical warfare defense. Nothing too serious.

To our scout platoon's great fortune, an extraordinary Platoon Sergeant Glenn R. Bollinger led us. In Lieutenants Bailey, then Morris, then Porter, we also had extraordinary platoon officers. An erudite man with a college education and from a solid Indiana family, Bollinger, with gifts of intellect and leadership, could have done anything in the world. In that era, the Fortune 500 fought over men such as he, and he would have been fast-tracked to an executive position, retiring wealthy. In the best traditions of our army, he was more than happy to lead, and he kept a solid family on the meager pay afforded to a noncommissioned officer.

On guard duty, with other men of the unit, I became acquainted with a salt in the Anti-Tank (AT) Section, Donald Bittner. He had biker tattoos and could quote Shakespeare. He'd been two years in the 504th Parachute Infantry. A death cult to match the Thirty-First Infantry, they were called the Devils in Baggy Pants. Don had just finished a book, *Papillon*, by the original French author Henri Charrière. I'd seen McQueen blow it away on the big screen, and the book was even better. Bittner, and others who'd taken this book up, began denoting the salty, capable men of the unit as *mecs* in colloquial French. It stuck. Bittner is still my friend, and still a *mec*, top to bottom. Don Bittner is the only man I'd ever allow to hand me a grenade with the pin already pulled.

One autumn afternoon while on a foot patrol in the northern Chorwon Valley, we encountered a Korean farmer and his wife gathering rice straw. As we approached, I could see they were middle-aged and stooped from farm labor. South Korea was in mid-transition from third world to first world, with most farm tasks still done by hand. Scars covered both of their faces, hands, and any skin showing, such that it appeared someone had shot them with birdshot in an earlier life. I incorrectly assumed it to be some sort of acne.

"Those are smallpox scars," mused Sergeant Bollinger, tipping his hat to the farmer. Moments like that served as a gentle reminder that I'd had it good in life, to be certain. That couple had seen things I'm sure were nightmare-like, between the wars, starvation, disease, and suffocating poverty.

Our patrol mission in the DMZ involved reconnaissance for North Korean activity and ambushes of North Korean troops probing into South Korea. Some of the mission meant long hours, manning listening-and-observation posts, and reporting on the North Korean Military directly opposite our positions in the DMZ. We studied and trained and conducted operations calculated to interdict the infiltration of North Korean Special Warfare units.

Patrolling the DMZ could be monotonous beyond belief, the ultimate test in patience, which was the best sort of training for my future work in surveillance. At one point I spent almost ninety days working an observation tower at a place called Guard Post Collier, ringed with concertina and prepositioned claymore mines. We had night vision equipment and technology for detecting infiltration.

I spent days on end behind "ship-to-shore" binoculars, scanning the horizon, and reporting every aspect of North Korean movement that could possibly be observed. On very clear days, we could see an enormous bronze statue of Kim Il-Sung, the premier of North Korea, erected to his murderous honor in the city of Kaesong.

That's part of the drill, securing the country from a large-scale shift of their forces toward the DMZ, in which case we would respond in kind. I know now this is not so different from the work of an investigator on surveillance, performing intense observation for extended periods of time. Hours. Days. Weeks. In wait. Watching, understanding, and knowing every detail because any change in action or behavior, however subtle, has implications and is noted, recorded, and often reacted upon.

There were several times that South Korean forces neighboring us on Hill 167, the Ninth Division White Horse troops, intercepted North Korean scuba men coming out of the Imjin River, close to Geumcheon-ri, and killed them all. These North Korean frogmen carried Czechoslovakian Scorpion VZ 61s, 7.65mm submachine guns. They also packed Czechoslovakian plastic explosive called Semtex. These North Koreans, what the hell were they up to? Who were they going to attack so equipped? Civilian targets, to be sure.

The North Koreans have a huge asymmetric warfare capability. They even use an unconventional stealth aircraft, the Antonov 2, exclusively for insertion of special forces. What makes this weapon unique is that it's a wooden biplane. Flown low, the aircraft can be almost invisible on radar and deliver eleven trigger pullers. You have to listen for the engines. This sturdy aircraft has been used all over the world. Nearly forty thousand Antonov 2s were produced, and many are still in use today. It is a fantastic airplane, but not one you'd think of as a stealth aircraft that can deliver bad guys.

Whether they attack by air or water or underground, infiltrating South Korea using tunnels, the North Koreans will try anything.

They've dressed as South Korean troops, using captured uniforms, carrying US weapons—M16s pilfered from Vietnam.

They were dangerous then, and they are dangerous now. In 2006, Barbara Demick, writing in *The Los Angeles Times*, reported that two million North Koreans had starved to death in the preceding year. Their food problem is endemic and cannot be addressed without foreign aid. Show us a country that has, in this modern era, a starvation issue, a food problem? I'll show you a country with a government problem.

Kim Jong Un, despite *Juche*—their grotesque pride and insistence on saving face—knows that North Korea must eventually change as a nation, as a political entity, and as an economy. They can't take on South Korea and win, politically or militarily.

Sometimes it can go the other way. One night we had an American defect to North Korea. A soldier from Saint Louis, PFC Joseph White did the unimaginable and ran across the military demarcation line with his M16 over his head. He danced his dumbass way through the minefield, yelling to the North Koreans, "Don't shoot! I surrender!"

While I didn't witness White's defection that night, I saw my fair share of gunfire exchanged between both sides. From those high pieces of land, you can command the fields of fire, and everything is visible. To the south of us we could see Hill 167, still occupied by White Horse. There was no shortage of activity over there. They'd fire a mortar illumination round, and you'd see red tracers flying north and green tracers flying south.

Aside from my job to observe and report on the DMZ, we did field exercises. We functioned as an infantry outfit where we'd go force-on-force and simulate war. We practiced river crossings and marched for the sake of marching. The work was physically demanding, a six-day work week with a twelve- to twenty-mile road march every Saturday.

This kept us all in peak physical shape. I left South Korea after my first tour of duty there, six foot two and 172 pounds. I could run two miles in a little over twelve minutes. Under twenty years old and

I thought of myself as a real salt, a stud warrior. Nothing bothered me, apart from boring fatigue details and the silliness of garrison life.

My second tour coincided with a series of extraordinary occurrences internationally and politically. In June of 1983, a North Korean pilot mounted his supersonic MiG-19, broke away from a training exercise, and crossed the Northern Limit Line above Yeonpyeongdo Island headed for Kimpo Airfield.

He flew so low his wings clipped the treetops and so fast the sonic boom rattled windows all over Paju-ri. The sirens of the South Korean air defense systems went off with the whole nation running for cover. When this occurred, I sat at a local watering hole having a drink or three, and suddenly emergency notifications blared out over the radio, leaving everyone distraught and evacuating to the nearest bomb shelter.

Then on September 1, 1983, a Soviet Sukhoi Su-15 interceptor with air-to-air missiles destroyed Korean Airlines Flight 007 with 269 passengers and crew on board. The flight strayed over prohibited Soviet airspace. Russian Air Defense assumed the commercial flight was a US spy plane. The Russians reacted precipitously and looked like monsters. Political tensions worldwide sizzled like a spicy Korean hot pot of *jeongol.*

Just over a month later, on October 9, the North Koreans attempted to assassinate the leader of South Korea, Chun Doo-Hwan, while on a visit to Rangoon, Burma. Their Special Warfare Team succeeded in killing fourteen of his cabinet ministers with a bomb concealed in the roof. The explosion killed a total of twenty-one people, sparing the president, who had been delayed in traffic. Naturally, this escalated tensions around the world, and especially along the DMZ in dramatic fashion.

South Korea teetered upon a precipice, the razor's edge of saying, "Fuck it! We're going to take care of House of Kim now, once and for all." Shortly after, Caspar Weinberger arrived in Seoul to confer with President Chun and reassure an important ally.

A few weeks later, on October 23, 1983, 241 marines and other US military personnel were slaughtered by Hezbollah (Iran's proxy) in Lebanon with a truck bomb at the Marine Corps barracks in Beirut, Lebanon. Minutes later, a second suicide bomber killed fifty-eight French paratroopers. Two days later, during Operation Urgent Fury, our largest military action since the end of the Vietnam War, the US invaded Grenada, the small island country in the West Indies, to overthrow a military junta that seized power in a bloody coup the day before Hezbollah's attack on our embassy in Lebanon.

All these major destabilizing world events occurred over a short period. On the DMZ, we studied each other across 153 miles of razor wire. Come November, our brigade hosted a visit from the commander in chief, Ronald Reagan. We paraded in combat equipment at warrior base after the president paid the DMZ a visit of his own.

The South Korean military was not in tatters like it was in 1950. Their army got its ass kicked badly in 1950. In 1951, a stiffening occurred where the South Korean Army turned it around, and the South Korean Marine Corps modeled itself after the US Marines—something they still do right down to the starched cover and marine swagger.

Their army had a few units taken over by officers who served as battle leaders in the Japanese Army in World War II, and notably, one of them is Korea's Ninth Infantry White Horse Division. Named after the Battle of White Horse Mountain during the Korean War, White Horse has a reputation, to this day, for kicking ass, taking names, and inflicting serious death upon any foe.

During our conflict in Vietnam, our ally South Korea deployed units to Vietnam to directly engage North Vietnamese and Viet Cong troops. White Horse was one of the outfits sent, conducting combat operations with Tiger Division. Dan Rather, a young CBS News correspondent at the time, stood in front of a blurred background, and when the camera panned out, it revealed a South Korean sergeant lighting a mountain of dead bodies on fire. Dan Rather said the Korean effectiveness in Vietnam bordered on atrocity.

That is the Asian ethics of war. There are no civilians. When they encounter opposition, they deal with that opposition the way they always have: They kill them. That's just the Asian way. The

Japanese in China, the Chinese in Korea, the Koreans in Vietnam, the Vietnamese fighting off a Chinese invasion, so on and so forth. My father, as a postwar marine, had to hose Japanese out of the caves in Guam in the late '40s after the war ended. For all this, he maintained a tremendous reverence and respect for the Japanese.

And despite being badly wounded in Korea and scarred physically and emotionally forever, he didn't hate Korea. He just said it was a horrible experience juxtaposed with the beautiful, just like the societal engineering, the up and the down. Just as the red and blue ying-yang, a *taegeuk* circle symbol in the center of the South Korean flag, indicates—the great duality, the good and the bad.

So, too, was the experience for me as a soldier there, though mostly good, even in a time that appeared on the cusp of cataclysmic war. The last time I phoned my dad from South Korea, over Christmas, he asked me where I was. This wasn't a security issue, so I told him my location, Uijongbu, a city midway between Seoul and the DMZ.

Norman replied, "The last time I saw Uijongbu, it was flat and on fire...."

The Korean War is mostly forgotten now, and some have suggested it was a waste of resources and lives. Thousands of Americans were killed in the three years of that conflict, and thousands more remain missing in action. My view, looking at South Korea now, is that it was worthwhile.

Today, South Korea is a developed nation with every comfort and advantage of a Western democracy. But still, to the North, their neighbors—speaking the same language, with the same history and culture—are impoverished in second-world Marxism.

On my flight back to "the world," as we called it, I flew next to an air force senior NCO. He was going back to the US, his tour concluded. Unlike forces on the DMZ, an air force tour was an accompanied tour, and his wife and children were asleep next to him. They'd lived in base housing, far south of our area of operations. He asked me what it was like, my tour, and I gave him the bland, brief version of things, first tour and second, lest his family be listening. "I've never had to sleep in a rice paddy, winter or summer. Things were pretty easy for us, and I didn't know it until speaking with you…."

Back at Fort Benning, a second time, I landed in a battalion that had a great commanding officer and a corrupt, treacherous sergeant major. Once, to curry unnecessary favor of our officers, the sergeant major called a formal dining-in of the NCOs, for which he insisted that our guests be the officers of our battalion, with their wives.

The notice on a disposition form stated that attendance for any man ranked sergeant and above was mandatory, as was dress uniform, in accordance with army regulation 670-1. This regulation, vital to every ponce and martinet, governed what was required and what was permissible in any circumstance or event. Some senior NCOs had dress blues, but the modification most would use was dress greens, with a white shirt and black bow tie.

The regulation stated that other dress uniforms in summer months were permissible, such as dress whites. No one had dress whites. As it happened, the prior year, drunk and lost in Seoul, I'd purchased a set of tailor-made dress whites from a Korean haberdasher. They were exquisite, with gold-bullion sergeant's chevrons and my single hash mark denoting years of service. Hungover, later, I'd kicked myself for spending the money. There was zero chance I'd be wearing them to the Blue Angel Club in Yonjugol.

My dress uniform issue solved, I'd only to find a date. The SOP (standard operating procedure) on the disposition form required each NCO to pay in advance for the dining-in, *and* that he must have a date.

One of the problems with Fort Benning, which made it such a dull duty assignment, was the 30-to-1 ratio of men to women. This left the odds so lopsided that local women had ceased any effort at feminine pulchritude sometime around the WWI armistice. No Chattahoochee County woman of attraction, poise, or letters would be seen dead with an enlisted soldier such as myself.

Tuesday night, I rode my motorcycle down to a strip club—not for a date, but to seek out the sage counsel of Bill Daugherty, alias

Wild Bill Kelso, once of Terre Haute, who was out of the army and tending a bar. He listened a moment to my tale, snickered, and said, "Maybe go over to Main Post Bowling Alley, see if you can get a date with a dependent girl…."

With my luck and winning looks, I'd have been asking out my no-good sergeant major's daughter. No go. No good. Back on my Yamaha, about to kick-start it, I observed an opportunity arriving in a wrinkled, rusted blue Ford station wagon. A beaming woman pulled up, leaned out the window, and asked me if I wanted to party. This was strictly code language, a clear solicitation for pay to play.

"I'm Velma Mae. What's yo name, honey?" she asked, stepping out of her car. Her dress was too tight, her age north of forty to my twenty-one years, and her perfume may have been motel disinfectant. But I'll admit now, the woman had style.

In that moment, I spied a solution to my dateless Friday situation. "Are you available Friday night?" I asked.

"I'm free," she said, "but not all night, not until the cock be crowin.' What we fixin' a do?" She was beaming.

"It's nothing bad, Velma. I need a date for an event, and I like the cut of your jib," I counter-proposed. She thought I said *giblets*, but that's another story.

I pulled twenty dollars from my wallet and promised another fifty if she'd meet me early Friday evening, in her best dress.

Velma Mae agreed to meet me, but on the condition that I bring a second helmet for her to wear on my bike, and that I have her "freed up" by eight thirty.

"I'm working Friday. You feel me?"

We had a deal, but I had no intention of "feeling" her.

That Friday, Velma came through. I pulled up on my Yamaha at our agreed-upon meeting spot, and there sat the same shitty old car. She stepped out from the vehicle, dressed to kill: a tightly cinched girdle, high heels, and a nice peach-colored dress that radiated against her dark black skin. Who am I kidding? She looked like she'd had more marines on her than Iwo Jima. But little did I know this would be the beginning of a perfect night, and perhaps the beginning of my career undercover, or at least working covert operations.

I looked resplendent myself in dress whites, right down to the white bucks on my size thirteen feet. Had I known I'd survive into my thirties, I might have saved more photos of my handsome self. I really am a beautiful man.

I handed her the helmet. She climbed aboard, and we roared off to the Kelly Hill Recreation Center for the dining-in. Velma Mae hung on to me, a little too tight and not right, but I tried not to notice.

In the receiving line I introduced Velma as my date to the battalion commander and his wife, as well as the executive officer. We made our way right down the line, with no problems. Then, there he stood. The asshole of assholes. The crooked sergeant major with his lovely wife, and somewhere, somehow, Velma Mae—my date—*knew* him. A most amazing coincidence.

I grinned.

It turned out Velma also happened to know my first sergeant *and* the motor sergeant *and* a few guys in the Mortar Platoon. Somehow, to my credit, I'd met and presented a local woman who *knew* her way around military men, if not their wives, as if she worked at the local ice cream shop and they'd all been in for a sample or two.

The first sergeant—already in the bag, sloppy drunk—grabbed my arm, took me aside, and hissed in my ear, "The fuck did you find *that* bitch?" He also apparently didn't care for my dress whites, adding, "And you, out of uniform!"

I scanned the vast room, Velma, and well over a hundred souls. No one else had dress whites on. No one. Just me.

"It's within regulations, Top," I said, and then added, "I checked."

Those could have been my famous last words, but I excused myself to catch up with Velma, who already had a cocktail in hand. I grabbed one for myself and waltzed Velma to our assigned table, where she proceeded to down a few more. She had a rather nice time of it, flirting her way from table to table, saying hello to men she knew and introducing herself to men she didn't yet know. Perhaps a few wives as well. Very social, my date.

When the time came for the sergeant major to raise a toast to our officers, Velma Mae, who might have had a few too many, stumbled in her heels, and I caught her as she nearly fell to the floor. That didn't slow her down. She toasted our battalion herself, in finest style, and after everyone else had found their chair.

True to my word, I delivered Velma back to the parking lot of Little Richard's on Victory Drive, right as the clock struck eight thirty. She planted a kiss on my cheek and went about her weekend. I chained my bike to the railing outside the bar, knowing I'd need a taxi, and made my way inside for another drink. Monday would come soon enough.

Braced after work-call formation, the first sergeant informed me, "Sergeant Major has a case of the ass for you, Sergeant. And don't give me none of your shit about no army regulations with your dress whites!"

We never had another dining-in, which surprised me considering how cordial and elegant that Friday had turned out. And that is how a well-intentioned noncommissioned officer of the US Cavalry can adhere to every regulation, rule, military custom, SOP, and order, and yet still be a tarantula on the wedding cake.

Later, after an exercise in Germany, I was not in any way surprised to learn that our esteemed sergeant major had been caught embezzling thousands of dollars in maneuver-damage funds. This was German currency used by mechanized outfits to placate the local farmers after a company of tanks churned up a wheat field and broke down a wall, rehearsing for WWIII.

That shitbag sergeant major's life in the military would come to a halt while my own would take a somewhat unexpected and unique path. Midway into my second tour in Korea, I would find myself receiving a devil of a proposition—a dramatic and interesting twist, with a choice that would send my own military calling into a clandestine and covert world I knew little about.

CHAPTER 4

MILITARY INTELLIGENCE

Upon returning to Korea, I landed "extra duty." I can neither confirm nor deny this had any connection to my date with Velma Mae, but my extra duty involved convincing Korean prostitutes with penicillin-resistant clap to be treated and tested.

A certain number of soldiers made the walk of shame into the clinic every Monday, bearing the symptoms of gonorrhea usually—sometimes syphilis, too—and other things.

And when their infection couldn't be immediately treated with penicillin, it was time to use the army's own special provisional treatment for gonorrhea—one the army created with its own clinical trial and treatment when infections resistant to normal treatment progressed.

I would sit down in my office across a nondescript desk from the soldier involved with obtaining the sexually transmitted infection and ask, "Sergeant, where did you happen to encounter this?"

Inevitably, I would get the same reply from every infected soldier: "This? This what?"

I'd lean in, either their new and most trusted confidant or the man who could make their life a living hell, and say, "Come on."

And without further ado, the standard answer would lead me to a club, and I'd have a name—Miss Kitty, or something of the sort. From there, I would link up with a Korean public health officer, go off to the Lucky Club or whatever ironic name the place had, on the hunt, searching for Miss Kitty before she shared her infectious meow with the rest of the platoon.

Once we identified Miss Kitty, we'd escort her back to Camp Edwards to be treated and tested. The leverage I had to get the info and cooperation I needed was that the club would be placed off-limits for all soldiers by Command Sergeant Major if the owners didn't cooperate. Their mitigation for this was to make me an offer, as this is a bribery culture.

It didn't take long before someone offered me a good sum of money to go away, with a similar offer extended to my counterpart, the South Korean public health official, who was conveniently always looking away when these conversations took place.

Ultimately every guy assigned to this extra duty prior to me, sooner or later, caved and took the jack. Time and time again I refused the bribes, but nevertheless, the sergeant major pulled me in one day and said, "They're going to put you on the box. CID wants to talk to you."

I didn't know what was wrong. Why would the Criminal Investigation Division of the military police suspect me of anything? Initially they were quick to allay my concerns. They told me they were sorry for calling me in. Nothing to worry about. "This is routine," the poly man said. "We do this with all the guys who have that extra duty just to see if they're taking bribes."

They put me on the poly, being examined once again, just like when I was ten in my father's shop, and I passed. I hadn't accepted any bribes, and I didn't need to cover for myself or anyone else.

A week later, they seated me a second time. This time it was because I didn't take the money. Something was wrong. Something *had* to be wrong. *Why* wouldn't I take the bribe?

And why didn't I?

Why? I knew, with my luck, they would catch me. The temptation was certainly there, and perhaps at some level I am that sort of guy who would consider a good offer. I have the heart of a bandit. But

I knew it'd be more trouble than it was worth, because there is hard truth in the army: They don't fuck around if you get caught stealing.

If you get popped for having your hand in the cookie jar, and there is no hiding from a sentence of five years hard labor. I knew I'd be there patching roads in the hot Kansas sunshine, at USDB Fort Leavenworth, just as Sergeant J.W. Parrott so artfully prescribed in basic combat training. This is the result of a trial by court martial: hard labor followed by a bad conduct discharge (bad chicken dinner!). Even worse is the dishonorable discharge. I guess it was at this moment in my illustrious career where I revealed some aptitude or a recognizable or discernable level of competence, or let's say—to improperly use an oxymoron—military intelligence.

I'd passed on the bribes and was subject to a second routine polygraph after refusing any graft, bribes, favors, or perquisites one might conjure in fencing with the operators of brothels. All these temptations were common to the posting.

About a week after that, a forty-something-year-old man dressed in a coat and tie shows up at our PT formation. He stood watching us, and based on his age and appearance, I could make a fair assumption for him to be either from the Criminal Investigation Division or some civilian from the Red Cross or some similar organization. My assumption was off the mark.

The first sergeant pulled me aside, narrowed his eyes, and said in a snide way, "I don't know what kind of trouble you're in this time, but..." He paused, gestured over at the suit, and added, "*That* man wants to talk to you."

I approached the man in the suit. "Yes, sir? What can I help you with?"

He gave a half grin and rubbed the stubble on his chin. "Well, Nils, I have what I think is an interesting proposition for you."

His use of my first name, and no rank, caught me off guard. "Am I in trouble?" I asked.

"No," he said, nodding his head the direction he wanted me to follow. "I want to buy you breakfast at the Officers' Club."

"I'm just a sergeant, sir," I replied. "I can't go into the Officers' Club."

He chuckled as if he could dismiss any concerns I might have but clearly loved the fact I had no idea who the fuck he was or what was going on. He continued, "I said, I'm going to buy you breakfast at the Officers' Club. Go on. Get dressed in your uniform. Shall I meet you up there in twenty minutes?"

I stood frozen for a second. Still a bit stunned. His demeanor was all soldier, but his clothing civilian. I didn't see that I had much of a choice, so I did what he said. I trotted over to my platoon sergeant and told him something was up, and I didn't know what. He automatically assumed the worst.

I donned my uniform and found myself quite out of place at a table with him at the Officers' Club. He looked me over and asked me, "Do you know what counterintelligence is?"

"I have a vague idea." But I didn't share that my knowledge was based on what my father had said and what I knew from the ridiculous Colonel Flagg on *M*A*S*H*, a popular TV show about the Korean War. For some reason, my father never found *M*A*S*H* amusing.

Flagg was always looking for communists and attempting to make the protagonist, Doctor Hawkeye Pierce, out for a Chinese spy. He had some classic lines like, "Nobody can get the truth out of me because even I don't know what it is. I keep myself in a constant state of utter confusion."

Between a superior breakfast and decent coffee, the man in the suit informed me in the simplest terms, "This is what we do," he said. "We catch spies."

He paused, as if considering something in me again. Took another bite. Followed it with a sip of coffee and continued. "We catch people spying on the US Army. And I can't describe it any more than that."

I nodded. As if I understood, which I did—philosophically. The actual way this might be done in a military organization was then external to me. That part I'd no idea of.

"So, Nils," said this strange man wearing a suit, sitting across from me in the Officers' Club, in a dining area not allowed by my rank. He concluded our short meal with a not-so-simple question. He asked me, "I just want to know if you're *in* or you're *out*?"

How does one answer a life-changing question like this on the spot, with no more information than what he gave me, a satirical television character, and my father's words lingering in my mind?

After what might have been a few heartbeats or twenty minutes, I answered in the only way I could: "I'll think about it," I said. I was already thinking about it.

He gave me his contact information, and I made my way back to formation and my unit, my head aswirl with a sudden new and strange door of possibility opening in a life where the doors I was choosing led into bars. I can only imagine what my stunned face probably looked like as I returned from the Officers' Club. The platoon sergeant took one look at me and asked, "Well? You going to jail?"

"Not yet," I said, "but we'll see, right?" It could still happen.

In my last months at Fort Benning, I began to prepare myself for training in counterintelligence, which was rather different from the tactical requirements of a scout in an infantry outfit.

CHAPTER

5

COUNTERINTELLIGENCE: TRUST NO ONE

Any device of security, or encryption, whether it is electronic, mechanical, or a codified protocol, that is devised by Man, can eventually [be] defeated by another man.

—SSG David F., Counterintelligence Instructor

I gave my bows of goodbye to the Koreans I'd worked with and befriended, uncertain if I would ever return, and more uncertain about my new career path in counterintelligence. I boarded my flight back to Fort Benning, and the only thing I knew for certain was the process to becoming an agent would take a while. I needed to first get a security clearance and then go through rigorous training.

They placed me briefly in the tank outfit, second of the Sixty-Ninth Armor, still as cavalry scout. Every tank unit, every cavalry unit, every infantry unit, has scouts as their eyes and ears. My job as a squad leader in scout platoon took on more meaning in the context of my pending indoctrination in counterintelligence. You're observing, and everything you report on goes up the chain.

Obtaining a security clearance started with a statement of personal history, detailing where I was born and to whom. From the statement, they vetted me for involvement with foreign governments, travel to foreign nations, and my friendships and affiliations. The questionnaire covered drug abuse and criminal behavior and anything that could suggest foreign allegiance, emotional instability, bad judgment, moral turpitude, or vulnerability to blackmail.

Of the jobs undertaken in counterintelligence units, I will state that there is an anodyne description available in any reference library. In essence, it involves the passive and active identification and neutralization of hostile intelligence services as well as nonstate actors, then an elaborate term for terrorists or revolutionaries.

Operating in the shadows, counterintelligence is constantly on a war footing, conducting operations even in peacetime. In counterintelligence, the very first thing they introduce you to after you have security clearance and have your formal training comes full circle—back to security. What is security? How do you protect information? What is confidential? What is for official use only? What is secret? And the big kahuna, what is *top secret*?

Operatives learn what security levels are based on, and that it's not enough to have a clearance; another component exists, and that is a *need to know*. What information are you authorized to access, and do you actually have a tactical or strategic need to know the information in order to do your official duties? We were taught to think of security in degrees, rather than in terms of infallibility.

To beat this into your head, you hear a litany of war stories: security failures of the highest order, the fuckups and the near-fuckups. The courses were taught by dry, acerbic counterintelligence agents who had seen it all, and you could feel as if they could see right through you. They each had an innate sense of skepticism and wanted double, triple, confirmation of information, yet this always came with the axiom, "When we ask someone a question, we are also stating something to them in text, context, or subtext."

Later, under the tutelage of a low-key warrant officer, I learned how to bury my true line of questioning in a series of contextual questions. On the other end, in reporting, he showed me an unwritten bit of tradecraft, which I came to know as "Slap-Stick." If we got something actionable from a source we were not supposed to know, or be in contact with, it might go up the chain attributed to a source who *might* have reported it, but with which it could not be vetted. "Slap it on this source, and watch it stick. . . ."

Another role of counterintelligence, generally, both ours and theirs, might include clandestine work like extrajudicial extradition (*rendition* in post–9/11 vernacular) or maybe snatching a troublesome fellow off the street, putting a bag over his head, and socking him in the kidneys. Let him fall from the car at a moderate speed, so he can later sort out his future, unclear as to whom may have borrowed him for a few hours. Nothing too serious, eh? There have been more ominous consequences in the past of nations and security, but I am writing generally.

By the end of a six-month course, counterintelligence by water hose, I knew a bit and felt ready to be sent out into the field as an agent. The training was arduous and challenging, but the work very interesting.

The people I worked with in US Army Counterintelligence were intellectual, analytical, thorough, and considered the posting as nothing short of holy. Within the US Army, for a mere careerist, it was a backwater where none were expected to have great promotions, where often particular "cases" went on for decades. Many of the officers and civilians to whom I reported were outstanding and thoroughgoing professionals, often women.

Here, many decades later, I must be circumspect in what I say about counterintelligence, because sharing sources and methods could endanger people still in the field. The nature of a counterintelligence case, an example like Robert Lee Johnson, perfectly shows what counterintelligence agents do. That was an eight-year case where the man's drunk wife kept telling people, "My husband is spying for the Russians." And because she was a drunk, no one took her seriously. Until someone did. Once they determined Johnson was in fact spying on the US for the Soviet Union, they had him under surveillance. Then when Johnson finally landed in prison at Leavenworth for treason, spying, and espionage, his own son, a grunt in Vietnam, comes back to visit dear old dad in the can and lets the air out of the motherfucker, stabbing his father to death.

CHAPTER

6

THE DARK ARTS

A counterintelligence case can run upward of thirty years. One lesser-known example of an army counterintelligence agent comes from a young sergeant, a German immigrant during World War II. The United States Army needed men who were above reproach, and who could be trusted politically, yet were fluent German speakers. They enlisted this sergeant as a counterintelligence agent. And in the immediate aftermath of the war, he controlled a whole province of Germany. He began running a former Abwehr (German Intelligence) Organization, a secretive espionage network. This US Army sergeant stepped in and ran the network and supervised German officers, picking and choosing between the spies who were compromised because they'd been turned by the NKVD (the Russians), and those in whom limited operational trust could be vested…among other things.

That man just died a few years ago, and his name was likely a name most Americans will recognize: Henry Kissinger. Counterintelligence is a unique thing. Today, when we think special forces, we think of Green Berets, Delta Force, and SEALs. They're tier-one operators, for certain.

These people are specially selected and fantastic at what they do; they're the trigger pullers. But there is also a vast system of asymmetric warfare conducted by women and men of great intellect who must be shrewd, rational, cunning, and treacherous motherfuckers in order to get shit done. Sometimes they direct special operations forces (SOF), sometimes they kill by remote control, and sometimes counterintelligence operatives will settle someone's hash themselves.

After the global war on terror in 2001, you can only imagine the sacrifices made by counterintelligence people and their work with other human-intelligence networks like interrogators. The interrogators bring in a subject and expose him to what could be darkly characterized as "holy baptism" to find out what he thinks, says, does, knows, where he's been, and where he's going to go. Torture—the use of force to erode a man's will to emotionally and intellectually resist—works and works very well. Otherwise, no one would trouble himself with it. "Baptism" in the form of waterboarding is but one effective technique.

Then you're comparing this information to signals intelligence, whether it's internet or phone intercepts, or anything else. Meanwhile the counterintelligence agents are running operations where maybe somebody *is* compromised, but they're really working *for* us. And so that person is under surveillance and tested by polygraph occasionally, not because polygraphs reveal the truth, but because polygraphs intimidate people into the belief that truth and fiction can be sorted out on the Box. Any good polygraph operator is first and foremost a good interrogator. The box is just a machine made by men.

On the subject of interrogations, post–9/11, there have been a lot of wild accusations of torture—specifically, American intelligence operatives engaging in the proscribed practice.

The ACLU, National Lawyers Guild, and other Marxist fronts operated by lawyers would define *torture* as any line of questioning which results in a frank confession. They, having no burden of securing our nation, conflate criminal justice with counterespionage and counterterrorism. Only US persons are protected by the Fourth and Fifth Amendments. Foreign actors, whether part of a hostile intelligence agency or a stateless terrorism group, enjoy only limited rights under the Geneva and Hague Conventions. Fuck them.

Like other aspects of intelligence, when a man starts providing information, it is all taken down and categorized, to be compared to similarly categorized information, so as to arrive at a more complete picture of what he knows, what he doesn't know, what he might know in the future, and what he is holding in reserve. Were I to debrief a man from a deprivation culture, like North Korea, I'd go at him in a counterintuitive way: I'd have him in a comfortable room by himself, with bedding noticeably changed twice weekly by modest yet attractive women. I'd feed him adequately and afford him brief exercise twice daily and two cigarettes a day. After two weeks I'd provide him two South Korean Newspapers on Sunday, and pipe in pleasant music. His food would be tainted with an SSRI that doesn't impede sexual function and has no discernable side effects.

At sixty days—and not before—I'd introduce myself. He'd already know that I am US Intelligence. I might have a South Korean with me, to whom I'd defer to in his language, with the South Korean being a pleasant, avuncular boss.

While his bedding is changed, he has a tower view of a city park, with families playing and recreating. He may or may not speak with me. At this point, I'd tell him since his capture, it's likely his family in North Korea is endangered, if not already executed. He's an intelligence professional, so he knows all of this. The larger point being that he'd never expect kindness upon being captured. He comes from a state where food is rationed, with mere coffee a luxury item, with no access to outside media or entertainment. His own intelligence service would deliver the rubber-hose treatment, pull out fingernails, burn flesh with a tool.

Eventually, he'd cooperate. Not fully, at first. But over a period of months and years, he'd give me nearly everything. None of them give up every single thing; all hold a bargaining chip in reserve.

On the other hand, Al-Qaeda, the Taliban, and ISIS are not deprivation cultures. Quite the opposite. While the people around them suffer, they fully indulge themselves. Upon capturing one of these men, I'd isolate him in a dank cell with too small a blanket and bring him two cans of Belgian dog food a week. His water would taste of chlorine, the better to masque the SSRI added to the water that completely impedes his sexual function, denying him even the ability to jerk off into his fetid sheets. I'd visit him twice a week with an Arabic speaker in an IDF uniform and ask nothing of him. In the third week, he'd undergo holy baptism. Eventually, he'd either give me everything, or kill himself from despair.

When an espiocrat goes in front of Parliament or Congress and sets a tone of seriousness, testifying that "torture" doesn't work, he's providing a bullet point for academics and media morons. Lawmakers can pose and strut and make grandiloquent speeches about democracy. Every mec who's ever plied the trade, in any service or language, is snickering. The statement "torture does not work" is their alibis. Since it doesn't work, they never do it. Never.

In counterintelligence, I was introduced to a dark art. It's easy to laugh about such a phrase, but I don't use it lightly. George Clooney made an idiotic movie called *The Men Who Stare at Goats*, which suggested we use remote scientific viewing, which is a myth. There is no one who can sit there and say, "Someone in the Alaskan wilderness took a dump behind that tree while a bear watched three and a half weeks ago, right?" Remote viewing is a fantasy. This is not the dark art I speak of.

I was indoctrinated in neurolinguistic programming. With neurolinguistic programming as an expositive tool, I learned to read how a man or woman communicates, whether they think in tactile, auditory, or visual terms. Then I might subject them, in casual conversation, to a series of questions calculated to warm them up, to relax them. They might not guess to what extent they're being elicited. What is even better is that there's a way for me to determine using neurolinguistic programming whether they're recalling a situation or inventing a situation, which is crucial.

Now in the intelligence pie chart, the big slices are signals and cyber intelligence, then imagery intelligence—meaning satellite imagery or some other covert photography. Human intelligence is the narrow part, the tiny slice. And because human intelligence has a small market share, for intelligence people, it's a dead end. You're not going to have a great career in military intelligence if you're in counterintelligence. It's not the most important, or it is seemingly unimportant, but I can tell you it's the most exciting aspect of intelligence there is. This is for its ability to predict future acts and reveal the true intent of an adversary. For this, it cannot be replaced.

Some people call the signals intelligence guys (folks like James Clapper) "spooks." I use this term of art advisedly, as for some it conjures an image of racism. Within the argot of special operations, spooks are HUMINT Operators, rather than uniformed trigger pullers. A spook wages war from the shadows, often in civilian clothing, with cover. Men such as Clapper and John Brennan, former head of CIA, are not spooks. A *spook* is a mec, an operator, who adopts an alias with forged or artistically sourced documents to cross a hostile frontier, knowing he can be tortured, processed, and killed for his status and actions. Whether or not he pulls it off, he has nuts like church bells, and *that* agent with huge balls might even be…a woman. Clapper, and the other suits who have homesteaded at National Security, are not spooks. They're espiocrats, with no more grit than the postmaster.

As a calvary scout, I was no Audie Murphy, and as a counterintelligence agent, I was no James Bond. My off-duty behavior would land me in even more trouble than my soldier days, but in a different way because the culture of counterintelligence is completely different from the infantry or cavalry.

Work as an agent was more esoteric, more refined. Some of the people I worked alongside existed as straight-up tattletales, sycophants there to step on each other to make the vapidest of careers. My thoughts were simply, *Whatever, fuck them*. I didn't care.

Nearly all the agents, even the assholes, were intensely dedicated, devoted, and highly intelligent people. Most of them were, but some were shitbags. No line of work is exempt from people like that. While I cannot blame my upbringing, my mother or my father, I'm the guy, the square peg, hammered into the round hole every time. I'm always going to make trouble.

And I did.

Me and my affinity for booze—I'd get drunk and shoot my mouth off. While I would never expose secrets, I sure as shit would tell people what I thought of them.

I got away with this in the infantry because I was tactically proficient and able to manage my men. I knew how to lead and handle myself in that realm.

Well, these attributes had very little value in counterintelligence, especially if I was going to be sloppy drunk. One slipup when I landed back in South Korea for my third tour nearly cost me everything.

At the time this little faux pas occurred, I found myself dating a very attractive woman—a fashion designer and daughter of a retired South Korean government official, a wealthy, well-connected banker in South Korea. I'd already spent the early evening having too much to drink at a bar called the Embassy Club. The place served a martini that tasted like dry cleaning fluid. I had probably already downed six, eight, or ten of them. Who counts?

Dressed to kill, in a suit and tie, I dashed off to meet my girlfriend, who awaited me in a distant city. I needed to catch the express, or I'd be late for her.

I arrived at the train station in Seoul, half in the bag, running late, and searching for the express line. I spotted a train preparing to pull away, and without hesitating, flashed my credentials to the platform attendant. I identified myself as a member of American intelligence and told him he needed to hold the train so I could board. When the door opened, the guy standing before me was part of a protective detail for a very high-ranking South Korean official. I don't want to identify the government official who was on board the train, but let's just say it was *his* personal train.

To say this sudden realization sobered me instantly wouldn't be much of a stretch of the truth. I bowed politely and stepped back into the crowd, losing myself quickly because I knew I'd be in an avalanche of shit if anyone figured out who I was.

This train fiasco occurred on a Friday night, and by Monday, an uproar consumed the whole unit. The first sergeant and the operations people tried their best to figure out who had stopped the train.

When questioned, I of course said I didn't know anything about it, and I asked if maybe it wasn't a criminal investigation issue, because the army does something the navy and air force doesn't: the army separates counterintelligence from criminal investigation.

After five or six days, concerns dwindled, the questioning died down, but the first sergeant kept coming around, demanding to know if it was me, as he knew I had a reputation for booze-related chicanery.

While they never got me for flashing my credentials and discrediting US counterintelligence, I was always their primary suspect.

This was my fault that anyone even had to bother investigating. That's not on them; that is my responsibility. Had I not been a drinking guy, I probably would have been head of SOCOM, or something consequential as that. Even as I started out, as private first class, a very considerate platoon leader, Mike Ford, offered me a shot at accelerated consideration for West Point. I declined because, at age eighteen, I knew I'd fuck it up. I had to find my own way—my own difficult path forward.

I wasn't a good fit in counterintelligence, even though I could do every bit of the work. Always the square wheel on the shopping cart, I'm forever the author of my own problems. Sometimes because I would see things that I thought should be investigated or covered, and there were others who refused to listen to me. It's not that I'm smarter than everybody else; I just saw the world differently. That's all. And so, in many ways, I was even a failure at that.

I then concluded active military service. My goal upon completing two enlistments was unclear to me, and I fell into the bottle as if it was an open sewer main.

Out of the army, I cast about looking for jobs. Unsure what to do next, I harbored the idea that I'd enlist in the French military and lose myself in that. The French Army has a long-standing program for men like me. There was something awry that I couldn't quite see. For all my ability and experience, ordinary life was corrosive and degrading. Falling in love felt like the onset of a fatal disease. If someone else had done to me what I had done, I'd have killed him on sight. But it was always just me. I didn't need a "worst enemy."

Here I was, with this vast skill set, and I felt utterly directionless. I could cross borders, obtain a fake passport, make a bomb from ordinary things, scale buildings, pick locks, install a wire or listening devices, operate any vehicle or weapon, learn a language in a few weeks, navigate by compass and pace count, send and receive Morse code, encrypt and decrypt secret communications, operate a MINOX or Robot Star camera, adjust mortar and artillery fire, evaluate a man's perception of truth without a polygraph, but I couldn't balance my checque book, keep household utilities connected, or know a girlfriend committed enough to hold my hand while my father died.

CHAPTER

7

THE PINKERTON AGENCY

When I left the army after serving as a counterintelligence agent, I'm found myself sitting there wondering what the hell I was supposed to do. My resume included seven years of military service, most of it as a soldier overseas, then as a contractor. I thought about becoming a cop, but then I thought about those years in uniform. Joining a police agency felt like more of the same. I never enjoyed being told what to do, especially not by people with a hidden agenda or deadwood, martinet time servers.

In my hunt for a new line of employment, I interviewed for a job at a detective agency, National Loss Prevention Associates, in Pasadena, California. I spotted a classified employment advertisement, expressing a need for an industrial undercover operative, and phoned their number.

George Schweitzer—at least ten years my senior, charismatic and affable—interviewed me. He took in my resume, had me fill out an application, and sat me down. The office felt stuffy, with fans blowing the hot air around, doing little to cool the room. As he looked my application and resume over, I sat before him in coat and tie, as if I was still in counterintelligence, as if I might have something to represent.

In his very first question, Schweitzer asked, "Do you speak Spanish?"

I shook my head and responded, "No. But I do speak some Korean, German, and Russian." (I speak a bit of Spanish now, but not so much then.)

Schweitzer was amused and directed me into the office of his older partner, a retired deputy sheriff and detective. Dressed in polyester slacks and a guayabera shirt, portly, balding, and a bit moist from the heat, this old lawman shook my hand, and upon hearing of my inability to speak Spanish, shook his head.

"You don't got no chance in a business like this," he said. "What are you trying to do? Don't speak Spanish? We looking to place a Mex in the loading dock at a shipping outfit, catch the guys stealing cargo. I wouldn't waste my time if I was you. You gotta have experience. Skills. See?"

I saw, and out I went into the afternoon heat.

I stood in the shadow cast by the building. I lit a smoke, looked north, looked south, and said to myself, "That wasn't so good."

I understood that in the short-term, they were looking for a specific type to fill a role, almost like an actor, but who could infiltrate a theft ring, identify the players, and help them make a case: grand theft, receiving stolen property, embezzlement, and conspiracy.

In the long-term? What Schweitzer and his partner meant was that I had no connections to municipal or county law enforcement. This seemed to those men a requirement for success as a private detective. They could rely upon someone in their old police agency to look up wants and warrants, a driving record, and booking photos. That is how the business was done then. Today an officer accessing this data is a proscribed offense, with cops losing their jobs for the very act.

Now, ironically, when a cop needs a license plate run or a man identified, outside the context of an active police investigation, he calls *me*.

In the interim I took a position as a skip tracer and assets investigator for Greater California Financial Services and occasionally ran down bail jumpers for an older bondsman. I was in good shape, and thought for twenty-five, I could make it in the detective business. It hadn't yet occurred to me to open my own agency, as that seemed such a daunting prospect and far out of my league.

I learned the job skip tracing—locating people who had skipped town. The job provided a great training ground, and the skills I acquired then, I still use now.

The Skiptracing Unit was run by a paralegal named Stephanie who was crafty and precise and prided herself on producing results for the legal unit. We were expected to close eight cases per day, one per hour, day in and day out. Using scant information such as name, last known address, and date of birth, each debtor being targeted by the amount owed, status, and client was to be properly identified and located for the service of a lawsuit, and their suitability as a prospect in litigation.

Men and women who owned nothing, or of limited means and ability to pay, were poor prospects for collection, post-judgment. I learned to read all three types of credit bureaus, collect and analyze information from bounced or even negotiated checques, obtain telephone numbers and addresses, and identify hidden assets. We were using the term *checque,* as opposed to check, to avoid confusion or ambiguity (and so will I throughout this book).

In commercial accounts, we would identify and define a business by the type of entity, whether corporation, limited partnership, sole proprietor, or others. Then, the status of the company. Were they viable? Where did they operate? At which institution did they keep their accounts? Who owned the company?

For me, the ancillary benefit of this regime of training and operation was twofold: First, I learned to evaluate information quickly, decide what the next lead was, and to cover that lead. Second, nothing was ever opaque to me after this. There is always a lead, a way, a woman or man pulling the levers of power in any company or concern, or quite possibly a group of them.

Real estate records were another avenue of information. Who owned the land when the problem occurred? Where did the tax bill go? Who notarized the deed? Was the sale of the property a sham? Why? Stephanie demanded that all leads be answered, and that in closing a case for action by the legal department, there be no ambiguity as to name, alias, status, or location.

While grateful for the work, the training, and the pay, I needed more action than sitting in an office, so I pressed my suit for detective work.

Then one day, nursing a hangover, I spied a classified employment ad in *The Los Angeles Times*, advertising a need for investigators. The advertisement included a phone number on a Los Angeles exchange, in Mid-Wilshire.

There was a pay telephone that the boss at Greater California Financial Services kept under intermittent surveillance, close to the office. If a man was seen on that phone at lunch, it was a given he was phoning around for a better job. That employee could be assured he would be given his last checque that day.

When I rang the number from the ad, I made sure I was half a mile from the office, in the portico at a tire store. A woman answered, "CMS Management."

She asked if I had any experience, and if I'd a resume. Getting time off from work for a competing interview felt dicey, but I managed. To my surprise, when I showed up for the interview, I learned that the investigative job was for Pinkerton's National Detective Agency.

Founded in the 1850s by a Glaswegian expat in metro Chicago, the Pinkerton Agency started as the first detective force, investigative agency—private or public—of any note in the United States. The founder, Allan Pinkerton, ran counterintelligence operations during the Civil War, and his agents protected President Lincoln until nearly the end of hostilities. Was Pinkerton a "trained law enforcement professional"? No way. He was self-trained. In the same way that the founding members of the British SAS Commandos taught themselves to parachute by jumping from the back of a truck, Pinkerton taught himself and his men and women how to ID crooks, to suppress crime, to infiltrate criminal organizations, some of which were communist-run "labor" unions.

The difference between law and customs is that customs are far more powerful, as they endure within a given culture. If one was to change the customs of a city, he could also change the laws. Pinkerton did this. At their offices in Mid-Wilshire, I came to learn the investigations boss was retired from LAPD Organized Crime Intelligence. The woman I'd spoken was efficient, pointed, and mid-forties. The overall boss was another woman, a bit younger than the woman on the phone, and very capable, with exceedingly high standards, I'd soon find out.

The Pinkerton Agency has at all times operated secretly, and as part of indoctrination in the service, they directed me to sign a nondisclosure form. Out of loyalty to the service, to my profession, and to the clients who have every right of secrecy, I'll address my work in that organization only in general terms.

The Pinkerton people called me in to the interview for a specific project, at a public agency. I handed in my resume, filled out an application, and found myself ushered into the office of the retired LAPD detective. There sat Russ Mancini, iron-haired and perfunctory. The younger boss and Russ looked my papers over and conducted the interview. There was nothing conclusive to our meeting, come the end. As I left, the woman I spoke first with on the phone instructed, "We may be in touch. Do not abrogate the agreement you signed, as we shall likely hear of it."

A week later, she called me and shared that the boss didn't think I was right for the assignment, but then added, "We may have something for you in the near term though. Do you have a narrative of anything you've worked on that I could show as an example of your work?"

I did, and using the secret methods of communication insisted upon by the Pinkertons, I sent it to their Mid-Wilshire office for her attention. This interaction occurred long before the internet's common use outside of academic and defense organizations. The Pinkertons employed a means of analog secrecy in communications, which was simple. I'll not reveal these secret methods, as it would be a needless exposition which could cost an operative's life.

My exemplar was a five-page report, executed by myself, on a device that was state of the art at that time, an IBM electric typewriter.

My report described measures I'd taken to identify and locate a real estate swindler for the Bondsman. I asked him if I could use his fancy typing machine, and if I could describe in narrative an investigation he'd put me on. He had no objection.

There was no way I could describe or identify anything I'd done in army counterintelligence, an organization that operated along lines similar to the Pinkertons, also to which I owe my silence. Like a report in counterintelligence, I wrote the report in the third person, past tense—a style of writing calculated to remove ambiguities, make the facts plain, and remove the investigator from the action in the investigative narrative.

I described what was known of the subject, his common Spanish name, last known habituation, former place of business, and why he was sought. Each lead was directly addressed in its own paragraph, including a summary of what was learned of the subject's whereabouts, activities, and status, and from what source or witness the information was gathered.

A week after receiving the exemplar, the woman from Pinkerton rang me up at Greater California Financial Services, by prearranged code, and asked that I come to the office in Mid-Wilshire during evening hours.

"The boss was impressed with your ability to detail aspects of the investigation you conducted and has elected to engage you as an operative," I was told. She went on to train me in accounting for case hours worked, expenses, and issued me an ID card and a pager. I did not yet have a permit to carry a gun. Next came the standard indoctrination homework, and they subjected me to the same background investigation and psychological screening I might expect going to work for LAPD. The Pinkertons resembled the realm of counterintelligence, but because the organization operates at a profit, they're very hard-nosed about billing. Everything gets documented.

One of the skills I picked up in counterintelligence was report writing. The standard was the third-person, past-tense report, which it turns out Allan Pinkerton himself first insisted upon. Army counterintelligence adopted this method around World War I. This type of written narrative brings the facts to the fore and reduces the author to the background.

At the time I could type thirty-five words a minute on a manual typewriter with four fingers using the Columbus Method: explore *and* land. I came in as a Pinkerton already knowing how to do surveillance. My skills also included the whole scale of interviewing: elicitation, interview, interrogate, tactically debrief. Add to this background investigations, and now missing persons, commercial fraud, and similar tradecraft.

I knew the cursory elements of technical surveillance countermeasures of looking for bugs and hidden cameras. I knew how to handle myself physically. I hadn't had my ass kicked since the eighth grade, and nobody was going to do it then…or today, for that matter.

As I'd done a fair amount of surveillance by foot, train, bus, and auto in the army, my first assignments involved physical surveillance with detailed report writing.

The work began with surveillance for theft, for diversion of cargo, and other commercial goods. Sometimes I sat on surveillance to establish the identity of an *unsub* (unknown subject) making threats, or a person involved in activity that posed a threat to a client.

An example of surveillance for theft might involve patronizing a saloon, owned or managed by a client. Once in the establishment, I would find a seat where I could study what gets entered into the cash register. Under the pretense of being any other after-work drunk, this sort of detail can go two to four hours. I'd memorize my drink transactions, make small talk with drunks, and fend off women, all while watching the bartender steal or not steal.

How does a barman steal? He uses a system, whereby he rings up three of four drinks on an order, usually "well" drinks, meaning a generic brand of booze, which isn't accounted for so tightly as compared to something more desirable to the liver. He might make a tick mark on a scratch sheet by the register for each well drink not rung up, all of which will be charged in the same amount. Simple math toward the end of the evening, and the thief knows how much scratch to palm from the till. Surveillance cameras are great but were rare in those days. Also, a camera cannot catch every nuance or detail.

Another way a bartender might steal is by pouring the booze heavy, which can lead to the drunks tipping more. Sometimes a regular customer or two might even be in on the theft. In a bar with regulated pouring, such as an anonymous lounge in an airport concourse, the barmaid might sneak in her own neutral spirits, grain alcohol, and have a syphon or bladder with which to discreetly enrich the cocktails—all to get those larger tips.

My reports were expected to be accurate as to time, drinks poured, amount seen on the register display, and if possible, amount tendered and change returned. To up my investigation, I might buy a round for a couple, to see if each drink is accounted for in the register display and accurately reflected in my change.

The more thorough a report is, and accurate, the less likely the eventuality is that the agent is called to testify at a labor board proceeding after a thief gets fired. Are these thieves prosecuted for embezzlement? For grand theft? Almost never. In these matters, a small business can go broke, and the bottom line of a publicly traded corporation can be badly dented—absent the work of a knowing private detective.

Usually, management lets their staff know that they'll be checked up on by either an operative like I was or an audit by a manager. That's where the boss comes in, middle of the shift, pulls the drawer and register tape to see if there is a difference between what is reported on the tape and what is in the machine. If there is "extra" money in the register, management knows the barman hasn't been making mistakes in favor of the house: He was stealing and was audited before he could complete the act.

Within our offices was an "inside man," a master of what is called *pretext work*, obscure and public data, methods for employing and detecting surveillance, who had tentacles into public agencies, private companies, and records units of every court. He later left detective work and turned his skills as an agent to trading equities. I consider him, and two field men, acerbic—skilled surveillants who'd attended school together, among the best the Pinkertons employed.

Injuries? Disabilities? These subjects, or *claimants* in the vernacular, are often placed under surveillance. *Res ipsa loquitor*, the notion is that there is negligence in an accident. There are bland, barely effective outfits that call themselves "surveillance" companies, and as they charge very little in fees to insurance and claims-management companies, they're the adjuster's fondest dream. Their operatives are paid little above minimum wage, are barely trained, and usually move on shortly to other employment. What was initially a bargain for the insurance adjuster often blows up when they cannot find their former operative two or three years later to offer sworn testimony on the footage, photography, and context of the investigation.

In instances where an individual actively threatens a client after an unsub was identified, we placed them under physical surveillance by myself or other operatives of the Pinkerton Agency, both men and women. I worked alongside two powerhouse agents, both young women: one Irish, with a bent for literature; and another vivacious, French. These two were armed with brains, beauty, and bullets.

Eventually my time came to be placed undercover. But, again, this was secret. My reports had to be securely and regularly sent, and I always had emergency communications methods for getting important information back to the office, or for requesting support in a matter. Careful and thorough work was necessary, as well as secure, secret delivery of our reports.

During this time, I kept two nights per week as a bartender at a place in Pasadena. The pay telephone was a convenient way to make and receive anonymous calls. There was no caller ID, and things were rather opaque in all matters of communication.

In my work at Greater California Financial Services, I'd learned about commercial data, reverse phone directories, credit reports, and how to use the post office to run some leads. The Secretary of State and Board of Equalization were a wealth of intelligence on companies and businessmen.

Earlier work in counterintelligence involved background investigations quite necessarily, and I'd long experience in vetting a man or woman for identity, criminal wrongdoing, foreign loyalties, lawsuits, indebtedness, and moral turpitude.

As a Pinkerton operative, I commenced to establishing a network of informants, of resources, and of data, which I am still using decades later. This is best business practice in my profession.

Much of the work as a Pinkerton was so secret that we did not know the identity of our clientele, or what else might be going on in the case. Sometimes this compartmentalization protected the interests of the client, and at other times it tested our operational effectiveness and organization as detectives.

There is not so much romantic or thrilling about the details of some of this work, as often I found myself in a rough neighborhood, pissing in a bottle and passing hours, an entire day, into an evening with nothing occurring—then a sudden rush of action when the subject went mobile. But for a field agent, surveillance is where a guy like me made his bones (industry vernacular for bona fides). An operative who can't do surveillance, with minimal instructions and minimal support has only peripheral value in operations. Usually, these capers came with almost no warning order. A page would come in from the chief of investigations, and twenty minutes later, I'd roll out, meet up with another operative at a rally point out of sight of the objective, and using what information existed, we'd make an operational plan and check in by telephone every few hours.

A client never wishes to know that operatives have lost the Subject, even for an hour, as often happens. Even with vast resource surveillance, with multiple autos and second operatives in one or more vehicles, taking advantage of carpool lanes, a Subject can be lost. A tracking sensor? In the 1980s, the technology existed, but those trackers were expensive and unreliable. Use of such technology now has been rigidly governed by privacy laws.

One of my many standard details involved placing men under surveillance at Santa Anita Park, and at another called Hollywood Park. The men we watched operated as known loan sharks, bookmakers, and flimflams who presented themselves as touts with claims of race knowledge in for a share of the winnings. Charles Bukowski—the famous poet, novelist, noted drinker, and sports fan—was often in our operating area at Santa Anita. When Bukowski became wise to me being a Pinkerton agent, he would shadow me, grumbling about fixed races, and demanding whatever inside information I might possess. On one particularly irritating day, I picked up a tout sheet from the newsstand, advertising the expert racing picks of a handicapper who called himself the Duke.

In the vicinity of the betting counter, I let the miserable satyr see me making crib notes next to the touts of four or five races, check my watch, look at my pager, weigh my balls, and check my watch again. I then absentmindedly allowed the marked tout sheet to flutter to the cement flooring, to nestle in with sports pages, cigar butts, and abandoned hope. In the mirror I could see Bukowski retrieve the sheet, compare it to his racing form, and off he sauntered to the counter to make his bets.

That Charles Bukowski won money in three of the races meant I could hardly rid myself of him after my prank. As I recall, the long-shot horse that Bukowski bet the bank on was gifted with the unlikely name "Carol's Beaver." Lesson learned. One day, I was called into the office to organize a report from notes and logs in a complex investigation. The staff member I worked with accidentally handed me the administrative file. When I opened that file, I observed that Pinkerton was billing my time to a corporate client at a rate more than ten times my hourly pay.

When the day was over, this kept returning to my thoughts. I knew better than to resent it. This is how business works: The medium pay goes to managers, big pay to executives, and dividends to stockholders. But it did make me realize that I could be billing corporate clients at an identical rate, or even more.

How would I get clients? I was in my twenties, had little business education, despite whatever tactical skill and tradecraft I'd mastered.

Over the weekend, I ruminated on the idea further and even tested it with my father. Norman didn't think much of Pinkertons

Service, or their services. When I enlisted in the military, my father reconciled himself to my fate, but when I started working for the Pinkerton Service, he told me, "You're wasting your time *and* Pinkerton's will never pay you anything. That's a union-busting organization. How could you possibly work for those assholes?" A creature of the Great Depression—despite his family's established, elite origins—he considered himself a working man, and Pinkerton had once counterorganized, spied upon, and waged violence against labor unions. He took a dim view of this, despite the certainty that in his own lifetime, some labor unions were little more than adjuncts of La Cosa Nostra, the Mafia, while others engaged in Marxist terrorism as a means of organization.

With the violence he'd seen in the Korean War and his tenure in journalism at the *Little Rock Gazette*, the *NAACP Newspaper*, *The New York Times*, and *Terre Haute Tribune Star*, Norman's fondest hope for me was that I'd one day be an engineer. His dream was doomed from the start as I couldn't master abstract mathematics.

In my first week undercover, I got a page while at work, from my father. When I rang him on a payphone, he told me of an article in *The Los Angeles Herald Examiner* about the vast need for private investigators in Los Angeles. The business section carried an article about how Los Angeles private investigators often make more than $100,000 a year, and that was in 1989.

"So, you now approve of the idea?" I asked.

He not only changed his tune about my job prospects when he found out how much private detectives earned in California, but he also said something that would be a bit of a gift to me. A subtle approval, you could say, but also something *more*, when he commented, "I think you're on to something, son. I think we should probably become business partners."

I was an able hand as a Pinkerton, but alcohol was a problem. A booze-related incident would spell the end of my time with that storied agency. About twenty of the US and Canadian Pinkerton agents descended upon Washington, DC, to learn some sensitive training involving military cargo. Pinkerton had a contract to observe private firms hauling ammunition, missiles, bombs, other weapons around the country, with our work geared toward making sure those haulers complied with the government regulations. As agents, the training included pulling trucks over and inspecting the vehicle and cargo.

I stayed dry all week. Zero drinking. But then, to celebrate, because I maxed the test and scored 100 percent on the closing examination, I accompanied my fellow agents into Old Town Alexandria, and the drinking started. My last conscious thought that night was, *This woman is gorgeous*. A Pinkerton agent from a Midwestern office, her behavior was questionable, and suggestive, and I was there for it with some suggestions of my own. I'd consumed far too much alcohol to harbor a shred of good judgment, and before long we found ourselves back at my room with the evening appearing to be heating up.

Out of nowhere, she shifted gears, and she started asking me questions, the uncomfortable sort of questions. Not questions about what might occur with clothing off, but my old line of work: counterintelligence.

I'm thoroughly drunk, not using good judgment, and every alarm bell you can think of went off inside my head. Right then and there I decided, *This woman is a KGB agent*.

An insane thought in retrospect. Outrageous, my inebriate thinking. But that ended the night for me. I invited her to leave my hotel room, and when she wouldn't, I called security.

The next morning, before I could reach out to my supervisor to explain the situation, she'd contacted her own. I found myself suspended and reporting to the office of my boss, Russ Mancini. The boss all but repeated what my last operations officer said to me in counterintelligence. "Nils," he said, "You're damn good at what you do. But your ego isn't your amigo." Then his tone shifted, and with a note of both care and concern, he said, "You've got to do something about the bottle."

While Mancini's assertion was right about my boozing, it would take more than a pearl of wisdom from the old OC detective to quelch my devilish relationship with a good, or even a bad, cocktail.

What was certain was that my fondness for the bottle was becoming more of a liability.

What it would take would be an unexpected punch to a heart I didn't even know I had. A loss that would at first push me deeper into the bottle but ultimately breed some sense and purpose into my life. If I didn't die grieving and fighting my own devils, I could start fighting for those who needed someone with my abilities.

CHAPTER

8

BACKUP

Three days after Mancini suggested I quit drinking, my father died. It took me a year to disenfuck myself from the bottle. I could go a week dry and drink for three days straight. I didn't get better in that year. There were some days that I needed a beer just to get across the room for a beer. I didn't learn anything to help me moderate or change how I felt. His loss combined with the alcohol made me crazy. Booze had lost its magic—the ability to change how I felt. Yet I still tried, valiantly, to bring it under control.

Coming out of a blackout, I finally had a moment of clarity, and I begged God—although I didn't believe in God anymore at that point. And in that moment of desperation, I cried out, "God, if you really exist, please help me to make it through this day without a drink."

And the God I didn't believe in pulled the thing out of me that was obsessed with alcohol. I still wanted to drink, but the obsession departed, and I haven't had a drink, ever, since then. I've wanted to drink, but the burning, uncontrolled obsession has never returned, contemporaneous with the desire. I realized then I had to make something of myself, strap my life back together. I'd a highly refined skill set, which seemed almost useless in civil society. That was when I said screw it, I'll become the lawyer my mother always wanted. Go to law school. Become an attorney, a successful one, like her.

That's why I started in on the thinking of, well, what am I going to do to pay for law school? I applied for a job with a detective agency in Pasadena that had about eight or nine full-time employees, doing mostly insurance work, disability, and accident claims. The owner was prim and professional, and she'd been on the cover of *Los Angeles Magazine* for being a successful female entrepreneur in a man's world.

A powerhouse of a woman, she looked my resume over and said to me, "Let me think on this."

A few days passed by, and I didn't hear anything. Two weeks. Nothing. On the third week I thought, *Fuck it. I'll call.* I'd started back picking up the bail jumpers and being a bouncer at a coffee dive. I'd been sober for months.

I called her, and when I got her on the phone, she asked, "What can I do for you?"

I replied with all the confidence a fool could muster. "Well, I want to know when I can go to work."

She paused a moment and then hit me with, "Sir, I would not send you across the road with five dollars for a bag of groceries. You have the worst reputation as a drunk that I have ever heard, and I'll ask you to never contact me again."

She wasn't wrong. But I burned with resentment, tinted with regret.

I knew I'd been a complete fuckup, but I felt like a changed man. I entertained the idea of going back in the army, but I couldn't see a way of getting through law school while enlisted in the military. I looked over everything, thought about what my father said about starting my own business, and I applied for a private detective's license.

A year from the day I sent the application package, I received my license.

Though I would never be afforded the opportunity to have my father for a partner, that simple suggestion was more than a nice thought. He left me something powerful to ruminate on for the rest of my career: a rare nod of approval.

Some nights, when I'm out on a case, riding solo, I'm armed up, carrying my 1911 or a .357, and I'm driving the dark streets or a rural highway, listening to the radio, or maybe not, I can *feel* him there. As if he exists, just beyond my peripheral vision. I can almost hear him speaking to me, "Slow down a little bit. Keep your eyes open." Or he might remind me, "This guy you're going after could be pretty bad, son. Mind your six."

I'm sure it's my imagination, but that's the essence of spirituality. Believe in the possibility, and to know, then to try the idea on, before arriving at peace with my father. I never worked a case with my dad, but every once in a while, I hear and feel him. His spirit is often the only backup I have, or need, and that is a beautiful thing. He and my mother now lie, forever, in an exalted state of grace. Perfect parents at last. This is all that is left of them.

CHAPTER

9

FIRST CLIENT

My very first "private job" was a one-off, which fell upon me when I was still a sergeant in the army. I had finished my second tour of Korea and was at loose ends, studying beer, whiskey, and a barmaid at Peter Monahan's on Lake Avenue.

Peter had purchased a cop bar, called the Bayou, and made it into what passed for an Irish pub. It was still a cop bar, and there were usually lonesome, thirty-something secretarial types who didn't mind a younger man getting up them. Whiskey was ever able.

I was having no luck with the barmaid, and was counting my change when a man I knew only as Tom, a sheriff's detective, looked over to me and asked, "You want to make a couple of C-notes for a job, man?"

I wanted. The matter involved me showing up the next night, sober, at six, and ready for work. Tom was there, already a bit juiced, and handed me keys to his department Plymouth K car. It was beige, like county government. "You drive. Get us to the Long Beach Freeway gone south, man." He swigged from a flask, and I motored us south.

En route to the "job," Tom told me of the 173rd Airborne Brigade in Vietnam. Tom was stocky and hard, with a lantern jaw and receding hairline. His necktie was always loose, because his neck was too big for his shirt. He'd been on the sheriff's department after that—first the jails, then the streets, and now…major crimes.

Major crimes. Maybe we were going to *do* a major crime, and a sheriff's detective needed a man from a scout platoon to get it done. He had another pull off his bottle, and when I asked him what we were going to do, he replied, "It's a secret."

We landed off the Long Beach Freeway and the sun sunk into the Pacific, in a nice stretch called Bixby Knolls. At the curb, two hundred meters off a large apartment development, Tom said what I already knew: "Never roll right up on your objective, kid. Get close and make the scene on foot." He was brightening up and checked his piece, which was a magnum revolver. I was armed only with me.

"When you get up to the phone console in the vestibule, ring 7-0-7, and tell him you were sent by Stevie." Tom was ready, and my adrenaline started to flow. This was like chambering a round at Guard Post 128, to enter the DMZ on patrol. I was twenty-one and this was already a familiar, comforting jolt. I took point coming off the elevator.

"No matter what happens, who happens, you don't let no one get on my back, man," were Tom's murmured instructions just short of the door. If he was still loaded, the adrenaline seemed to have overridden it. I planted my feet and knocked the door. I could see the fisheye of the security port go dark as someone peeked out, checking to see who may have arrived.

The moment the door cracked, Tom was shouldering it open, taking short, choppy steps as a linebacker would to move a guard aside and make a tackle. Within the apartment was a fat, large man my own age, wearing a Hawaiian shirt, gold chain, and the look of unbridled horror. Tom brought his gun up and struck the fat man across the side of the head, and he fell to his knees and elbows.

"Keep 'im down, man." Tom cleared the rest of the apartment and came out of the bedroom with a cigar box while the fat man wailed. "Get him in a headlock!" Tom directed, and with feet planted, I encircled his neck with my right, hauling his bulk to his knees. "I told you I'd be back, didn't I, motherfucker?"

The fat man choked and wailed. Tom cracked him over the head, again, with the revolver, and now shoved the gun past his teeth, into his wetted, bleeding mouth. "You just make me come back again, me an' my buddy here is going to make you a coroner's case, savvy?"

Fat Man pled agreement around the blued steel-gun barrel.

We left him in a heap, on his floor, the white powder contents of the cigar boxed emptied upon him.

"Gimme the keys," Tom said, shoving two hundred-dollar bills into my shirt pocket. I moved the money to my jeans and got in the passenger side while Tom drove. We took the bridge over to San Pedro, and then the Harbor Freeway, north, a different route, just like leaving a heavy objective.

Halfway over the Vincent Thomas Bridge, I asked Tom, "What's that guy's problem?"

Tom handed me the flask—it was a quarter full—and lit a smoke. "Can't tell you, man. But this is what you could know." He drove a minute, thinking what to tell me. "That fat motherfucker won't ever, never ever sell no more cocaine to (insert name of dead politician)'s niece again. You feel me? You like that?" He was still riffing on the adrenaline, and so was I. The flask went out the window, and I renewed my failed attempt at the barmaid, with five more days to report at Fort Benning.

My first private case. How's that for experience? The next time I saw Tom Hageboeck, he was tossing Eddie Murphy through a plate glass window in a bit part as a bodyguard in *Beverly Hills Cop*. And the Fat Man? Next time I met the Fat Man, he was on a State Parole Board and under a different type of investigation. That's our Golden State. The Americans "stole" it from the Mexicans; the Mexicans absconded with California from the King of Spain; the Spanish had it from the American Indians; and the American Indians took it from God himself. Now the Kool Kids are throwing paradise away, in the name of saving it all.

Private Jobs. Private. Easy work. Anyone can do it.

At the end of the kinetic, analog age, when the WWII generation were retiring, metropolitan Los Angeles loomed before me, a tough proposition for a younger man to contemplate opening a professional practice, especially one as demanding, vice-prone, and hazardous as a detective service.

I was twenty-nine years old and had already been a soldier, a contractor, a bail enforcement agent, and a Pinkerton. That summer of June 1992, with a crisp new State of California issued private detective's license in hand, I didn't have a clue what was to come. I had plenty of experience, working the world over, but not a single client.

There I sat with that piece of paper saying I was a private detective, but I started at zero. I couldn't even afford a phone when I first got my license. I had a pager and a calling card. I drove a twenty-year-old automobile that leaked oil. I also had a bad attitude in a lot of ways, but I knew that there was only one direction: up. It has been said that there's always room at the top, and the top was where I intended to land.

The first time someone hired under my own aegis, licensed, and ready to start my first investigation, I found myself on the phone with a lawyer. He needed me to find someone who had fled the scene of an accident and left behind pieces of his car—a hit-and-run with a badly injured victim. The attorney asked, flat out, "What are you going to charge me for this?"

I'd already set an hourly rate in my mind that seemed like kind of a premium to me, but I lacked the confidence to spell it out. I didn't want to lose the work.

"Uh," I began, hesitating with my brain swirling, "I'm going to charge you a day of work, eight hours."

The momentary silence over the phone could have been a second or an hour. Then he asked, "What can you guarantee me for those eight hours?"

My confidence restored, I thought for less than a half a second. "Sir," I replied, "I'm guaranteeing you that I'm experienced enough that I think I can get the job done. I can't promise you anything beyond that. But I'm willing to take the case on if you want me to work it."

And then, without hesitating, he said the magic words, "Do it."

So began my first case. I started with some simple clues from the accident and took them and ran with it. I identified the guy based on the license plate still attached to the mangled front bumper left at the scene. After a record search, I located the address of the vehicle's owner, and within an hour, knocked on the man's door. The man stood in the entry way reeking of booze. I could recognize a terrible hangover when I saw one. Six hours after the accident, and the man was still drunk.

After I confirmed he owned the vehicle, he asked, "What's the problem? Is something wrong?"

"Yeah, something is wrong," I replied. "That woman that you hit last night is very badly injured. And she's actually being treated over at the hospital where you *used to* work."

This hit him like a right cross to the chin. "What do you mean 'used to'?" he asked.

"Where you used to work," I said.

I recorded a statement from the poor bastard while he sat weeping, choking down a can of beer, and confessing to me he's an alcoholic.

While booze fail was something I could identify with, my job was to protect a client. I took his recorded statement back to my office and transcribed the confession, incorporating this into a report. Then I faxed that document off to the attorney.

Case solved. But would I get paid?

Later that day, I sat back at my office, staring at the invoice I was about to submit, and I thought, *Damn, that's a lot of money.* I knew this would be the real test. Was this guy really going to pay me? I took a deep breath and faxed the invoice over. I winced. No one was going to pay me to do this work.

Twenty minutes later, my phone rang. I recognized the voice on the other end as my first client's secretary.

"Mr. Testa," she began, "wants you to come over to his office and pick the chequue up *before* you decide to bill him more." I brought the tape recording to him, picked up the chequue, and kept him as a client from that day until the day he died—*twelve* years later.

CHAPTER

10

FALLING UPWARD

Within two weeks of hanging up my own private detective shingle, I was earning my way. But it took a few years before I went past living "from hand to mouth." Any PI in Los Angeles will say the business is feast or famine, with days and weeks with little new business, then a rush of cases. The money? It is good enough to have a bit of freedom, which is sometimes just the ability to turn down a case, refer it to an hombre just starting out. I love the work.

In some cases, I found myself amidst the dumbest, simplest investigations you could imagine: Find a certain witness and interview him. Find this witness, interview her, and serve her with a trial subpoena. Or perhaps a trucking outfit is missing a trailer from their inventory and think an ex-employee took it. They would give me an $800 budget at $50 an hour and say, "Find the trailer." Some clients would want me to bounty hunt, meaning they're not going to pay unless I find the person or object. Those cases I refused and still do. That scenario means I would be stumbling over three other operators; all offered the same deal by the same client. It also means that I'm working for a client who views me as a cutout for the next mec he burns. In analyzing this kind of proposition, I've determined that the client is always a *sharper*—withholding key information about his own dirty hands in the matter and wanting me to take on more risk than is commensurate with the pay.

Within three months I found myself making nearly $1,200 a week. Not terrible money in 1992. This was a living I could get by on, and the business was growing. But I didn't do it for the money. I had to support myself, and the money was good, but it was the hunt, the pursuit, that held me and that just got better and better. Wealth can be defined as having time and funds, simultaneously. Its synonym is *freedom*.

As my book of business grew wings, I signed up for the Rio Hondo Police Academy, which is a high-stress academy, training to, and above, the State Peace Officers Standards of Training (POST) Commission. I learned more of the street skills I'd need, and made meaningful, lasting connections with law enforcement, but more importantly, found my mind a bit more focused.

In 1989, an actress named Rebecca Schaeffer was murdered by a stalker, a man who had obtained her address by engaging a man ostensibly in my line, who used DMV records to identify her address for the killer.

Within this profession, men and women like me owe the public a duty of care. Even the people I investigate are owed that duty. Schaeffer's murder cast ripples through the pond.

The next event, the Rodney King Riots, colored the business climate as well as the eroding culture of metropolitan Los Angeles.

During those riots, I spent three straight days and nights protecting property in the Los Angeles garment district. Rioters and looters inflicted enormous damage to business, with small, family-owned operations bearing most of the burden. This riot was needless and seemingly urged on by political and media voices.

City government did the bare minimum while citizens were murdered, robbed, assaulted, looted, their property burned. The *Los Angeles Weekly* was gleeful in its coverage of the mayhem, with innocent people the primary target for the rage emanating from criminal elements in the Black and Latino communities. Add to this the malpractice of Los Angeles city government.

The message was very clear to business and property owners: In the event of an insurrection, your rights and ownership mean nothing compared to our need to appease the criminal class in the city of our creation.

This was a very busy time for me.

I kept saying to myself, *Law school was still in the offing*, so I signed up for city college. I first took Criminal Investigation, English, and Business Law. It turned out that Business Law would probably be the single most important civilian-training course I ever took. Business Law starts with the US Constitution, detailing the finer points of contracts, bailments, guarantees, commercial fraud, truth in advertising, and the Uniform Commercial Code. Boring minutia, like promissory estoppel, justified reliance, fraud versus mere puffery…and intricacies of business and civil-legal maneuverings most will never know or understand. I took a year of those courses, working toward a baccalaureate, so I could land myself into law school. I figured I'd take an LSAT and see the result. The typical strategy in taking this examination is to enroll in a course that teaches an applicant how to dope the test. This is vitally important, as law schools are selective, wanting exemplary undergraduate grades and a high LSAT score.

Further, an applicant's LSAT scores are averaged, should he take the exam more than once. I looked over the study guide handed out by the State Bar of California, and decided to take the LSAT cold, with no preparation other than a good night of sleep and some black coffee.

I did better than most of the people I took the exam with, despite the fact most of them had taken prep courses and were all fresh, bright-eyed undergrads with degrees already secured toward an eventual *juris doctor*.

I attended my classes but could feel myself losing interest. My competition were recent undergrads, all enrolled in the preparatory courses, with long years of good study habits and less a history of bashing themselves with booze, getting hit over the head, or shot at. My reasoning for pondering dropping out included the certainty that I had never been a great student, and if I lacked the ability to gut law school, I shouldn't waste my time (or theirs).

For comparison, I'd scored very well in the foreign service's examinations, finishing in the top 1 percent. I lacked only a college degree to further damage America's standing abroad.

The results of the LSAT were that I scored higher than 86 percent of the people I took it with, which was an adequate score. Adequate meant I'd have to enjoy perfect grades in my baccalaureate studies in order to gain admission to a decent law school.

Then in the middle of the night in Orange County, I was sitting in the darkness, my eyes locked on the driver's side mirror, surveilling a pervert, a suspected rapist. In that moment two things occurred to me as I hunkered down low, my head level with the dash in a beater, a Mazda pickup truck that I couldn't even get insured.

The first flash of realization as I observed the man sneaking into the bushes and peering into the window of a woman's home was that the guy wasn't just my suspect, but likely a serial predator.

And with the recognition that I'd broken a client's case and uncovered a dangerous rapist was when I thought to myself, *This detective shit is pretty damn good work. Important work. Fuck it, I'm going to do this.*

Right then and there I made the decision to withdraw from college, my degrees forgotten. I knew then that I wasn't going to be a lawyer. My mother would be enraged, then disappointed when I dropped out, but she was always pissed off and disappointed in me about something.

In this life and line of work, I did manage to redeem myself, a bit, with my mother. My sister Louise, with a lifetime of drug addiction, abandoned a newborn at Los Angeles County Hospital. My wife was fearful as hell, but for good cause. Our social welfare system is corrupt and fractured.

Her greatest fear was taking this baby in, raising him, only to have him stripped from our home by a capricious judge on the recommendation of a naive social worker. My wife had experience in these things, being a county employee, and later a social worker. The most daunting part of the job, first week, was the detox from narcotics. County Medical put addicted infants on a low dose of methadone to make them manageable. He was given a last dose on the morning of discharge and was handed, screaming, to us.

The detox is physically painful—pain a child cannot understand. When he wasn't sleeping, he was miserable, and we got no rest. On the sixth day, I went afield on a case, and some hours out, my wife rang me. "I can't take it. Really need a break."

When I got home, it was 106 degrees, and the baby was wailing in a sodden diaper. "Take the day off…" I started to say, but she was already gone. I rocked him, changed his loaded pants, and fished a fresh, cold boob from the refrigerator. Dodgers baseball was on TV, and I turned a fan on us and fed him. He went to sleep on my lap, the volume of the TV extinguished.

Some innings later, I heard a gurgling noise, looked down, and saw he was awake—for the first time without hollering his discontent. He smiled up at me, and I saw the face of my long-dead father. I took this as a sign from God, and from that day to this one, I have never doubted His providence.

When my wife and I took this child in, my mother, in her sixties, took his four-year-old brother in and made great sacrifices for that boy.

Statistically, these guys—born to an addict mother at County Hospital, already addicted—are supposed to fail at school, supposed to gravitate toward criminality, are likely to have learning disabilities. It's all the worst a man could imagine.

As I write these pages, one is a combat medic in a cavalry outfit, whose life goal is to study cardiothoracic surgery. This boy finished school, never came home drunk, and has always been unstinting to this family. The other had some ups and downs, but enrolled in college, and on a January night in 2025, rescued my sister Alice and her husband from the Eaton fire which wiped out Altadena. This boy, tattoos and all, wants to be the lawyer I could not be.

"There are some things that are the exclusive Province of God…." said Carl Jung.

CHAPTER

11

RUNNING AND GUNNING

One of the things cops are accustomed to is quick backup, hopefully with a single help call over the radio. I'm usually solo, and must be very deliberate, tactically, as a result. If I get in over my head, it's all on me. Many private operators, here and abroad, have been killed in the pursuit of a man or men. Once, long ago, I was checking my gear—shotgun and 1911—to take up pursuit of a cartel heroin dealer, lamister from a bail bondsman. He was supposed to be at an address in Antelope Valley, per a shaky informant. Just as I was going to saddle up, my phone rang. At the other end of things was Tom Lange, justifiably famous for arresting O.J. Simpson on a double homicide. Lange was retired and working an insurance desk.

He was introduced to me by his former partner, Bob Souza. We'd some things cooking. "What are you up to, Nils?" Lange ventured.

I told him of the heroin man and my idea to take down a door in Lancaster, get him in irons.

Lange paused at the other end of the line. "Hold up. I'll join you. This. This is something you shouldn't do on your lonesome." Here was a kind offer. Lange had done a couple of tours of Vietnam, as a marine grunt in 1/9 (First Battalion; Ninth Marines), a.k.a. the Walking Dead. He'd been a patrol man, then homicide specialist at LAPD. Tom had many dangerous capers under his gun belt.

I'd go it alone. He was ace—the best—and I was flattered for the offer. But if shit went heavy, he could lose his thing at the insurance company. If he got killed, how could I face his family? If I got gunned down, I'd deal with it my own way, probably face down. As much as I valued Tom's sincere offer, I couldn't accept. I went afield that night, then again the next, but never got the heroin man. Later I heard he was retired by his employers, a liability in the dope trade. It was an October evening, still in the late 1980s. The college student son of the bondsman had called me, needing help. He had to protect the interests of his family's bonding agency. A man had been bailed out, on drug charges, only to miss a whole series of court appearances. The bail would be forfeit if he wasn't found and surrendered to the county jail.

Frank went to West Covina's police to let them know we had him cornered, and that we'd be taking the fugitive into custody. Our quarry was a young Black man, whose trade and cause was field sports. He was a recognized sprinter and hurdler named Carl. As of that night, we'd learned from the young woman who'd paid the bail premium with her father's credit card that Carl was hunkered down in the office of an auto wrecking yard, close to the San Bernardino Freeway, sleeping on a pallet. While Frank was trying to contact the watch commander, I kept watch on the wrecking yard. The sun was long set, and between a bright moon and streetlights, I could see a bit of the yard through the slats of a cyclone fence. It had plastic strips threaded through the steel weave, obscuring much of the operation from street view. A light had come on in the office of the shop, and I could see movement. Human movement.

A few minutes later, I heard footfall and the breathing of a man. "What do you need?" came his voice from the other side of the opaque fence.

"Hello, Carl. I've got a good idea for you, man," I responded.

"Idea?" he blurted out.

"Put your hands atop the fence, and do not move. I've got a shotgun, and I'd hate to shoot you, shoot your legs, Carl."

"Say what?!" he breathed.

"It's done, man. Give it up. This is your chance to start over. No more running. You get shot, that's the end of it—everything. Hands on top of the fence. *Now*!"

And his hands were at the top. I could hear him, smell him and the fear in his chest that radiated across. I clicked a cuff on one wrist, and the other around the top pole of the fence.

Climbing up, I hauled him over, still cuffed. He was all bone, muscle, and sweat. His eyes were wide open, but he never noticed I was without my shotgun. It was only me.

Frank was exiting the police station when I walked up with Carl, now cuffed. I sat in the back seat with our man while Frank motored into downtown, so we could surrender him at inmate reception and get the surrender signed by a deputy. "Anything you don't want them seeing when they inventory your property, Carl?"

He had a pipe and a rock, which I tossed from the first street bridge as we closed in on the jail. He wept. This man was in the jaws of a monster. The cocaine epidemic was in full burn, and he'd erased much of himself. Frank paid me and dropped me off at a bar so I could erase some of myself. This was when I was still lost in the bottle.

In 1873, the US Supreme Court, in a case titled *Taylor v. Taintor*, cemented the rights of bail bondsmen to hunt down, arrest, and deliver to the courts or jails those whom they've bailed out. The way this works: Clyde Barrow gets arrested by Texas Ranger Frank Hamer. Bonnie Parker calls a bail bondsman and says, "My boyfriend has been arrested for robbery, and his bail is set at ten thousand dollars. Can you post a bond for me?"

The bondsman gets Bonnie over to sign a contract, guaranteeing the face value of the bond, and collects a nonrefundable premium for the bond equal to 10 percent of that value—in this case, $1,000. The bondsman goes over to the jail, posts the bond, and Clyde is free to go, pending his court date. If Clyde does not show up to answer the charges, his bail is forfeited, and the bondsman must make good on the amount of the bond.

If Clyde did show up, or if the case is dismissed, the bond is exonerated, and the matter disposed of. But Clyde Barrow, not to mention Bonnie Parker, is a Psychopath. And the bondsman has to hire a mec like myself to locate Clyde Barrow and bring him in. I am paid a percentage of the value of the bond by the bondsman.

Being a clever fellow with much at risk, the bondsman has a clause in the bond contract that Bonnie Parker signed, which obligates Bonnie and Clyde to ultimately be responsible for my fees, in addition to the value of the bond and the premium. It is a good deal for criminal justice and for the accused, provided Clyde has sand enough to show up and answer the charges. Before I was licensed and running my own detective agency, I was rounding up bail jumpers, mostly for a man named Frank Repetti, and later for his sons Frank Jr. and Paul—both fine men.

Frank was a World War II veteran who kept a modest office behind the Pasadena Jail and lived for his family. He was one of the few bondsmen who would extend credit in the ghetto and was well-regarded by that community as a man who'd inconvenience himself, do favors, and take on risks other bondsmen would not.

This was Frank's way of protecting his own operation. When a man (or woman) failed to appear for court, it usually only took him a phone call or two to extended family, and they'd surrender their wanted relative. His was a connection none of them wanted to lose. From Repetti, I learned how to locate men who had no credit, no driver's license, no job, and no fixed address.

"Hookers make great informants and are a lousy risk." Wisdom from a man who'd been a Pasadena police detective, only to retire early after punching the lights out of his lieutenant in the Bayou.

Called into Repetti Bonding one morning, I was to operate with a very experienced hunter of men: Archie Berry. Frank Sr. had hired Archie off a construction site in the mid-1970s, and as of this writing, Archie Berry is still in the saddle. Every bondsman in Los Angeles knows the man, and I've never seen Archie drop a case, back off, or get scared away—by anyone. A warm and friendly man to colleagues; otherwise, his heart circulates ice water.

Frank and Paul had a case involving a very interesting young woman, a hooker, and an attractive one at that. She had several men competing to be her pimp and her lover. She had been made by sheriff's homicide for solicitation of murder and had been bailed out for six figures.

Out in the wind, it came to the attention of Repetti Bonding that the deed of trust on an Altadena home, which had been used to collateralize the bond, was forged. The pimp who'd presented the collateral neither owned the house nor had permission to encumber it. The network of informants their father had established through goodwill in the ghetto had paid off, it seemed.

Would the court system see this as a problem for the pimp? Not likely. This was a liability for the bondsman. Paul Repetti was fresh out of USC with a degree in finance and had great street sense to match his brother's sense of law and business.

"I see it this way. Our hooker hasn't skipped town yet, but every dude in this area code is vying to own her. She could take a powder any minute, and if they get a hint of a setup or investigation, she will disappear immediately. Based on her perceived value as a street commodity, her ability to go underground and evade is almost unlimited," Paul reasoned.

Paul and Frank figured the pimp wouldn't let the hooker out of his sight, lest another man come along with a bigger car, better offer. He would protect his investment. Frank grinned across his battered desk within the offices at the American Legion Hall on Marengo Avenue. "We will page her pimp, telling him he has to sign the bail posting so that his girl's bail remains valid…new thing from the county jail. If he comes in here, there's a high chance he will have her with…"

It was as solid as these things get. Archie and I made a tactical plan: The Repetti's office was off a walkway, on the south side of the American Legion Hall on Marengo Avenue. It had a back room, which was dark and cavernous, directly opposite the entrance. Once both of them were in, I'd secure the door so no one could join the party once the play started. Frank and Paul were seated at their desks, facing the entry, weapons in their laps. Once we heard Frank yell, "Hands on the desk!", we were to secure the door and emerge, guns drawn. If the Repetti brothers had been forced to engage either subject with pistols, Archie and I would've had to take a fast dive to avoid crossfire. We waited at the appointed time, in darkness, armed. And within twenty minutes, we heard the booming voice of a man and the dulcet tones of a woman. Once they were seated before Paul and Frank, their escape route was cut off. We locked the door against any who might venture into to route us, or with a competing appointment.

Approaching from behind, with Archie looming over the man, the Repetti brothers drew pistols from their desks simultaneously, and Archie rested the muzzle of his pump gun on the enormous pimp's shoulder. Archie is somewhere between twenty and forty years my senior, hard as they come. He was duded up in loud 1970s polyester "cheap clothes you don't mind getting bloody in a fight" from the Salvation Army.

"I'ma tell you jus' once, here, you don't move. I'll scatter your hash all over this room." Archie grinned as the man looked up. I had my .45 leveled on the hooker, who rolled her eyes. Paul holstered his gun and moved to the side to be out of the line of any fire.

"Hands on the desk," I commanded her.

"Cedric, that deed of trust is a piece of shit, man." Frank had the file open in front of the pimp. I stood the girl up, frisked her for weapons, and cuffed her fast. Archie was still covering Cedric. "Ain't this some shit?" exclaimed the pimp, offering cash collateral to keep his girl out. Paul had anticipated this and looked to his brother, as if a bet had been made as to Cedric's next gambit.

She was attractive, and I looked at her ID. She was all of nineteen. Nineteen and as dangerous as it gets. Even though it was a brisk California January, our girl was dressed for sucking cocks on the boulevard. Hot pants, heels, tube top, hair extensions. She was a very fair-skinned Black woman with freckles and red-tinted hair, with great huge cocaine scoops for fingernails and eyelashes like Japanese fans. Men of a type would murder each other for her, and she was flattered to set it up. I dumped the contents of her purse on Paul's desk. Typical hooker items rolled out: ID, condoms, lube, pager, KFC wet-naps, lip gloss, noxious perfume, and a lighter for a crack pipe. No hand grenades, thankfully.

"No cigarettes?" Frank asked.

"Smokin' bad fo' you," she mumbled, studying the floor.

Her purse bagged, we backed out, unlocking the door while the brothers shook Cedric the Pimp down. He was in a leather coat that must've claimed the hides of five cattle, so large was his bulk. Archie drove, and I sat in the back seat of his Monte Carlo. If she minded having been laid low, this girl didn't let on. As we got on the Pasadena Freeway for the drive to Sybil Brand Institute, she finally spoke. "You know we could just get off to a motel, settle this here thing 'atween us, just take care of it, you know?"

I looked at the hooker, and she smiled at me and then addressed Archie, who'd adjusted his rearview mirror to see her in the back seat of the Chevrolet. "Maybe my partner and I haul your hoe ass to a motel, fuck you real good, and take you on to the jail anyway? You ever think of that, honey?"

"I know you would do some shit like that, okay. We could do that too." She squirmed in her seat against the handcuffs, knowing we were having none of it. Last I saw her, Archie was getting the surrender signed off on, and the hooker was getting shoved up against a cement wall by two female harness bulls from the sheriff's office. They'd toss her purse again, do a gloved examination of her often-used places, issue her jail clothes, and assign the hooker a module, pending trial.

A single man, flinty and able, armed with a sidearm, can hold off three or four with his pistol. Two can hold off twenty or more, provided neither bend. Armed with automatic rifles, a pair of trained men can stare down fifty, and so on. There are some with grave reservations about using firearms to protect themselves, to secure a scene, to keep the opposition ducking, or at least in doubt, long enough to get a fugitive under control and on his way. There are those of principle, opposed to weapons of any kind. I'm opposed to dying, so I keep myself trained and tested and have done so since I was a youth. A more objective view is that the gun is a tool, and the man is *the weapon.* Once a course of action has been chosen, to stay alive, one man or twenty must remain committed to it—even as the situation unfolds in unforeseen ways.

Back to Junior, our robbery suspect in Watts. He was bailed out of the Inglewood Jail on a $10,000 bond. The bondsman was based out of South Gate, and I'd never done business with him before. "I'm hard up against a statute, a forfeiture on this guy, have to get him into irons within five days." It wasn't a huge forfeiture, but I needed the money.

From the zip code, the charge, and the age of the defendant, I knew he was probably a gang member living in Watts. It's illegal to say so, but this was the very seat of South-Central Los Angeles. I had a certified copy of the bond, a Polaroid photo of the guy, and two addresses. One was his grandmother's house, in Norwalk, and the other was an apartment building at Ninety-Second and Avalon, where the defendant I'll call Junior was staying with his girl, two children, and a younger brother. The only informant in the case was his grandmother, who'd pledged her house for Junior's freedom.

"Junior stay up, all hours, every night, then he crash at four the morning. He runnin' the streets, selling dope, stealing from the dope man…." This was what she told me. Of course, I'd never burn his grandmother as my informant. She described a battered Nissan Z car as Junior's bronze-colored one.

Grandmother also told me that the steel security door was flimsy, could be easily pried. It was a ground-floor apartment in what turned out to be a three-story building, nestled between two other apartment buildings.

Taking the Harbor Freeway south, I landed in Watts with the rising sun. A turn around the block where Junior was supposed to be living revealed the bronze Nissan Z. The building Junior was in was tagged up with gang graffiti—nothing artistic about it. I pulled the stem from a single tire on the Nissan so Junior couldn't go mobile and went about looking for a functional pay telephone.

The neighborhood was as quiet as it was going to get, and I had to work quickly.

Five blocks east, a Korean market let me use their phone, and I got Seventy-Seventh Street LAPD on the line, then asked for the watch commander. A short minute later, Lieutenant Earl Paysinger came on the line. "What can I do for you?"

"I'm making a bail arrest over at Ninety-Second and Avalon. Defendant is—" was all I could get out.

"Get on it, boy. Don't call us. You get yourself in no trouble, hear?" was Paysinger's reply. We weren't legally required to notify the rollers where and when we were operating, but the idea is to avoid getting shot by the police when making an arrest.

"Stat." I hung up and went to work.

Parked on the sidewalk so I couldn't get boxed in, I had more sunlight to work with, and the smell of breakfast was in the air at Junior's building. I found apartment 3, jammed a tire iron in the steel security door, and pulled. It was loose, shaky, jarred, and junky, but it took my best pull to fling it open. Then, I was at the inner door, the second part of the portal after the steel security gate. The door didn't even have a knob. I stuck the tire iron in my belt, lest anyone wield it against me in what was picking up.

After I pulled him out of his apartment and I weighed my options (and counted my rounds), I got the break I was hoping for in the form of the high-pitched whining noise distinctive to Kawasaki police motorcycles when they're running full-out, at redline. I only heard the sirens as they jumped the curb in the front part of the building, with Mr. Mouth and his cohort making for the rear of the building.

Shortly after I discovered a Mexican lady had looked out her window and saw what she thought was a police detective in trouble, so she'd made a 9-1-1 call, and Seventy-Seventh Street had responded. They took Junior off my hands, and I holstered my sidearm. Two more were in custody on the sidewalk and then I met Lieutenant Paysinger in person.

"I told you, warned you, not to call, when you get in trouble!" He was mad.

"I didn't call you, but as it happens, I'm glad you could make it."

Taking Paysinger's signature on the warrant and card, I went to the Inglewood Courthouse to memorialize the fact that Junior was surrendered. It was then that I discovered that the bondsman had Junior out on a bond for $10,000, and also a bond for $30,000. I took a copy of it with me, hanging on to the surrender and making tracks for South Gate. Informing the court would wait.

Of course, the bondsman didn't want to pay the vigorish on the second bond. "I got a lot into this business, been doin' this a long time. I can make it up to you next time."

He already knew I had Junior in custody and was off the hook and out of danger. That was the hardest $500 I'd ever earned, but I learned my lesson. Repetti Bonding would never do any such thing. It was incumbent of me to examine the record before taking a job, rather than after. Like the man said, "Dying ain't much of a living."

I never worked for *that* bondsman again, and I took a fair amount of delight in learning he'd been run over and retired from the business some years after. There was a bit of temptation to visit him while in the hospital and step on his oxygen line, but I was too busy minding cases.

Well after I'd established myself as a detective, I'd get the occasional bail case from Repetti Bonding, and others. Once I got a commission from an agent in San Francisco, who'd been referred to me by former Chief of San Francisco Police Department Tom Murphy.

"I've got a cocaine cowboy lam. Don't know for certain where this guy is, but I've got some intel where he's going to be," came the call.

The bail jumper was a Mexican national, tied to a drug cartel, who'd been bailed out by a woman who styled herself his "fiancée." She was an American and had put up a deed of trust on a house to secure the bond. Things started heading south for the bondsman when he discovered the fiancée recorded a quitclaim deed on her house four hours after her cowboy, Hector, had bailed out. The property now belonged to another woman, with the tax bill being directed to a private mail drop in San Ysidro, California, mere meters from the Mexican border.

The house in question was in Stockton, San Joaquin County. Two months had passed from the recording of the deed and Hector taking wing. The amount of money at risk was enough that when I asked for a retainer, the bondsman wired it immediately. Don Moon and I made the drive to Stockton, up the San Joaquin Valley. Don was exactly a day older than me, had been both an enlisted and an officer in the marines, and could match me for size, strength, speed, and analysis of a man. I was free to act with Don aboard, as I never had to worry about him losing focus or dropping his gun. He was a stud warrior—a mec.

We watched the house in Stockton for two days, with no one coming and no one going. The mailbox was stuffed, and when I intercepted the letter carrier a couple of blocks distant, he stated, "No one picked up the mail in that house for two months. Haven't seen no one."

It was a single-story ranch house, built in the late 1950s style, in a middle-class neighborhood, mostly Hispanic. Athwart the driveway was a sliding wrought-iron gate with cinderblock corner-posts and fence encircling the home. We waited until 0300 hours, then with Don keeping watch at the end of the cul-de-sac, I vaulted the gate. The garbage cans were stuffed with clothes. The only vehicle in the garage was a motorcycle with flat tires. A light was on in the kitchen and on the porch. The power, gas, and water were all still connected in the name of Hector's fiancée.

The kitchen door had a portal for a pet. A large one, like a rottweiler, but judging by the dried-out state of the dog shit decorating her driveway, I was certain there'd be no dog. I've been luckier. Having let myself in, I saw dirty dishes on the kitchen table, mingy food stuck to them, and more in the sink. The downstairs toilet was running, and a Spanish language radio was announcing news to an empty upstairs.

The beds were unmade, and open closets announced whoever had lived in the house had departed in a hurry. The floor of the closet had carpet, and one corner was curled back. That corner covered a floor safe, the lid of which had been removed. It was empty.

"We got good information that Hector's going to be in Van Horn, Texas, in the next two weeks." We heard this from the bondsman. I didn't know the source of his information, but I was sure it wasn't the fiancée from Stockton.

With Moon asleep in the back of my car, I motored south to Pasadena, working on a plan. We didn't know what night, but within the subsequent two weeks, Cowboy Hector was going to show up, to meet a buyer of cocaine at a cantina in Van Horn, West Texas, due east of Ciudad Juárez, on Interstate 10.

Don still groggy in the back seat, I stopped by C&H Surplus and put some hundreds into land surveying equipment, used hard hats, and reflective vests. When I dropped Moon at his house, I told him, "Be ready in ninety minutes. Dress as a highway engineer. Boots, flannel, all that."

Weighing our options, it was decided that we'd take Don's SUV, which looked more in line with our cover, as surveyors for a nonexistent utility company. Driving overland, we found a cheap motel, overlooking the cantina, which I'll call Rosita's. It became our HQ for nine straight days. During our days, we'd drive out, dressed in reflector vests and hard hats, and get Don's car dirtier, exploring the area around Culberson County, Texas, and working on a farmer's tan.

Nights were spent at the cantina, eating slowly, and being amiable with the locals, any of whom could be a friend or compadre of our subject, Hector. The company went from sedate and polite at the dinner hour, growing more raucous as the nights wore on. Rosita's had nine tables, and at a certain point, after the kitchen closed, cards would come out, and people were casually playing poker.

The cantina ran on Mexico time and would close at, or about, 10:00 p.m. Our guns under our vests and a takedown shotgun in the tool bag, we'd shut down for the night and lug our hardware back to the motel. No one was the wiser as to the stakes we were playing in their midst.

"I'm thinking we're chasing our tails," Don lamented one morning, maybe six days in. There was no sign of Hector, and it wasn't as if we could afford to go overt and start trying to collect information on our subject.

Late that afternoon, just before we were to arrive at Rosita's, a call came in from our Bay Area bondsman. "You ready for this?"

We were ready. Hector's fiancée had rung the bondsman's informant, claiming to be in Fresno, but the caller ID had been Nuevo Laredo, Mexico. "What'd she have to say?" I fished with the bondsman. It was obvious to me that he didn't wish to identify who the informant was.

"Made a threat on my informant" was the information.

"And?" I had to ask.

And nothing. He hadn't heard further from his informant and couldn't get ahold of her, or him. It meant that Hector could be wise to his meet in Van Horn being blown. We had already exhausted our retainer, days before, and had quite a bit into the case. Moon had a Mercury dime he carried as a reminder of the Great Depression, as if it might visit us again. He called, "Heads," so we committed to three more days.

It was our eighth or ninth night at Rosita's. We'd occupied a table in a corner, close to the wall, with the jukebox between us and another table. The special that night was chili *verde*, and to save expenses, we both had it. The clock turned slowly until the kitchen closed, and then the cards came out. Don and I were grumbling when I looked past the jukebox to the table on the other side. As if by magic, Hector had joined the two Mexican men at that table and was seated with his back to the wall. I checked a mirror on the next wall to get a better look at the man, without being so obvious in my observations.

Don Moon was grousing over the cost of dinner, and I tapped his forearm, then made eyes toward our man. Moon fell silent a moment, and his vision visited the mirror as well, as if to confirm.

"Yeah, buddy. That's him."

We got ready for action. Don grabbed the tool bag from under the table and exited the back door. The plan was he'd position his SUV in the alley and put the pump gun together for the apprehension. I watched Hector in the mirror, all the while my hand on my 1911.

Don poked his head in the door and nodded that he was ready. I took to my feet, casually stepping over to the jukebox, my back to the room and Hector to my right, ten feet distant. If he suspected anything, our man didn't let on. At that point there were about twenty men in the room at the various tables.

Working fast, I unplugged the jukebox; Don stepped into the room at port arms with the shotgun, turning up the lights. The room immediately fell silent. My gun was out, then, and I stepped to Hector, along the wall, and buried my gun in the angle made by his collarbone and neck. "Keep your hands on the table. *Manos arriba*!"

Under Hector's left arm was a 1911, from which I dumped the magazine. On his right hip was a two-inch .38, which I also unloaded with my left hand, dropping it on the deck. Don had the gun leveled, and no one was moving, or talking, other than Hector. "Shit, man!"

He was a Mexican national but spoke perfect, unaccented English. Holstering my 1911, I cuffed Hector quickly and stood him up to finish searching him. He had two wallets, which I retained. In his front pocket was a wad of hundred-dollar bills, which Hector later claimed was $50,000. I left it on the table and backed him out the door, to the car, with Don Moon covering the room and backing out himself, to make sure no one would be on our heels.

The phone in Hector's jacket pocket started ringing, the theme of *The Good, the Bad and the Ugly*. I answered it, and it was Hector's fiancée. "You can visit him in jail, honey," I said. I pulled the battery and dropped it in the seat pouch. Don was up front, and I was in back with Hector, who suddenly grasped that Moon and I weren't police.

"You are dead men." He smiled.

Anticipating a possible routing with other men wanting to get Hector from us, we motored north instead of taking Interstate 10 west. If they came after us, the logical way would be to blast down that highway. We'd left our surveying equipment and toothbrushes behind at the motel, as getting out of dodge was the more important move. When we got to Carlsbad, New Mexico, Don turned west. We swapped positions, and I drove for eight hours, our objective being Las Vegas, Nevada—the court where Hector was to be surrendered.

We were pretty tired when we got to Las Vegas, but we didn't want to waste any time. The longer we had Hector, the greater the chance one or more of his friends or family would try to get his freedom at gunpoint. We walked Hector into the United States courthouse on Las Vegas Boulevard just before quitting time. The US marshals took him off our hands, signed the bail surrender, and took his phone into custody. Three days later, awaiting final payment, Don took a call from the San Francisco bondsman. After several minutes on the phone, Moon hung up and said, characteristically, "You won't believe this."

Hector had bailed out, again, thirty-six hours after we had surrendered him. That fast.

"I guess that settles it." Moon believed, and so did I, that Hector was an asset of the DEA or some other federal law enforcement agency. For getting paid, it made no difference. Our work was concluded successfully.

A bondsman in Whittier called me about a year after I'd established myself. He had an embezzler out on $50,000 in bail, with forfeiture pending. The absconder was a mec I only remember as Carlos, who'd created fake vendors at the company he worked at and controlled the PO boxes to which payments were sent.

The bondsman had two disconnected phone numbers for Carlos, and his only address was a mail drop, which was dead by the time I was called. Of course there was no photo of Carlos in the file. No automobile description or license plate. All quite thin.

In the file was a cosigner and guarantor on the bond, Carlos' girlfriend, Tanya. This is the usual "informant" who aids the bondsman, or his operative, in getting the absconder rounded up.

"What does Tanya say?" I asked the bondsman.

"Tanya says she don't know where he is, even though she's on the hook." Tanya had no job, no house, and the only collateral she held was a new Ford Mustang. This was curious to me, how a woman without assets could afford such an auto. "We got the title for that car, but you can't go take it, please, because we need Tanya cooperating" was the bondsman's word.

Tanya had lost a leg in an accident, and the Mustang she had purchased with settlement funds. I found Tanya, paid her a visit at her mother's house in a grimy suburb called El Monte. Her Mustang didn't seem to be there. Wasn't in the backyard, garage, or around the neighborhood. "I ain't seen Carlos, an' I can't help you." Tanya wouldn't even open the security screen of her mother's house to have a pleasant conversation. Rather curious.

The employer, from which Carlos had stolen, had a decent photo of the man: short and stocky. Carlos looked more like a construction laborer than a bookkeeper. "His lady dropped him off to work most days, unless he was driving her car."

I cleared the decks and placed Tanya's home under surveillance the next day. A long day, I pulled off at 10:00 p.m. Next morning, I arrived at sunrise, and the garage was uncharacteristically closed. The home could be entered from the garage, this was plain. Approaching indirectly, discreetly, not driving or walking past the house, I waited a block away, watching all day in my rearview mirror. At 6:00 p.m., the garage door opened, and the Mustang pulled out and headed toward the Santa Monica Freeway. I could see there were two people aboard, with Tanya driving…and a man in the passenger seat.

Maintaining cover and distance, I stayed on their six, from El Monte into Central Los Angeles, a section west of USC, which was densely populated. Off the freeway, on city streets, I got close enough to see that Tanya was driving Carlos in the Mustang. I stayed with them in traffic, then Tanya powered through a yellow light. My choice was obvious, and I ran the red to stay caught up, nearly getting broadsided. Two blocks further, and I jumped another red light, going around congestion in the right-turn lane. She made me!

It was obvious when Tanya picked up speed and Carlos craned his fat head around.

I was driving a compromised Volvo that could barely pace the Mustang. To make maximum use, I was shifting the automatic—by hand—and beating more acceleration at high RPM. Traffic slowed Tanya down a bit, and we were in an area of the West 50s, Tanya pulling over several times, with Carlos trying to bail out.

Then, in front of a three-story apartment setup, Carlos was on foot. I was undoing my belt when Tanya changed direction, lost control, and clipped Carlos with the fender of the Mustang. From behind. In the left hip. Sending him cartwheeling.

He flew akimbo, first a thud when the fender got him, then like a sack of garbage dropped off a roof. Tanya couldn't stop and ran his legs over. Her car came to a halt on the sidewalk, and she sat screaming. Carlos was silent. I got to Carlos and saw he was still alive, with at least one compound fracture to the lower leg. Carlos was blinking, trying to make sense of what had just happened. The blow from the car had rotated his pants, half around, and his shirttails were out, both shoes lost. A compound fracture bleeds and is an ugly wound. Carlos was observing his Miranda rights, not that I'd to recite them.

The adrenaline had him such that he didn't yet feel the pain, said nothing as I handcuffed him. An older man was on the sidewalk, massaging himself with his hands in his pockets, marveling at the mayhem spread out across the sidewalk. Before much time could pass, I told him to get on with 9-1-1, for police and EMS. He stumbled into the building, looking back every so often, not wanting to miss any of the fun.

Paramedics arrived first and wanted me to uncuff my charge. I searched Carlos for weapons and was about to accede to their demand when a patrol unit of LAPD pulled up, code 3. They didn't know me or my status, so I had to be cautiously circumspect.

"Why'd you do him like this?" asked an officer who looked to be fifteen. He was probably probationary, just out of academy, with a senior lead as a training officer. Showing the two stripe the warrant from the bondsman, I got his signature and badge number so the bond could be exonerated. Carlos was in their custody.

By then, Tanya, prosthetic leg and all, was wailing over a shattered Carlos as he was being worked on by LA City fire. Her face was distorted in furious tears, and she was limping circles on her prosthetic leg. The keys for the Mustang were on a fob hanging out of her purse, and I slipped them. Naturally Tanya was distracted and didn't notice my move until I'd locked up the Volvo and was pulling the Mustang off the sidewalk in reverse.

She hobbled over, a furious cast to her tear-streaked face as I put it in second gear and headed toward Whittier and a payout on the bond. The bondsman was due in court for the forfeiture in mere days, so he paid me on the spot, surprised I also had the Mustang, complete with damaged undercarriage and a leaking oil pan. No good deed ever went unpunished, though. When I got a ride back to the scene two days later, someone who had been sleeping, drinking, and eating in my Volvo left a solid dump in the back seat. "Probably made it more valuable," said Paul Repetti when I shared that detail over lunch.

Most of these cases were less complex and less fraught with danger. Before I knew Don Moon, Robert Ferris would occasionally sign on. We once took a commission to round up a fraternity member from a suburb of Los Angeles, who'd made a series of pronouncements about never going to jail. What this young man may have called "partying" looked a bit more like a drinking problem to the classmate who'd guaranteed his bail.

Ferris showed up in a leather jacket with a Walther PPK holstered. It wasn't intended, but he looked like a character in a le Carré novel. We scooped up the frat boy at his girlfriend's house, where she lived with her insular parents, on Thanksgiving eve. He didn't put up a struggle and made as if the whole thing was a lark. Ferris had him in irons in the back seat of his Volvo while I drove. When we went right past the exit for the Pasadena Civic Center, heading for downtown, our charge sat up. "Hey, where are you going, bro? Pasadena police is that exit."

"Going downtown. County jail." I drove. He was silent for a minute, for two minutes, then the thrill of the lark left him. He shuddered with tears, as Carl had some years before.

"How'm I supposed to do this?" He looked to Ferris.

"Do your own bit. Mind yourself and don't try to make friends. Time will go faster." Robert looked out the window at the passing signs. To his credit, or maybe because he was out of cred, the frat brother didn't offer to buy us off and stood stolidly waiting the jailer's search as we did paperwork. The sun was gone, and we were behind cement walls, with long chains of inmates on either side of us. Last I saw of him, he was being walked into a module by a deputy in rubber gloves, with another eight men already in the tank. Maybe that was his night to grow up. Well, party's over.

Being routed or losing a prisoner by the intervention of others is a legitimate consideration, and not just from the standpoint of losing a commission. What if the person trying to take my arrestee wishes to do violence to her? If she was in my control and I allow another to take her, I am responsible, to some extent. And just as I should safeguard and control my arrestee, I should also make all haste to either the criminal court with jurisdiction or to whatever jail he was bailed out of. Any delay on my part could be misconstrued later.

In most cases, delay isn't a concern: As soon as I have my man in irons, searched and secured, I'm getting him into the custody of the Man. I once staked out the arraignment court of a tiny county close to the Oregon border, awaiting a woman who'd jump bail on a drug charge, and took her into custody right in the courtroom. The bailiff was briefed in advance. He took no offense to an armed agent sitting in the gallery of the court he was responsible for. Of course, she was the last person in that afternoon, accompanying her cannabis-cultivating boyfriend to be arraigned for assault with a deadly weapon. My female subject was easily recognized, and I put irons on the upset woman, only to have an eight-hour drive, overnight, to Los Angeles.

I turned on a digital recording device to protect myself. But, in any case, it was not necessary. I booked her, forlorn and jonesing, into inmate reception center, Los Angeles County Jail. Awake thirty-six hours, I was so fatigued I was about to sleep on my feet. Don Moon once had two women attempt to strip him of a man—the son of one woman, and husband of the other. The women attacked Don with mace or pepper spray—I can't remember the details of it—but he did manage to keep control of his charge and surrender that man at the jail, even drenched in noxious chemicals.

One of my more memorable commissions was a man who'd jumped bail on a series of domestic violence cases. These acts of domestic violence involved the woman who'd bailed him out, sworn collateral on his bond, and then moving her husband so as to evade arrest. Most would view this as bizarre, as it was not in her apparent interest.

My first phone conversation with her went something like this: "Hello, Bernice. I work for the bondsman, and—"

Her furious response was, "You can get on and fuck yerself. I ain't tellin' you shit!" Which is pretty salty language for a public-school teaching aid.

Bernice had changed jobs, but I managed to find out which school she was working at and trailed her home. Her car was a beater, and she flung cigarette butts out the window all the way home. The apartment building she was living in looked like a stationary version of her car: faded colors, battered siding, and poorly maintained. In the alley, I could see a light come on in a second-floor jalousie window, announcing which apartment was hers.

The mystery of whether her husband, Clem, was living there was solved by the voluble, profanity-barbed conversation taking place between Clem and Bernice. Having fixed them in a location, I could wait for them to open the door and leap on them then, but that was a risk. They could open it in a few seconds, or they could never open it at all. Or, I might wait until Clem had consumed his entire nightly allowance of malted liquor before taking him down. I'd already had enough of the two for a whole lifetime, so I got my nine-pound sledgehammer from the rear of my auto, walked past the pool in the littered courtyard, and mounted the lone set of stairs to the second floor.

As I approached the door I could hear them, smell their tobacco, and glimpse their TV blaring in the living room. I'd already notified the sheriff's office I was taking him in, so there was not much left to do but take the man. The door looked to have been kicked in a few times, the lock plate reinforced with a new installation of sheet metal. No matter. One single, hard strike with the hammer, and the door was wide open. So as to get immediate control of Clem, I dropped the sledgehammer next to the door and charged in, announcing myself and my cause.

Bernice got wide-eyed and started screaming but never lost the cigarette in the corner of her open mouth. She'd taken the trouble to go to work on her hair and had curlers in, the kind that look like pink barrels. Clem stood and tried to hide behind his wife, who was broad-hipped, and a solid 230 pounds of luxury-sized lovewoman. Clem was half of her corpulence , flitting behind her to a bathroom.

With Bernice screaming and flailing at me, I reminded the wife, "Bernice, I told you I'd be coming. We could have done this the nice, polite, easy way," which had no discernably calming effect.

In fact, it made Bernice louder. "Go fuck yourself get outta muh *house* you mother*fucker*!"

I shoved the woman out of my way and tried the bathroom door, which was locked. Of course. The whole apartment stank of tobacco, fried food, and rancid cat litter.

I tried the door, harder, and the portal of hell gave way to my boot. I fished my charge from behind a Hello Kitty shower curtain, with Clem gaping at me from a mouth that held four teeth. Thrown to the floor, I fitted Clem with irons and searched him. His whole kit was a cigarette lighter and a crushed pack of Salems. Then he was on his feet with Bernice no longer in sight, nor making any of the noise she had when the door came down.

Exiting the unit, with neighbors now out for the *Clem and Bernice Show*, the man's handsome wife was on the walkway with my own sledgehammer raised in both hands over her head. She was wobbling, in house slippers, and snarling around the cigarette. Taking no heed, I moved Clem forward, in cuffs and wrist lock, between myself and his winning bride.

She tilted back, hammer high in the air. I moved Clem forward. Knowing his wife's skill at arms, Clem was ducking and weaving, trying to give her a better chance of braining me. Just then, the woman lost her balance, the weight of the weapon taking her in reverse against the iron railing, between her and a thirty-foot drop to the cement, or the pool, or the cement and the pool.

Bernice let go of the hammer behind her back at that moment, reclaiming her balance as I advanced. My sledgehammer made a pronounced *sploosh!* when it landed in the murky green pool. With Clem still flopping left, then right, and Bernice backing up and trying to claw my face, I approached the top of the stairs. I still haven't recovered the hammer.

Bernice was planted like a pro-wrestler, her hands before her trying to grab at me, around her Clem. I could feel myself starting to tire, and to be tired in a fight is to slip, and to slip is to lose. I tightened my hold upon the arm of Clem and pulled him up between us. He screamed something about me breaking his arm. With my right foot, I found Bernice's left and stepped hard on it. With my free right hand, I grabbed ahold of an ample, unharnessed tit with all my might. And with it in my grip, she began to let go.

My grab became a clockwise twist, and Bernice yelled, "Leggo muh titty!", with authentic pain in her eyes. I gave her a shove to clear the way, and Clem's war bride went backward down the stairs, ass up, head down, and thumping and rolling, in a heap at the bottom. The stairs seemed to have a calming effect on her, and I got her husband buckled into my car. A crowd was growing around Bernice as I drove off.

On our way to the freeway, en route to inmate reception, I rang the watch commander again and let him know I'd to use force and that a citizen might be in need of help at the arrest scene. Clem bawled in the backseat, telling me that he was regularly attending church and had given up fortified wines. It caused me to recall a pinch that I'd made, early on, with the older Frank Repetti. We'd got irons to the wrists of a skinny burglar, whose last name was Merchant. This was ironic, as his modus was to fold his skinny carcass up and hide in a retail store at closing time, to caper after the employees departed. I was in back with Merchant who insisted, "I've found God, Mr. Repetti! I have the calling of God! Caint you *please* lemme go?!"

Upon arriving at inmate reception, while I unfolded, and unloaded, Merchant, Frank said, "I ought to show that back seat to our parish priest. He's the third man this year to 'find God' back there."

Upon arriving at the county jail, the booking sergeant was waiting for us, with two deputies taking ahold of Clem for the remaining, administrative parts of incarceration. He had forgotten the road to Damascus and was blackguarding the deputies who put him on tiptoes to toss his pockets again. Never rely on the word of a man you don't know that a custody has been searched. Not ever.

"I need a statement from you. Use of force." The sergeant handed me a legal pad. I described for him verbally what had occurred, and he nodded. "Make sure you include the part about her slipping."

Not every case is local to Los Angeles. Within a few hours driving time is a foreign country, which appears friendly for a man on the run. Mexico is a dicey place, for nearly anything. It is convenient to those wishing to evade arrest and avoid, or at least delay, criminal justice. But it is even dicey for a practiced criminal fugitive, unless he is protected and connected.

I've seen it happen in Mexico, as I have in Brazil and El Salvador. An American fugitive thinks he has money enough to hide out, evade capture, and enjoy his freedom. Do Mexicans enjoy having American criminals skulking about? They do not. One of the programs the locals use to dispose of American fugitives is to bleed them for money. Bleed them pale gray, until the fugitive can't wait to get back to the states. Sometimes it is the *policia*, but just as often it is the Mexican criminal class who, upon finding *un Americano* hiding out, starts looting him a day at a time until he is used up.

I've done it though. Gone to Old Mexico looking for a bail fugitive, American or even Mexican bailed out of American jail. Once, I rounded up a man in San Felipe, Baja, California, on the Sea of Cortez. His car was easily spotted: garish American paint scheme, but someone had stripped it of wheels and doors, and it was at a cheap, beachfront motel. The man I was after was an American citizen who spoke little English and was wanted on a narcotics trafficking charge. The bondsman had offered me extra, should I get this man to Fresno. Somewhere between the Sea of Cortez and Calexico, this fugitive smiled, and in poorest English, explained that I'd arrived just in the nick of time, that I'd saved his life. Whomever he'd been associating with in Baja intended to kill him when the money had run out.

Surrendered in Fresno a day later, I was paid by the bondsman, who chuckled and said, "It isn't much money for such a foolish act." As it happens, Mexican law respects so little and so few of our customs, procedures, and penal code. To arrest a man, even an American, in Mexico, is kidnapping. There are bounty hunters serving long sentences in the jails of that nation. They, too, can be bled gray for money.

Never ask me why I don't vacation in Mexico. Every trip, every case, every cause, has been fraught with peril. Often the greatest threat to a man in my profession, operating within Mexico, is Mexican law enforcement. I usually employ a Mexican colleague to accomplish anything in that nation. In this I must use all caution, as a plurality of the characters styling themselves private operators in Mexico are just smooth con artists.

Within my business education, I learned that if Nils Grevillius owes his bank a million dollars and cannot pay, Nils has a problem and is in financial trouble. But should I owe that same bank $100 million and be unable to pay this money to my bank, my bank is in trouble. This state of affairs came to pass with some companies issuing bail bonds.

There came a time when I was approached by executives of a surety underwriter with an extraordinary dilemma. An agency, operating out of multiple states, had loosened underwriting requirements in the bail bonds they were posting. They were not requiring collateral, nor was this agency taking the full amount of the bail premium up front. In fact, this outfit was "financing" the premiums, meaning allowing the party negotiating the bail bond to make payments over time, potentially earning interest on the unpaid balance.

Human nature cannot be removed from markets, and bail bonds were no exception. Not only were bail premiums defaulted upon, but criminal defendants—freed by dint of loose underwriting—felt no sense of honor, obligation, or loyalty to the instrument of their freedom, and what followed was a predictable and unprecedented wave of forfeitures. The bail surety had defendants scattered all over several Western states, provided the information submitted on the bail applications was true. This company wanted me to undertake a concentrated effort to ride the range and work around the clock rounding these absconders up.

Don Moon and I sat down, did some arithmetic, and decided that most of it made financial sense for us as two freelance operators. The bail surety was making a decent proposal from that angle. But there was an aspect to this that Moon and I agreed upon: To undertake this work, and concentrate exclusively on criminal apprehension, to the exclusion of all other matters, was what this project called for. Doing this would significantly increase the risk to ourselves and to the broad public. We would be taking doors down every single day, and so I consulted three different liability insurers for a quote.

Not only were Don and I operating without backup, entirely by our wits, our guns, and our experience, we did not have the sovereign immunity to liability that a police agency is shielded by. In short, Don and I could shoot it out with the worst men in the world, be absolved of any criminal charges, and still face a catastrophic lawsuit in the civil arena without this protection. We counterproposed, explaining to the bail surety our need for coverage, and asking only that their company indemnify us. We had this discussion with the same executives who'd approached me for this work. They understood the counterproposal and ultimately balked. That they rejected this told me that they did not want the risk that Don Moon and I were to assume in this undertaking.

And with that, I walked away from this line of investigative work. To this day the Repettis are my respected friends. To them and their parents, I shall remain forever grateful for their trust and generosity. I can report that I've nothing to prove as a detective. In my years I have been shot at; shot; stabbed; bitten by drunks, whores, and dogs, jointly and severally; run over; and fought more men than I can count—and a few able women. I pursued this for almost two decades, one or two cases a month. Every one of these capers was a learning experience, as was the response of the bail surety to my proposal. They made a series of unwise business decisions, so I was forced to make a smarter one.

CHAPTER

12

CONFIDENCE MEN

Confidence men are poorly understood by the broad public, and government types are no exception to this. This is by design—the stripes of the con man. In order to perpetrate sophisticated swindles, the typical flimflam has a very hard mien, coupled to an oily, flamboyant insouciance. The Viennese have a term for this metaphoric, oily coating: *schmeh.*

The con men I have gone up against were hardened, crafty, and always had a way out. They're great believers in luck—bad and good. A con is just as happy to hose a fellow swindler as to make good on a shared deal. All that binds them is their need to cooperate to take down a mark and make a clean getaway. If anyone in a grift fails, he endangers all, and it will take him rather a lot of work to restore his standing among the turds he considers friends.

Long ago, in the distant eon of pagers, phone booths, answering services, and exorbitant mobile comms, I was brought into an investigation involving a crew that had taken down an investment group that brokered liquor licenses. The con was unclear to me, as I was introduced, at first, to disambiguate whether or not a man identified by an informant was, in fact, in on the con.

The man directing me said, "He is often at the HMS Bounty, Mid-Wilshire, at happy hour on Thursdays." They didn't know much of him: male, white or Spanish, slender build, between twenty-seven and seventy. If he was the Man, he'd make a play in a particular way, involving low-interest, unsecured business loans. I wanted to use a friend I'll call Joe here as a foil, who was much my senior and a gifted raconteur. On the downside, this friend had poor eyesight and could barely drive—let alone make a positive ID in a bar. In his favor was his long experience as an artist, with academic credentials to match. I took this idea to the Boss, who said, "Joe is blind. Forget it. He won't learn anything we need learned."

Somehow my plan prevailed, with Joe and I posing as a wealthy Canadian real estate investor and his local agent, respectively. The bounty is a wood-paneled sewer, cheery enough for a drink or six. The music was going, and the cloud of cigarette smoke getting lower, when a man sat next to me at the bar and asked that I watch his sunglasses and smokes while he took a leak. I wasn't sure but studied him in the mirror behind the bar. Right build, about forty.

Upon his return, the mec asked if he could buy me a drink, and I said he'd have to buy one for Joe as well, amiably. "He's in town on some business, showing him the Bounty."

Let's call this man Flintcraft. As he ordered the drinks, got the eye of the barman, paid with a fifty-dollar bill, then changed positions to the other side of Joe and introduced himself. Flintcraft had abandoned the change on the bar, a pile of bills, after asking me to watch after his glasses and smokes.

In five minutes, Joe had Flintcraft warmed up to the notion he was in town to buy a Wallace Neff house in Los Feliz, to winter outside frigid Ontario. Flintcraft was apparently keen to work a sucker and stated, "I lend money. Lend business funds…myself. I'm an originator and closer…"

This was our man. I excused myself to the men's room for a spell, and he was on Joe like a wet dog. Joe passed me a note stating that Flintcraft had asked him for contact information, then asking that Joe not up me to the request. "Your manager might be a good man, but I am exclusive in my dealings. Personal money, you get me?"

Then Flintcraft changed gears and worked a cocktail server with the wet dog routine. She wasn't a mark for anything but possible sex. He was as persistent as a carney hustler. I studied Flintcraft further, and what I saw was telling: a fake Rolex watch, but a decent fake; immaculate blue cord suit; buffed wing tips; and a perfectly executed, half–Windsor knot in an amethyst-colored necktie. Over two hours he nursed two drinks and didn't seem to be drunk or whacked with cocaine, then a matter of style. Flintcraft was in control, and it was obvious his role was in identifying and steering marks to be played in a con.

On my second bathroom trip, I made my way out and briefed the surveillance team as to Flintcraft's description. Joe had a card from him, and the phone number on it was an Orange County pager exchange.

Our swindler downed his drink, gave a smile to the waitress, and made for the door. Joe and I stayed put. To have followed would've been a tell, and men like Flintcraft were always about the tell. Men like this possess true jungle sense for a tail or even a robbery. The other unknown was whether or not Flintcraft had an accomplice in tow. Next day we took stock and were debriefed by the Boss. I gave a full description of Flintcraft, right down to the ersatz Swiss watch, the necktie, and the embellishment of the bar change Flintcraft was unconcerned with. "It's all an elaborate act," said the Boss.

Joe sat down at an electric typewriter and pecked out three pages, almost verbatim of his interaction with our subject. For description, Joe included the apt characterization: "Subject is a waitress fucker."

"Brilliant," mused the Boss.

The surveillance team played it loose but managed to follow the operator to a car, parked two blocks distant. "Ran the plates, and it's a rental."

The Boss had a good source at airport police, who leaned on the rental agency. "It was rented at San Diego Airport with no flight information. Rented by a woman, lives in La Mesa, in an apartment building. We are running a make on her."

Overnight, the Boss learned the woman was a cocktail waitress named Sylvia Talbott, with a past jolt to prison for forgery. Sylvia was thirty-six, twice divorced, no children, and no known paramour. Her booking photo didn't look extraordinary. "You and Joe beat feet, get down there. Surveillance team is setting up on Sylvia," the Boss directed.

Two days sitting close by Sylvia's apartment, a second-story corner unit in an elegant-yet-threadbare edifice of the 1930s, revealed there was a man in residence with the waitress. From a block and a half distant, I could identify Flintcraft through the dusty porch screen. I also made out Sylvia. Auburn hair, always tied up, freckles, maybe fake tits, and an ass like a fifty-dollar cheeseburger. That night, Flintcraft went with Sylvia to work at a popular restaurant close to the racetrack. He sat with a view of all she did and drove home with her, in Sylvia's car. If there was a car belonging to our subject present, we could not ascertain which one it was.

Second day, dressed for business, Flintcraft bounced in Sylvia's car and made for downtown San Diego. He visited two pawn brokers briefly. On his third stop, surveillance team shadowed him at a coin dealer, buying gold coins with a stack of US currency. They could not get close enough to take the measure of this, nor could they be sure Flintcraft was familiar to the coin dealer.

Flintcraft had parked two blocks from each of his stops and circled the block twice before heading back to La Mesa and Sylvia. Two hours later, Flintcraft stepped out with his woman, her to work, and him to eye-fuck her, lest another waitress fucker take a stab at the girl. His demeanor suggested neurotic possession of Ms. Talbot. I didn't ask her if she liked it.

Next day, Flintcraft went solo in Sylvia's car to the racetrack—early. He watched the walkers warming the horses up, and one of the surveillants reported that Flintcraft seemed quite the handicapper. Our subject whiled away the entire day. Upon five o'clock, Flintcraft returned to Sylvia's apartment, blared the horn, and she came right out dressed for work. I briefed the Boss, while surveillance stayed on Flitcraft at the restaurant.

"Think you can do me a New York search warrant?" asked the Boss. A New York job is where a man like me lets himself into the premises, has a look around the place, and if there's evidence of the crime, or a crime, then he might get a bona fide warrant to toss the place while the skell sits on the curb in his boxer shorts.

The security signal—should Flintcraft head back for the apartment while I was working it over—was a page to Joe and a page to me from the surveillance team. Naught can be trusted while working a caper this way. Joe sat in a vestibule, in the second-floor hallway, reading the *New Yorker*, while I picked the lock. It was an elderly building with elderly locks. I could feel how loose it was when I put the tumbler under tension. Two passes of the rake, and it turned as if buttered. My set of picks looked like a billfold, a black leather one. It consists of various tension bars, "rakes," and flat pieces of flexible steel for recessing the pins in a tumbler. If my pockets were frisked by a municipal cop, he might ask if I am a 459 man (burglar), as possession of these tools without a locksmith's license is tantamount to possession of burglary tools—a common penal code section—across all states of the US and every province in Canada. As it happens, I never had to find out.

Sylvia's apartment reeked of a perfume of depilatories and ashtrays filled with tobacco. I worked the closets, the dresser, the medicine chest, the freezer—all the usual places. I labored cautiously, lest my entry later be detected. There was booze in the refrigerator and empties in the garbage. Nothing to suss out Flintcraft's actual identity, and no cache of coins. Had Flintcraft taken them with? Most thieves know in their thieving hearts that everyone else is a thief.

I looked under the bed, my penlight growing dim. My pager was still, no warnings. Each of the men's shoes in the closet was inverted, then his suitcases. Not even a luggage tag. I couldn't get a BB up this guy's ass with a sledgehammer. He was very disciplined. There was only furniture on the porch, and I checked each cushion of the sofa. Under the bed a second time, my light shining on the hardwood floor, there was a pile of fine white powder on the wood, right up against the wall. Gently, I pried the queen bed away from the wall, and there I made my discovery. A key detail I missed the first time, a void cut in the plaster and lathe. The headboard covered this. To maintain quietude, I slipped off my shoes and removed my belt, lest the buckle strike the wooden floor and alert the downstairs neighbors that a caper was unfolding above.

The void was an ugly, oblong cut in the plaster. Flintcraft had cleaned up his initial work on this, plainly. There was only a bit of telltale dust on the dark floor. In plain sight within the void were two small coffee cans, complete with tops taped on. Each was filled with a mix of Krugerrands and gold sovereigns. None of this was American bullion. Gold was worth north of $400 American at the time I found these. Each can weighed a few pounds. This was real money. The Krugerrands were familiar as I'd seen these South African coins once, in the army. Of gold sovereigns, I'd only read about and had never held so much gold in my hands.

As I was on scene with no phone, my options were few. Getting Joe down to a market to call the Boss for guidance would take too long. I used Sylvia's landline and called the Boss's toll-free pager. There would be no telltale charge on Sylvia's bill. My page included the digits "8-6"—my operative number—so the Boss knew who was paging him from a strange number.

But a moment later, her phone rang, and I answered, "Yeah," as if I might be Flintcraft, asleep, just in case it wasn't the Boss ringing in.

"Talk to me," the Boss said.

I briefed him about the gold and asked, "Do I put it back, or take it with?"

The Boss answered yes and hung up.

Thinking quickly, I chose to resort to an aggressive form of direct action in my closing: confound and confuse. I'd leave Flintcraft bewildered as to whom may have taken down his heist gelt. In my wallet, like any conscientious bachelor of the 1980s, waited a Magnum condom, which I removed from its foil. From the refrigerator I secured a blob of mayonnaise, then worked it into the unwound rubber. This I knotted, and draped over the edge of his cache space and then carefully repositioned the bed. It spoke for itself.

Joe and I motored to Los Angeles, exhausted, leaving with the surveillance team on Flintcraft. Two days later, we received a report that Flintcraft, in a taxi, hastily departed Sylvia's pad, getting a ride to an auto body shop in San Diego. Then, at last, our subject was in a car, later identified as his own, and he was tentatively named an Argentine national from San Diego. Flintcraft was tailed all the way to the Stockton area, to a house he owned. His identity was verified by past grand theft charges, and an airport service had sent delayed luggage twice to his home. "The house is in the name of someone that doesn't exist," the Boss said. It was owned, outright, by an alias.

This may be momentary security for the man who thinks himself a smooth operator, but what it really means is that a thief more enterprising than he can just sign the house away with the original thief having no recourse, nowhere to turn.

Years later, in casual convo with the Boss, no longer my employer, he enquired, "D'you remember that flimflam you took down in San Diego?"

I did.

"Clients got the gold, then sued him under his real name, then the fake name. Kinda ruined him. They got back most of what he hosed them for. Good caper."

I remembered. "What's doing? A new case on him?" I had to know.

"No. My informant that first tipped us he might be our man tells me he drank himself to death, down in Mexico, a resort called San Miguel de Allende."

For a man who lives by his wits and his wiles to discover a spent rubber in place of his take-money could only have wilted the man. I am sure, from that moment forward, he didn't know who'd set him up, who'd laid him low. Not being able to get a name or explanation out of Sylvia only compounded the weight upon him. Men like Flintcraft are used to always having a way out, the final word, a parachute, a safe house. Being on the bent, hurt, broken, and hosed end could only have staggered him. "Funny thing, my informant says he died washed up…never had another score, another caper again. Like he lost his juju…"

Lost his juju.

What is the "juju" of the confidence man? It lies in his ability to not just talk his mark into doing something expensive and unwise.

No. Neurolinguistic studies suggest that it is far deeper. The con infects his mark with a persistent bad idea. The infection has taken hold when the victim believes there really is "something for nothing." Treading on the greed and vanity buttons, and providing a partial payout, fires the endorphins, and the emotional experience of the victim, in this moment, is like unexpectedly hitting a jackpot. That the bad idea is persistent is borne out by the number of otherwise intelligent, educated men and women who are serial victims.

David Maurer, Professor of Linguistics at the University of Louisville, wrote a book decades ago wherein he delineates each stage of the process. This all predates neurolinguistic studies, but the scholarship is still sound. Among the criminals Maurer studied were Harry Gondorf, Joe Furry, and "Yellow Kid" Weil. The book is titled *The Big Con*, and it is the partial basis for the 1972 film *The Sting*.

> *I never cheated an honest man. All the men I took off were rascals. They wanted something for nothing, and I gave them a whole lotta nothing for a lot of something.*
>
> —"Yellow Kid" Weil, as quoted in
> *The Big Con*, by David Maurer.

In my years I have investigated many confidence games, a few of which I can enumerate, all operating in the greed/vanity vein:

1. The Badger Game: Older man meets younger attractive woman of ambiguous age, who convinces him to come to her room. She partially disrobes, whereupon her "uncle" walks in, often with a camera, taking a photo of the old lech and the young woman. "Give me some money so I can forget all this, or I will call the police." Very common in the Chinese community.
2. The Prime Bank Note: Person with money is approached by a stranger at a resort, summer or winter. "Don't you hate how the government limits how working guys can invest?" I sure do. "Great. You know that there are secret investment

programs, available only to the very connected." Really? "Of course. They get seventy-eight percent interest on their money, quarterly." How do I get in? "Well, I can introduce you, but you have to be very discreet. Is this something you can do without asking the wife?" Yes. How much do I need? "Everything you have." This is now largely overtaken by cryptocurrency cons, presented in some variation.

3. The Offshore Bank: We operate a bank offshore, in the Caribbean/Isle of Man/Panama, which used to only be available to the high-net-worth individual. But you must keep this quiet. We pay 8 percent on deposits and report to no government. Once the money is deposited, the "bank" disappears. I found a pair of jokers who'd set up three of these in twelve years, and both were Canadian lawyers.
4. The Wire: We can delay the race/board of trade/crypto results for 28.9 seconds, every other Thursday, because we have a man on the switch…and so on.

Sometimes the police are sympathetic, but usually not. I have had moderate success in identifying sharpers like this, but hosing the money out of them is the hard part. Usually it is a Pyrrhic victory, because the moment they steal your money, they blow town for Monte Carlo, or Vegas or Macau, and invest heavily in hookers, booze, and cocaine. When the jack is gone, they go jack someone else up.

If I call the FBI and report that I have given a cocktail waitress in Curaçao, whom I met on the internet, $3 million by selling my house to invest in crypto, he takes a brief report and says he may call me back—which he will never do. Why not? Too many victims, too many man hours to break a case, and…the victim deserved it. It's almost government policy. Within the US Attorney's Office, this is called *pig butchering*. "He was hiding money from the government, and it serves him right…"

There is a very familiar con game, often played long-range, called the Nigerian 419, so named for the Nigerian government code section on fraud.

"Very pleased to inform you that your family/church/company invested a modest sum of money in petroleum exploration, in the Gabon Malagasy Republic, which our government has now fully developed. There are very substantial royalties to be paid to you after you pay back taxes, and a government registration access fee to my cousin, the minister of official petroleum explorations. Big celebrate." That is a loose descriptive of the always varied and, somehow, often successful approach.

Very exciting. How much are the taxes? Take a checque, or do you require an international swift wire? How rich am I? Some would be surprised how many people fall for this. But they have even hosed big financial institutions, like Banco do Noroeste, on a much larger scale than just the equity in your home. The bank had enough capital and gunpowder to go after the Nigerians who hauled this in and made a modest recovery. But this is the exception.

Within my profession, there have always been those operating outside the edges of legality, often as fixers, bagmen, extortionists, and swindlers. The states license us to protect the public. Historically, a plurality have been cops who were caught up in graft or vice of some sort but whose crimes were swept under the rug with an early retirement in lieu of prosecution. But a guy doesn't have to be a corrupt officer to become a corrupt PI.

Some style themselves private operators, but are straight-up confidence men, like Nick Barone, for instance. Barone died in 2000, none too soon. First I heard of Barone was from a supervisor at Pinkerton who asked if I'd ever worked with Nick during indoctrination. This was without context. Later I learned Barone was an extortionist, whose con was often like this:

> Barone: What can I do for you?
>
> Dumb Client: I need my ex-husband beaten up. He owes me money.
>
> Barone: This can be done, but it ain't cheap.

Dumb Client: How much?

Barone: Maybe ten to the large…or more…

(Waits to see if she flinches at the price)

Dumb Client: I can afford it.

Barone: Ten now, five when done.

Dumb Client returns with cash. Two months pass. Dumb Client calls Barone: he answers.

Barone: The Silver Fox, how may I help you?

Dumb Client: Why isn't my ex beat up yet?

Barone: Meet me at (insert some cocktail lounge in Encino). We have a complication I need cleared up.

Later, in quiet corner of cocktail lounge…

Dumb Client: What's the holdup?

Barone: You got money on you?

Dumb Client: No, why?

Barone: The district attorney is wise to you, and I gotta pay someone off.

Dumb Client: What?! How?

Barone: Listen to this. (Plays tape recording of Dumb Client commissioning Barone to commit a felony.) We gotta make this go away. You could have big trouble.

Dumb Client: How much?

Barone: Ten to the large.

Oh yes, $20,000 for nothing, other than lost sleep and wonderment as to who set her up, other than herself.

I don't know if this is what Nick Barone did to Erin Fleming, Groucho Marx's surviving lover and secretary. In the early 1990s, I was brought in, as I had another case involving Barone swindling the estate of a music producer.

A noteworthy and entirely noble actor, a white knight for Fleming, engaged my services to help the old girl. Erin, somehow been talked into executing a power of attorney in favor of Barone, who promptly took loans against Erin's condo, which had fallen into foreclosure. Nothing could be had from Barone, who wasted the thousands on repairing his Jaguar Vanden Plas, booze, cocaine, and a transvestite hooker.

Erin Fleming wound up evicted, homeless, and died on the streets as the partial result of Barone hosing away her home. Damn him for that.

Barone was fond of using an electronic voice-distortion device, making himself sound like Darth Vader on the telephone. He drifted from motel to motel, often living out of his car between boosts. The next encounter with Barone's wormcraft was a conversation with a respected journalist, who had First Amendment issues, including an early-morning search warrant from the FBI. He recounted being contacted by Barone for a sit-down, in, of all places, a cocktail dive in Encino.

"Look, man, you're being wiretapped by Tony Pellicano," was Barone's hustle. There was a long-standing rumor around investigative circles, back in the era of analog switching equipment that Pellicano, a PI, was wiretapping for hire. The first to warn me of this was a man, much older, who was our occasional wiretap expert at Pinkerton, an eminence named Fred Otash. Otash, also a PI, had run his own private wires in the RFK–Marylin Monroe era.

Otash could find an analog wire rather easily. Sometimes he needed me to climb a pole, cross a roof, then pick a lock to ascertain the beginning and end of the connection. The journalist, made paranoid for his experience with the feds, paid Barone "ten to the large" to switch the wire off. Was Tony Pellicano wiretapping him? I do not know. I do know that tabloid news was after the journalist and that Tony kept a close, consanguineous relationship with the tabloids.

Barone was a Psychopath, with no assets, who lived hand to mouth to nose with his cocaine habit. When I discovered he had never registered his Jaguar, I disappeared it and sold it for parts. Erin camped at a motel on Fairfax with that jack, but that was all. Later, Pellicano, well into the Digital Switching era, had been caught by the FBI…wiretapping. This arose of Pellicano being paid to intimidate a journalist named Anita Busch off of a series of stories unfavorable to a once-powerful man named Michael Ovitz. The ensuing matter had me trying to determine, for quite another party, exactly whom hired Tony and why. I elicited from people in his office building, not long after his initial arrest, but got no clear answers. Some had been instructed by the FBI to not speak with anyone in these matters, as they were building an extortion, wiretap, and weapons case against Pellicano.

In the course of this, knowing that Tony was once connected with Anthony "Tony the Ant" Spilotro, a murdered figure of La Cosa Nostra's operations in Chicago, Kansas City, Las Vegas, and a cornfield in Indiana, I warmed up a mob informant, who closed a discreet meeting with, "You know, I think I seen Whitey Bulger the other day in west Los Angeles." Bulger was Irish mob of south Boston and wanted as a fugitive—ostensibly by the bureau, and by his own crimes for setting up rivals in organized *crimee* [partner in crime or codefendant] to be taken down by the FBI. Bulger had been a Boston OC informant for more than a decade when he disappeared. Next time, trying to phone elicit from a known agent in the FBI, I said, "Informant of mine says he saw Whitey Bulger the other day, in west L.A." This sentence was followed by five straight seconds of silence.

"Who told you that?" He wanted me to give up my informant. This struck an odd note. He wasn't asking me where, what time, what was Bulger driving, are you sure…anything I'd have asked.

Could it be that Bulger was a tethered goat, being run by the FBI as an ersatz fugitive? Bulger had suborned John Connolly, a supervisory special agent of the FBI, who'd disgraced himself by being Bulger's paid man, protecting Bulger as he committed crimes including murder. If this was so, the operation may have been calculated to ID other people in law enforcement friendly to organized crime. For now, this is unclear to me.

With notable exceptions, like Anita Busch, most of the people Pellicano wiretapped were of the ilk who'd be perfectly pleased paying Tony to wiretap their enemies too. There is no greater collection of people who are simultaneously hostile, delicate, and wealthy than metro Los Angeles. In my opinion, Pellicano isn't any worse than his best clients. He operated outside the law, did his time, and mitigated damage to his clients by never rolling over on them.

Batman.

School. Credit Chris Connell.

In winter. Credit Sally Davies.

Jack Sparrow. Credit Steve Gnerlich.

In the era of dress whites and dining in.

President Reagan addressing the 31st Infantry, on the DMZ, November 1983. Credit Marvin Ferrera.

Gunning. In my early years picking up fugitives. Credit Joe Ferris.

Photo of the author. Credit Wild Don Lewis.

Where Don Moon took his own life. Credit Aldo Grevillius.

The night we arrested Brian Harrington. Credit Nils Grevillius.

CHAPTER

13

THE POLICE!

Once, long ago, driving up the Central Valley, for God knows what, my wreck of a car lurched to a steaming halt with a blown water pump. A bootleg tow truck dragged me to a tractor barn, run by a father-and-son team. Son was my age, hulking, and an ace wrench. We worked out a plan and a price, got it done. While he labored, his dad, grizzled with half-grown gray whiskers and old prison ink all over his hands and neck, was giving me the eye.

"You a police, boy?" he asked.

No. No, sir.

"You got the look.... Sure you ain't police?" Again. Sharper.

Not police.

"What kinda shit does a man like you do to make him look a police?" He had to know.

Private eye.

"Gudammit! I knewed I smelled bacon on you!" He grinned and spat.

Don't care for the Man, eh?

"Small town cop is just like a preacher—too lazy to work and too yellow to steal." He muttered as his son grinned and closed out the job.

"Muh pop is one of 'em dust bowl oakies...don't mean anything for it..."

No offense taken. Upon a winter afternoon, I testified in a felony preliminary hearing at the criminal courts building on Temple Street. It wasn't an extraordinary case—just the usual cargo hijacking. I'd testified about incriminating statements of the defendant and his mother, seeing the proceeds of the crime in plain sight in their garage, recovering a stolen gun from Mom—who somehow escaped a felony filing—and a consensual search of the premises.

The young man's lawyer, a court appointee, had tried to break apart my investigation as well as that of the deputies who'd come in at the end of my work. The defendant was held to answer an eighteen-count felony bill, and my day was done. The courtroom was full of police and defense counsel and deputies of our district attorney. I boarded the elevator with a police detective I didn't know and two women from the DA's office. It was a long ride down.

"That was pretty good, dude. Why didn't you go become a policeman?" asked the officer.

"Well, I was going to do that, but I couldn't pass the drug test…" I stared at the buttons on the wall.

"Yeah?" The police detective turned.

"Yeah. Background investigation, Voight-Kampff test, psych exam, or polygraph. I couldn't pass any of it" was my reply.

"Yeah, got that." He chuckled, searching the ceiling of the lurching elevator for hidden meaning. The ladies of the DA's office looked on in horror, clutching their files close to their tits. It's easy. Anyone can do this. Private cases.

Pretty much anytime I'm riding in the front of a police unit with a cop driving, he will point out some hapless derelict pushing a grocery cart full of aluminum cans up the sidewalk and say, "There goes a retired police sergeant." Cop humor. The jokes they tell when I'm in the back seat are different. What defines a person's line of work as a profession is a recognized, enforced metric for malpractice. Within my profession, impersonating a police officer is prima facia malpractice. Impersonation is the primary of three offenses certain to cost a private detective his profession and freedom.

How can police malpractice be defined? For the individual officer, it might include being so inept that an innocent man is prosecuted and jailed, which is quite a different proposition than creating probable cause, in order to nail a guilty man. Could police malpractice include being physically inept, unable, or unwilling to wield the tools cops are issued and trained with to protect the public?

Is there organizational malpractice? Yes. You can bet the ranch on this. Maybe this would include looking the other way while a city falls apart. Soaping the backsides of greasy-mouthed jackals, elected to public office, so both the command staff of an agency is protected, and the political class are insulated from consequences. Maybe this would include one of those daisy chains, wherein the politicians and the command staff team up with a vacuous, feckless media to burn individual officers to the ground over decisions made in a second, the consequences of which last a lifetime. Is the city better? Are the people living in the city any safer? In writing this, any sentient man knows I am asking rhetorically, Socratically, and serendipitously all at once.

Interrogation, surveillance, background investigation, the polygraph, public records, news archives, evidence collection, forensics, and confidential informants are all tools and resources that a private detective has in common with the police.

In some of these, I have more access and ability to act than the police do. But I cannot get a search warrant without involving police agencies. At that juncture, my case becomes a public cause. If it is to the knowing detriment of my client(s), I must not expose my man.

But clients are not always honest. To protect someone engaged in crimes is to imperil my license. This is separate and distinct from doing criminal defense investigations, working for lawyers defending those accused of crimes. To strengthen my bona fides and establish professional ties with public agencies, I paid my way through both levels of police academy, obtaining POST certificates—the professional credential a police officer has when taking to the streets under a badge. This was a worthwhile investment, but it doesn't mean I am always welcomed or understood when I approach police agencies on a client matter. Often at the very moment I've identified myself and my profession, a sour, concerned, or skeptical look creases the face of the man across the front desk or in the bullpen of the detective bureau. Just as I am only as good as my last case with a client, the same is true of the police. They are right to be suspicious. In the past, a majority of Los Angeles private detectives were former police officers, like Fred Otash, dismissed for illegal activities. If the agency was so compromised or lacked sufficient evidence, there was no coinciding felony case. The former cop caught grafting, whoring, drunk, or indebted had no bar to a private detective's license and may be working for those with morals as low and lost as his own.

If I have good relations with a police agency, it means I have established my own abilities, ethics, and contacts with one or more officers. I go over and ask them what they know or what evidence they have in a case. The police detective smiles and says, "I can't tell you. What do you have?"

If the interests of public safety and the filing policy of our DA coincide enough, there may be collaboration. Whatever I provide my police counterpart has to be turned over under *Brady v. Maryland*, as a matter of constitutional justice. This means I must be circumspect in how I identify sources and methods. Much can occur downstream of a contact with police detectives. Cooperating with me, a detective might reveal something she knows from evidence, from a sealed warrant, or some such, that could endanger her career. To maintain good relations with these officers and agencies, I must also be cognizant in what I ask of them.

Clients often believe it is a simple matter of me going over to the department with jurisdiction, opening my files, and perfect synchronicity will take place. This is a lofty dream.

There have been occasions where I am running a case, and the person I have under investigation has some hidden, special status with police, such as being an informant. If I am greeted by a stone wall, I can presume this is the case, or my client has not been perfectly honest with me.

Some years ago, I was contacted by a used automobile dealer—Ralph Rammage, let's call him. Ralph had been given a neoprene checque by a man who characterized himself as a minister, who'd used the bum checque to motor off in a late-model Cadillac.

"This guy comes in here, all dressed up. He was dressed in a white suit, on a Sunday afternoon, and wants to get a car. I showed him a couple of cars, and he played hard to get, saying his parishioners board voted to buy him a Cadillac. I had one on the lot that was worth having and he kept circling it. He was wearing lots of flash jewelry, a pinky ring, see?" Ralph held up his own pinky ring. He was out a valuable auto, and nothing checked out.

"When I got his checque, Sunday, his bank was closed, you know? It has the name o' this church on it, but I can't find it in none of the phone directories. His phone worked on Sunday two weeks ago, because I tried it then, but it don't ring now. It's disconnected." There was an address on the checque. Overstamped on the checque in purple ink was "ACCOUNT CLOSED."

Pastor Graylice Warren Bovingdon III was the name on the bottom of the failed checque and on the contract for the Cadillac. Calls to the secretary of state revealed no articles on the church as an entity. The address on the checque was a ghetto storefront, occupied by an Asian liquor store. The proprietor being Korean, I went in, introduced myself in Hangul, and asked the man if he knew Bovingdon.

"He was getting his mail here to pay his bill. If he gets money, I cash the checque, maybe, get him to pay what he owes me, but this isn't working. He gets more bad checques than good, and I'm out a lot," explained the Korean, with his wife nodding behind him. They'd rented Bovingdon a room for almost a year. Bovingdon never had guests other than a teenaged daughter, who smoked marijuana and played loud music. Bovingdon had complained of the smells of Korean food and was fussy about his use of the bathroom.

The liquor store owner's wife presented me with a stack of mail, including a letter from another car dealer about, surprisingly, a bum checque, and…another Cadillac. This didn't look so good. I called that dealer, and he told me that they'd hauled their missing car at a massage parlor in the San Gabriel Valley on pure luck. As an afterthought, the Korean man phoned me and said, "A couple of weeks ago, policeman left a business card here for Mr. Bovingdon. I paged him, gave Bovingdon the information."

Now I had a working pager number for my subject and the name of Detective 3 Bill Abbott, Monrovia Police Department. A Detective 3 is the highest grade of Detective in Police Service, fully the equal of a Sergeant. Was Detective Abbott the long-lost brother of Jack Henry Abbott? Not likely, nor was I going to ask. Monrovia is a small town, in the northern San Gabriel Valley, with about forty sworn officers most days of the week. It used to be a blue-collar residential community of teachers and tradesmen. Now it is considered prime real estate.

I proceeded to the Santa Anita Municipal Court, which served Monrovia, Arcadia, Sierra Madre, Baldwin Park, and a few other small jurisdictions within Los Angeles County. I gave the criminal clerk Bovingdon's name and date of birth, and a file came across the counter after some checking along with a presentation of my detective's license.

Bovingdon was an alias, and my suspect had a few others. Bill Abbott had enumerated them all in a probable cause filing, in which Bovingdon was wanted for grand theft, forgery, and worthless instruments. The arrest warrant was, as yet, unsatisfied, which meant he was still on the run. Using the stack of aliases, I rang up the Department of Corrections and learned Bovingdon was, "on paper," a polite, euphemistic way of stating that Bovingdon was a paroled felon.

Now that I could ask questions with a bit of knowledge behind them for comparison, I fell by Monrovia Police Department and asked for Bill Abbott. I was directed to park myself on an oak bench and wait. After twenty minutes, Detective Abbott introduced himself.

"Can I do for you?" He was about twenty years my senior, thick through the neck, and wearing an elderly summer-length shirt, with a polyester tie. It looked like it needed an oil change. I stood and stated my name and that I was a private detective.

"Yeah. I got all that." He was dry.

"Bovingdon, Abbott. I'm making a case on your suspect." I didn't offer my hand. Cops don't usually shake hands, even with each other, as it is how men get disarmed. Between cops, it can even be an insult.

"What do you have on him?" Detective Abbott perked up.

I stated my case and evidence, and proposed we work Bovingdon, run him to ground. "I want to recover the Cadillac before he wraps it around a tree or sells it in Tijuana."

"How do you propose *that*?"

I'd enlist my Korean liquor merchant to page Bovingdon about a checque mailed to the liquor store. Bovingdon was all about the checques. In fact, Bill Abbott's case went like this:

"Asshole I'm looking for goes to a car dealer, a dealer selling cars with a rebate involved from the manufacturer. This guy is slick, gets up like he's some kinda minister, some shit like that.

Anyway, he gets all funny and hinky about the financing, refuses permission for the dealer to run him for a credit report, has a hot checque off a closed account to buy the car. So, while the finance and insurance guy is in the next room trying to verify funds on the hot checque, Reverend Bovingdon heists the rebate checque from the deal package. When the F&I man can't verify his fake-shit checque, Bovingdon takes it back, cuts out of there, bangs the rebate checque at some liquor store."

The next day, Detective Abbott and I braced the Korean couple, who were sad-faced about having to set up Reverend Bovingdon. "It's the least you could do after pushing all that hot paper through your till." Abbott closed the deal, so we sat up the street and waited.

Not unlike another police detective I'd known, Bill Abbott instructed me, "When this asshole shows, don't let any of the locals get up my back, clear?" I knew what to do.

Ten minutes later, Bovingdon circles the block in a sky-blue Cadillac, a woman in the passenger seat. She was got up in a tight dress, like for a discotheque, only heavier, with iridescent green eye makeup on the hot afternoon.

Having cased the block, Bovingdon parked the Cadillac up a perpendicular street and approached the liquor merchant on foot. He was dressed, per the usual, in an immaculate white suit, white bucks for kicks, and a panama hat. Religion must have been good, kind, and lucrative for Reverend Bovingdon, who looked to be without a care in this world. Once he crossed the threshold of the store, which had one way in and the same way out, Abbott and I went in. Thrown over the counter with Reverend Bovingdon hollering as Abbott braceleted him, the contents of his pockets came up, including two checque books, a bindle of heisted bank cards, keys to the Cadillac, and his Department of Corrections parole ID. "Y'all can call my parole agent. I'm clean and in compliance!" said the Reverend.

Abbott handed me the car keys. "If you make anything in his car, get it to me at the department." He didn't have a warrant for the car, but I was lawfully impounding it, under the contract with Rammage. If Abbott tossed the Cadillac, there could be admissibility problems, problems that didn't apply with a private detective recovering a stolen car and taking inventory of its contents.

"The reverend needs your help, has to carry a box of money out of that store. Told me to tell you." I smiled at Disco Woman, who stepped out, leaving her purse on the white leather seat of the Cadillac. In my subsequent search, I learned her name and that she, too, was on parole…with a stolen gun in her purse. My kind of twist; a pity she was dating someone else.

Ralph Rammage got the car back with not too many more miles on it, and Bill Abbott sent two skells back to prison. Case closed.

Prisons, too, employ police officers and cops, only these are called *corrections officers*, or COs in the lingua franca shared by law enforcement and convicts. Early in my solo career, a law firm defending a property owner against a claim of wrongful death engaged me to identify, locate, vet, and hopefully interview a series of witnesses to the death at the center of the lawsuit.

"We represent the owner of a development, which employed private security officers, so as to comply with the zoning requirements of the city. There was a man long suspected of dealing narcotics on our client's property, without actually living there. Late one afternoon the security officers tried to apprehend the man, which led to a foot chase, and ultimately involved two police officers. The security and police officers grappled with the man, and he collapsed and died. The plaintiff's attorney has provided us a list of witnesses, whom the lawyer claims saw a choke hold being applied."

Almost three years had passed, and it fell to me to sort these witnesses out. One of them was an employee of the security company, who'd subsequently been convicted of possession of narcotics himself, as well as robbery. In pursuing this witness, I learned he'd suffered a major skull fracture sometime between his last job and going to state prison.

The probation report I got to characterized this witness as "brain damaged" to the point that he had trouble communicating. I put all this in a report to the law firm employing me.

"We can't take a chance on this guy saying something different at trial from the statements in his own report and the police report. See if you can interview him."

I learned that the plaintiff's lawyer had not even properly identified this witness and likely did not know where he could be found. Discovery between the two sides revealed this. My imprimatur was to provide a work product report to the law firm employing me. This is a term of art, denoting a report that is privileged between the law firm and its client—in this case, the property owner. If I took a recorded statement, formal deposition, or tape-recorded statement, these would all have to be handed over in the discovery process peculiar to civil litigation.

As the city involved also had a lawyer, outside counsel, engaged by their insurance companies, there was another private detective on the case with whom I'd been instructed to share information. This man was a retired homicide detective, not unknown to me. I rang him up and briefed him as to what I knew and that I was going to the state penitentiary to interview the witness. In the interest of cooperation, I invited him to go along. He listened a moment, chuckled, and said, "Don't waste my time. He's a fucking vegetable."

Having located the prison in which my witness, whom I'll call Big Howard, was located, I called the facility, and after a series of short conversations, was connected to a man whose title was *corrections counselor*. He informed me that Big Howard had been in custody over a year and had no visitors. I explained the purpose of my visit and was given a date and time.

"Look, if you just come up on Visiting Day and sit in the dining hall, it's too much noise, too much distraction. You'll look a cop to the inmates and their people, and Big Howard won't talk to you. He won't want to get 'jacketed' as a snitch. I'm not going to put you in the attorney room for exactly the same reason. Defense counsel could also make trouble, even if they are here on unrelated matters. Some of the court-appointed lawyers tell the Aryan Brotherhood, Mexican Mafia, who's snitching, talking to detectives up for a visit. I'm going to have Howard pulled in off the work detail, and you can interview him in an area closed off from the CO lockers and gym."

Either I was being greatly accommodated by this corrections official, or he was setting it up to fail. He faxed me instructions, permission, and a dress code. I was to be in coat and tie, no uniform and no jeans or T-shirt. On the appointed day, I departed Pasadena at 0400 hours to make my way over the Grapevine, into the San Joaquin Valley, to the state prison. When I got to the gate for the parking area, I showed my invite and was waived in. At the main entry, I showed the invite, again, as well as my professional credentials and was invited to secure my gun in the bank of lockers next to the desk. Then, I went through a metal detector and my first sally port, which is a chamber where one door is locked while the other opens, controlling who enters.

Then up a hallway, to a second sally port, where I again showed credentials, and when I was buzzed through the second port, I was discharged into the body of the prison, walking through a long cellblock with two tiers on each side. Cons were coming and going from various parts of the facility, and it dawned on me that I was unescorted, among the prisoners, with the COs behind glass and in gun towers.

I made my way a hundred meters through one part, out into the yard, following the directions for where I was to meet a sergeant who would take me to Big Howard. The prisoners were in varying uniforms of cheap denim, orange jumpsuits, and such, and I was given a way through at each stage. Only once did I hear a man snarl "cop!" as I crossed the facility.

"Once you in that there room with this inmate, he your responsibility, entirely. Are we clear?" The sergeant searched my face to make sure I understood his instructions.

Big Howard was seated at a table, wearing orange. Across his head were a series of scars, with one eye and cheek lower than the other. He was huge, at least six foot six and three hundred pounds.

"I got hit pretty good," Big Howard explained without my prompting him. Despite serious brain trauma, Big Howard was able to state what had occurred the day the man died, right down to the grappling.

"We were controlling his hands and arms, me and a police officer. He wasn't ever in a choke hold. Not ever. After we got him cuffed, we went to get him standing, and he collapsed. At first, I was like, 'Oh, he's faking, and it's on again,' but pretty quick the police got paramedics there."

As to other witnesses, Big Howard was able to provide reasonable descriptions of three men he described as gang members. These corresponded with what I already had of the plaintiff's witness list.

While I was talking to Big Howard, a double door was left open to a loading area. It looked to be outside the security perimeter, and Big Howard kept looking to it. While we were seated, he was not in irons of any kind and was drinking from a Styrofoam coffee cup. Suddenly, he was on his feet, ignoring me.

It took all my strength to get Big Howard onto the linoleum, in a hold. I wrestled him onto his gut and pinned the bigger man, pending the arrival of the sergeant. He was grunting and wheezing and no longer talking to me. The sergeant and another CO took charge of Howard as I tucked my shirttails in and caught my breath. "Tol' you he was trouble now," came the sergeant.

If I had failed to contain this man, I might never have been permitted another inmate interview by the Department of Corrections. I'd learned this agency kept a long institutional memory. Finished, I made my way out of prison the same way I came, with the sun setting in the western sky when I got to my car.

The next day, physically sore for wrestling with Big Howard, I got a call from the corrections counselor, who had to follow up after learning I'd used force. "That sergeant thought you were from a municipal agency, a cop. Otherwise, he'd never have left you in sole charge of a numbered man." This was the price of getting what couldn't otherwise be had in the investigation. By the time the plaintiff's lawyer was able to identify Big Howard and get him seated and sworn for a deposition, it came to naught. Howard had either become, or was pretending to be, a babbling idiot, probably the latter. And as to the death of the man they'd taken into custody, forensic science revealed that he'd succumbed to a heart attack, aggravated by cocaine, with no evidence of a choke hold.

One afternoon I got a call from the chief of police of a San Gabriel Valley City. "We haven't been introduced, but I need your help with something, something my agency cannot do." We met that afternoon. He'd been a cop for more than thirty years and was close to retirement. The chief had been referred to my office by Chief Neal Johnson, Arcadia Police Department, who'd also been academy staff at Rio Hondo Police Academy.

"A man came in, a tile setter, who did a tile job on a property owned by a doctor. The doctor stiffed him, didn't pay for the work, and sold the rental property before the tradesman perfected a lien," said the chief.

"This is a civil matter," I responded, stating what he already knew.

"Correct. It is, and if I could, I'd work up a case and arrest the son of a bitch myself, but I can't." The tile setter was a Mexican immigrant who didn't understand common law very well, however elegant and professional his work may have been. The chief was personally offended by the misconduct of the doctor and wanted it set straight.

"He got a lawyer, who worked a civil case, got him a judgment for fifty-five thousand dollars..." It must have been quite a tile job. "The tile man spent money for materials and labor and fuel. He is seriously out of pocket. Now he has to sit on the judgment, wait to collect it. I want to help speed this process up." Here was what his agency could not do.

The lawyer had prepared an order to appear for judgment debtor examination (ORAP) and had tried eleven times to serve it. The doctor was a heart surgeon, with admitting privileges at hospitals in San Bernardino, Riverside, Los Angeles, and Orange Counties. He lived in a gated, guarded estate community on the Pacific Ocean, and the Orange County Marshal's Office would not take civil services from outside Orange County (their discretion), nor would the security staff manning the gates at the coastal estate admit a process server. This had been tried and failed.

Their collection rationale was sound: the subject was an egotistical asshole who had hosed an immigrant tradesman of his money. The doctor obviously knew he'd never face criminal sanction for this casual act of fraud. Being served with an ORAP meant the doctor had to personally appear, at a debtor's cattle call, and be humiliated in detail. To ignore the summons could mean arrest for contempt of court. I took the case and went to work on it.

In studying the surgeon, I learned he was a tithing Catholic, active in an Orange County parish, and the social butterfly at golf and tennis with membership at an exclusive private club close to his coastal redoubt. From press releases related to charity work, I was able to identify a few doctors with whom this man practiced medicine. Ascertaining the doctor's work schedule was difficult, as he was committed to several hospitals, which is typical for a surgeon. My mother paged me and asked what I'd be doing for Easter Sunday. And this led to a solution.

I went to Stat's Floral Supply and got the stupidest looking Easter basket they sold, and a large Easter card. On the upper left of the card envelope I printed, in florid script, the name of one of the doctors the subject was actively engaged with in golf and charity. Dressed in my seersucker suit, bow tie, and saddle shoes, I motored down to the coastal community, the ORAP nestled in the Easter basket. The guards at the gate were uniformed and appeared to be off-duty police officers. When they asked for ID, I presented only my driver's license, explaining that I had an Easter delivery for the esteemed doctor.

Carefully eyeing the envelope, one of the security guards phoned the home of the doc. It was 0715 hours, and Easter services at his parish were at 0900 hours. After a sweaty moment of delay, they had him on the phone. He even asked who the delivery was from. Then I was waived in. The carefree doctor greeted me at the outer gates of his villa, a palace on the sea, wearing a bathrobe and slippers. I dismounted my Ford Bronco, smiled, and presented him the Easter basket. The card within the envelope was unsigned, and he found the papers right away.

"Happy Easter, dickhead" was my parting bon mot. I didn't invoice extra for this, or the illegal U-turn in front of his home.

He flung the basket aside and yelled, "*Fuck*!"

This was quite an intemperate reaction for a lay Catholic on Easter Sunday. It wasn't as if the doctor couldn't afford it. Coasting down the hill, I was stopped with a barricade by security guards who looked rather perturbed. "Get out of the car, asshole." I stayed behind the wheel, made myself most pleasant, and instructed, "Out of my way. I'm operating legally."

Five minutes later, local police arrived, lights and siren. For them, I dismounted and presented credentials. I was frisked, with one of the officers demanding to search the car. "You may not. If you suspect a crime has been committed, I can assure you men that no such thing took place." They handcuffed me and placed me in a police unit but did not search further.

Just then, their sergeant appeared. "What are you doing?"

"Happy Easter. I'm a private detective, sergeant. I used a ruse to identify, locate, and serve a civil defendant within the walls of this community. All quite legal."

A circular talk ensued between the sergeant and his troops, to the exclusion of the security officers. Then they uncuffed me, and under the glare of gate security, dusted me off and told me I could go about my Easter Sunday. The Mexican tile man had a cashier's checque by sundown on Monday, and the chief called me over to his office.

"Did you really call the doctor a dickhead?" he asked, writing me a checque on his personal account. I took the money, pleaded the Fifth, and went on to other, similar matters.

Not all interactions with police are positive, and a man doesn't even have to take an indictment to experience these. A referral came by my Marengo Avenue offices, having called first. Her name was Rocio, and she was an immigrant from South America. Rocio was more than presentable, well-dressed, and attending Pasadena City College.

"I got a problem. Anytime I am in my apartment, maybe ever thirty minutes, someone, they call me. They don't say *any*thing, they just wait for my answer, they hang it up. I'm at school, at work, same thing, maybe eleven, thirteen hang-ups on my answering machine."

This was just a couple of years before phone companies (TELCOS) launched enhancements to residential telephone services, such as caller identification.

"Is there ever a word spoken by whomever has called you?" I asked Rocio.

"No. Not ever." She was emphatic, nor was she couching the discussion in terms that might suggest paranoia or altered perceptions.

"Is there ever anything like background noise?" I asked for context beyond just time and frequency of the calls.

Rocio expressed a certain amount of fear. "There were a couple of times that they'd hang up, and I could hear the coins jingle the box." Rocio was referring to the sound made by a coin-operated pay telephone. At least some of the time, whomever was harassing Rocio was calling from a pay telephone. The young woman had called Pasadena Police Department and attempted to make an annoying calls complaint. With this, the TELCO could place a trap on the line, then notify police of the originating number or numbers.

Whomever Rocio had spoken with at the police department had told her, "We can't take a report if there isn't anything said." This was not true, but there was no way to make the department to take a report. I took Rocio's case. I asked Rocio as to her marital status, whether she was dating. Rocio was single, never married, was on good terms with a former boyfriend in her home nation, and had not dated anyone. Rocio was employed in retail and attended the city college. No coworker who had potential access to her home phone number had done or said anything about dating. To satisfy my own procedures, I checked Rocio out for any criminal or civil cases. She was as clean as the prairie parson.

"Has anyone, male or female, expressed romantic interest in you, asked you out, at all?" It was a logical question.

"There is a guy, but I don't know how serious he could be. He asked me to go to cinema six weeks ago. I didn't want hurt his feelings, so I didn't say no, exactly. Maybe I should have?" she asked and stated her final question.

The man in question was a tutor at the city college—and nearly eighteen years older than Rocio. The reason Rocio had not exactly taken the approach seriously was because of the age difference, and also because she perceived the man as a goof, not serious as a man in the context of men in her own culture. Rocio stated that the man spoke of himself as living with his mother, never married. He lived in Pasadena, she knew, because he often mentioned the neighborhood in which he'd grown up. When I asked how he may have obtained her home telephone number, Rocio recalled that the Student Help Center coordinated tutoring, which took place at the city college, and that tutors had limited access to student records. Rocio also had a pager for her job but had not received an unexplained series of pages.

From Rocio's characterizations of the tutor and description and phonetic pronunciation of his name, I was able to ID the tutor using an unknowing informant at the city college. I worked outward from there, establishing his name as William DuQuesne, with a complete date of birth.

Checking DuQuesne for civil and criminal, I discovered DuQuesne had no record of prosecution, nor did he have a driver's license. DuQuesne used public transit and an aged "ten-speed" bicycle, yellow, to get around Pasadena. He lived with his widowed mother, Dorothy DuQuesne, in the Chapman Woods section of unincorporated Pasadena. There was no history of divorce cases for DuQuesne, nor were there any prior restraining orders. Curiously, though, without having ever been employed beyond volunteer work as a tutor, DuQuesne had filed twelve small claims in municipal court over a ten-year period, all for small amounts with retailers, such as a dry cleaner.

Rocio didn't have a lot of money to blow hiring a mec like myself, for even a situation like this, so I made my approach as expeditious as possible. I surveyed the neighborhood close to DuQuesne's home and made a pay telephone next to a liquor store and laundry on Rosemead Boulevard, still in unincorporated Pasadena. I called Rocio from the pay telephone, and she stated that the coin drop and background sounded the same. She was going to the city college in the morning, then to work in the afternoon, so the very next day, and I staked out the phone.

Attired in a polyester jogging suit, yellowed cycling helmet, and thick spectacles, William DuQuesne arrived not long after Rocio departed from the college for work. He dropped coins, dialed, then left. Thirty-five minutes later, he returned on foot, repeating the process, and departing. I spent six hours, reading the racing form, listening to Right Wing Radio, and photographing DuQuesne as he used the pay telephone over and over again.

I compared the times with the hang-ups on Rocio's machine, and they matched. It was an obvious conclusion that the harassing calls were coming from DuQuesne, who either knew his mother would not like him making these calls from home, or that law enforcement could make a case on him for telephone harassment, hence his multiple use of the pay telephone. This is intent—mens rea.

Rocio attempted another crime report, based upon my findings, to Pasadena police. They weren't having it. That's when I elected to cut to the chase in this matter and wrote a letter to William DuQuesne, on my letterhead, informing him that I knew he was making harassing calls to Rocio, and warning him that legal action could result from this. I'm not a lawyer or prosecutor, so in my judgment, it was better to just leave this open-ended and allow the nebbish's imagination to inflict whatever informative damage was necessary to end the harassment he inflicted on Rocio.

I also copied the Dean's Office at the city college. They should know that a tutor was advantaging himself using the context of his volunteer position at the school. Rocio never received another call, nor was William DuQuesne a tutor at the college, ever again. But I got a call, about a week later.

"Hey, hotshot, when are you going to file charges?" came the hostile call.

"Oh, I don't think I've had the pleasure. How about you introduce yourself, ass-eyes," was as courteous as I could make myself.

It was a lieutenant at Pasadena Police Department, whom I'd first known a year before. He'd brandished his sidearm when I served a federal trial subpoena on him in the King's Villages case. Something about him only allowing himself to be served on Thursdays.

"I want to know when you're filing charges on this guy?!" the lieutenant snarled.

"Look, Lieutenant, did you ever consider it might be just as illegal for you to impersonate a private investigator as it is for me to make like I'm you?"

We said goodbye with the lieutenant screaming and breathing hard. Turns out Dorothy DuQuesne was his older sister. This wasn't the last of it, nor did I expect it to be. About seven, eight months subsequent, late at night, my home phone rang. The only person who calls me at home is my mother, so I knew I was in trouble.

"When? When you coming over?" It was an angry woman, but not my mother.

"Didn't know I was supposed to…" I needed to figure out who was ringing me.

"You got to come over to my house right now. It's happening!" She was adamant, and I didn't recognize her voice.

She was expecting that I'd come over and sweep her home for listening devices and cameras. Her neighbors were seeing her, nude, in the shower, through her microwave oven. The clock said it was after 1:00 a.m. I hung up and unplugged the phone. A week later, this happened again. Then two days after that.

"What kind of shit is this? Ain't you a detective?" She was distraught. Plainly, someone had given this woman my home phone number, maybe just as a cute gag. "I'm off duty right now, honey. Maybe on Sunday?" I asked her.

At 3:00 a.m., on the occasion of her fourth call, "But the lieutenant said you were available right now!" she hissed.

Police agencies, like I often do, get calls from distressed, deluded people, convinced they're under technical or actual surveillance. My antagonist police lieutenant had given this poor whacko my telephone number, with a suggestion that I'd do what his agency would not and could not. It's a funny practical joke. I could make a complaint against him. I'm never lacking for recourse. But a good joke should be shared, broadly. Others should enjoy it, otherwise it isn't much of a joke. Obtaining the lieutenant's home telephone number didn't take much effort. I'd tell you that I used a source in a TELCO, or someone at city hall, but the reality is he was such an asshole, one of the men on morning watch gave it to me in exchange for a walker's tip on a lame horse.

The next time the agitated woman called just before sunrise, I told her, "Listen, now, the lieutenant is just about ready to take up your case. You wait until 8:30 a.m. and ring him at this number. If a woman answers, tell her the magic password is 'cocksucker,' and she will put you right through." That was the end of it. I've made peace with him since—the lieutenant. We are actually reasonably friendly, like a lion and a hyena who enjoy the same muddy, carcass-strewn watering ditch.

Perhaps due to the contaminated wasteland offered by television, citizens can have an unrealistic expectation of what the cops are going to do in the face of a complaint.

Not many years ago, a realtor referred a friend of his to me: a sixty-something man residing in the estate his parents had left him, an only child. The place was situated in a very desirable neighborhood and resembled nothing so much as stately (threadbare) Wayne Manor.

Richard Headley had suffered a break-in to the estate, a palace on a hill, which was mostly unfurnished. I asked if it was up for sale, hence the relationship with the referring realtor. "No. I'll never sell this place! Are you kidding me, man?" was Headley's offended response.

He had it unfurnished so he could rent the place out to the studios, for film and TV production. While his circular driveway was large enough to accommodate a production crew, I surmised Richard's neighbors were not enamored of him and his business model.

"I was raised in this place, bro. My parents left it to me," mumbled my consultation.

The garage had a few highly polished classic cars and a Harley Davidson motorcycle. I was ushered into a high-ceilinged room with a stained-glass skylight. In this room was an enormous slot car track, elevated for play on an antique dining table that could have come from Versailles.

"In here is where they broke in," said Richard, showing me to an adjoining washroom, also with a stained-glass skylight. Whomever had broken in had done so through this skylight.

"They broke in a week ago, and the cops haven't done a thing!" He was agitated.

"What did they take?" I had pen and paper ready.

"They broke in, cut themselves. They got blood all over the washroom," Headley blathered.

"Do you have a list of what was taken?" I tried again. "You are insured, I'd imagine."

"They bled all over the washroom, then defiled the sink." He pointed to an early twentieth century sink, hewn of marble, which was carved to look like a clam shell. It was an ancient, pale pink color. It appeared unmolested to me.

"Defiled it?" I questioned, with no answers yet as to what had been taken.

"She…er, they, took a shit in that sink."

You don't say. Amazing. By Richard's use of the feminine pronoun, which he rapidly corrected, I formed the belief that my consulting client knew whom had relieved herself in his pristine, antique, pink sink.

"The cops sent their CSI team over and said it wasn't likely there could be fingerprints. I've called the detectives three times, and they haven't returned my calls. Can you believe this?" He was turbo with anger. Incandescent.

"I see. Now how about telling me what was taken." Nothing. Nothing was taken. All the more reason to believe that Richard knew exactly who the guilty party was. "So…what is it you'd like me to do, Richard?" I asked my final question, stitching up my notepad.

"I want you to collect DNA from the blood she…they…left behind, so we can prove who did this!"

I broke out a three-page contract, written for civilians, and started filling it out.

"What's this going to cost me?!" Richard glared at me when I handed him the document for signature. It includes a clause, wherein the client who omits material facts forfeits unearned retainer, defraying the liabilities arising of working for man-child liars.

"My standard retainer in cases such as these is ten thousand dollars. A personal or business checque will do rather well." I waited.

"You're joking, right? This is outrageous!"

And down the circular drive I went. From that day to this one, I've never heard from him again.

His expectation was a full-blown, scientific investigation to ID whomever of his lays had been offended enough to break in, in his absence, and drop a deuce in the sink. The reality is that the police reserve their large expenditures for homicides, ugly accidents, kidnappings, and protecting the thieving jackals you elect to public office. Not much else.

Just as not all agencies are equal, I can say the same for cops. Most are great men, great women, who push a patrol car around the city, rescuing people from situations they should avoid, even when the rest of us have the day off. I have the comparative luxury of firing clients, in more ways than one, like Richard the Man-Child, with his slot car track and a dump in the sink. Police cannot always properly "fire" a citizen making a complaint.

Are the police violent? I should hope so. Hiring weak, incapable people as cops has a direct, negative impact in the safety of a city and the people who dwell within it. Commissioning men and women who lack emotional fortitude, physical courage, and the ability to fend for themselves on the streets means that even the simplest confrontation with bandits, a drunk, an addict, a neurotic, or a mental case can escalate from an awkward, disjointed discussion to a fatal shooting, with no intervening steps. Police officers who cannot protect themselves cannot protect you, nor can they stand up to the machinery of a city government at cross purposes with citizens.

If you believe your police department is populated with bad, corrupt people, take a harder look at the filth you've elected to your city council. Your police are a direct reflection of what the majority have voted for.

While you're at Little League games, weddings, Christmas, and a bar mitzvah, the cops have to skip theirs and work the streets you've created. I've a solid friend, who served this nation in the air police as a female airman, then went on LAPD. She has more sand than many of the men that I know.

Her father was a combat veteran and a cop, and her husband is a cop. Working a gang task force, she was struck by a street criminal driving a car. She took early retirement to raise a family…with shattered legs, partially disfigured for the rest of her life. She earned every dime of pay, every benefit, and the modest pension she lives on with her husband still working the streets. Call these people corrupt at your family's peril.

And then, there's other guys. Bums who do the bare minimum. Deadwood. Couldn't find a burglar in a phone booth with both hands, a flashlight, and a butt-sniffing dog. Their agencies can define *corruption* as taking payoffs, warning criminals of a pending search, identifying informants. But those same supervising officials will *never* associate laziness, incompetence, and prejudice with corruption. This is job security for mecs like me. At the very moment these agencies get to be good at what you're paying them for, I'll be off the case.

There is a two-hundred officer agency patrolling a city I am quite familiar with that employed a man who called himself a burglary detective. Let's call him Detective Jose.

Jose was working a case, involving stolen property, being fenced by a shot-caller in the Mexican Mafia. After other agencies and competent officers had made a case on the gangster, Jose took up a hot and heavy affair with the gangster's gangster wife. The Mexican Mafia has its own intelligence network, comprised of defense lawyers and union officials, and they got the word to the gangster that his wife was sharing panties with Detective Jose. Then, they helped the gangster figure out where Detective Jose lived, with Detective Jose's wife and children. The gangster made a very credible threat about wiping out Detective Jose and family.

Did Detective Jose get dismissed? Fired? Board of rights? No. Detective Jose, his wife and family, got 'round-the-clock armed protection from officers of his own agency as well as the officers employed by the distant city in which Detective Jose lived. Did taxpayers ever hear of this? No way. The city attorney knew, as did the city manager. Who protected Detective Jose from getting fired? His labor union. The labor union that owns two city council members. Sweet deal. Try this at your job and see what happens.

Nearly as amusing was the call I received from a city manager, who asked me to take on a job recovering a police car, unmarked. It had been used by his city's unwise hire. They'd engaged a man as chief from out of state to demonstrate to citizens how inclusive they were. To call him incompetent, conflicted, corrupt, and distracted wouldn't do the man justice.

The city had lent him money to buy a house in the city, which he'd sold when he took an East Coast chief's job. The house had been sold, and he'd pocketed the money. He wasn't much of a cop, much of a leader, much of a chief, but he made city management look good and took a wise position in a piece of real estate. As far as I know, this loan was never repaid, not even from his trebled pensions.

My assignment was to recover the unmarked police interceptor, which had been his to use as chief. He drove it to the East Coast, casually, and was certain no one would file grand theft charges, mostly because they wouldn't. From the city attorney I muscled some funds, a release and authority to operate the cruiser, and a letter deputizing me as an officer of the city, for the purposes of recovering city property. Oh, and keys too.

I booked a flight east, landed in a neighboring city, took a taxi to the city where the chief was now the chief, and stole his car. I walked right into the lot, started it up, and drove off. There was a hot cup of coffee in the console and soothing music to enjoy on my way west. My work has a lot of pleasures—"French benefits," as my platoon sergeant called them on the DMZ, and stealing a police car, from a chief of police, counts as one of those pleasures.

Of course, I got pulled over, just inside the next state. A *felony stop*, it's called. After I'd been stretched out on the highway shoulder, frisked, cuffed, and identified, they fished the letter out of my jacket pocket. There were four state police units on scene. It took a phone call or three, but I had time, and the weather wasn't bad. I got dusted off and treated to a fresh cup of coffee before I was sent on my way. The lead officer was a pockmarked lieutenant of indeterminate age. He was laughing as I pulled back onto the interstate. I could've run

Code 3, "lights and siren," all the way back to my clients, but I was being paid by the hour.

In the course of my career, LAPD has fallen long and fallen hard. To best encapsulate this, I'll recount a very telling, emblematic anecdote of what this agency has become. There was a time when Los Angeles was patrolled and protected by an agency that was the model for the nation.

One night, about 9:00 p.m., in the early 2000s, I was motoring north through Highland Park, in northeast division. Ahead of me, a few car-lengths, was a gardener's truck…with a rack over the bed for rakes, branch cutters, and other tools, and a lawnmower caroming off the sides of the bed. The truck was moving at less than twenty miles per hour and weaving the lanes.

The man driving was drunk—*deuce*, in LAPD argot. I looked to my right, and equilateral with my car was an officer known to me from a few investigations into his off-duty misconduct, who was either deputy chief or still a mere commander at that point, in his department issue, plain-wrap Crown Victoria. This senior officer was in uniform, stars twinkling on his blue collars. The drunk was fifty meters ahead of him, and he did exactly, precisely nothing.

I put my window down, sounded my horn, which caused Commander X to look over. "Are you going to pull him over, or is it my turn?" An irate look puckered his face, and finally he turned on lights and siren and called for a patrol unit, and the drunk continued north, his truck veering toward the curb. Is there a time for mercy with a drunk gardener? Certainly. But that decision isn't made by ignoring the problem. Maybe Commander X intended to pull him over, summon northeast division patrol, but I doubt it. If I had called LAPD emergency communications, I could have been on hold for an hour.

Gone are the men like Tom Lange, Mac McClain, Bob Souza, Ernest "Curt" Curtsinger, Philip Vannatter, Serge Robledo, and Earl Paysinger. The women, too, have changed from cops like Betty Kelepecz and Peggy York. Now it seems all the command culture of one of the leading agencies in the Western US are risk-averse, glib, facile versions of Commander X. No one could argue that Los Angeles is a safer, better city than it was on the day that Daryl Gates took his leave as chief.

Lange and Vannatter took O.J. Simpson to trial for murdering his wife and worked the Wonderland Avenue murders with Souza. Mac partnered with Tom to haul Ed Nash in for murder after Souza retired. Curt Curtsinger was an original LAPD SWAT team member when no other agency had a SWAT team—real or imagined. Paysinger was the bulwark as South Central fell into a cauldron of drug and gang violence, knowing every single community leader for each situation. Betty and Peggy were pioneering women in police work, with Betty being the first female officer to earn the rank of commander. This is a history that is now ignored for the most part. But I remember. Once, in Mayor Bradley's outer office with Russ Mancini, my Pinkerton boss, I overheard Mayor Bradley bark at a whining Tom Hayden (state senator): "Of course the troops protect each other. Men who won't protect each other won't protect the city. Grow up!"

Working with Curtsinger and Souza can be illustrated so well in this way: I was working an informant, who seemed to have solid information on a group of characters hijacking delivery trucks, some of which were operated by a warehouse-distribution client. If he was what he appeared to be, we could suppress the whole crew.

I wrote a two-paragraph summary, which Souza walked in to Curt, who looked it over, polished his glasses, looked at Souza, and asked, "What time and where are you meeting this asshole?" Curt and Bob spoke fluent LAPD.

I am to meet him at a greasy spoon, a diner, in Commerce, off Interstate 5, where all the truckers stop for dinner. Rendezvous at 8:00 p.m. He is supposed to bring something, otherwise I could make seven felony cases on him.

"Okay. You'll be shadowed by Souza. I will go now and set up in there in case he's a bigger asshole than we might be thinking he is." Curtsinger departed with a 9mm Beretta, a two-inch .38 on his ankle, and a short Ithaca shotgun rolled up in the *Wall Street Journal*. Otherwise, he looked like any other working stiff in Los Angeles.

Souza covered the lot on the outside, armed heavy like Curt. I was strapped and seemingly on my own. The informant was there, jacked up on speed, and dancing around in his seat, gesturing in the exaggerated fashion suggestive of methamphetamine use. He kept hauling his hands from under the table and I was concentrating on three things all the time: (1) the information he was gushing; (2) what was in his hands when they came up; and (3) whether or not me, Curt, or Souza would have to dump him. It all worked out though. The forty-minute conversation had Curtsinger in the next booth, silently studying the *Journal*, and me wired. Transcribing the recording was arduous, and thankfully I never had to bring it to court. His information was straighter than he was, and we made several cases on people in the crew we were hired to suppress.

Chief Gates took his PI license exam with me, right around the time of the Rodney King Riots. Two weeks later I ran into the chief at a breakfast joint in San Marino. "How did you do on that test?" Chief Gates asked me.

I passed it; he didn't and needed my study guide. He and another senior officer were forming a police consulting firm and needed the license. There was a time when Chief Gates was a household word. Another good man…forgotten. And as long as I'm addressing municipal malpractice, the politicians on the city council? The Mayor's Office? They amount to little more than Lenin's kindergarten. At the time I didn't recognize that I was punching and batting above my weight and average. To work with and around these guys was like being in the batting lineup with Babe Ruth, or a stunt coordinator for Bruce Lee.

CHAPTER

14

MISSING PERSONS

In any police agency, of any size, in any place, in any country, the missing persons desk is where homicide detectives are lashed after admitting their own alcoholism to the captain. It's a form of rehabilitative hell, where a constant risk-versus-reward calculus plays out with each new, low-grade case he catches: Retire? Die in place? Cinch up the gunbelt, close cases, and return to rotation.

Often it is the grinding ennui of this detective, who cannot, or will not, work the matter that drives the citizen to me. Some years ago, an officer with a Native Indian tribe's police department shared with me a three-page questionnaire, developed by someone bright in the business, which was written in such a way as to jog the memory and or conscience of anyone making such a report. I was amazed how thorough it was, which is increasingly rare in public agencies.

Your police agency has an established procedure, triage of sorts, that they work through when a party walks in to make a report. Is the missing person endangered? Is that person missing and a juvenile? Are they a juvenile who runs away every week, to smoke dope and drink wine under a railroad trestle with Zeke and Cisco?

What is the status of the party making the report? A wife, whose husband never made it home from work, and she's decided a year later to figure things out? Is it the employer of a single woman who disappeared with the company checque book? All quite obvious. When someone comes to my office, wanting another person found,

I, too, have a checklist, mostly involving the motives and disposition of the prospective client, as well as whatever may be known about the party being sought.

If the client makes noises about violence, it is important that I abstain. Sometimes people who intend violence will send a proxy who can be innocent or just part of something more elaborate to put violence to someone.

"Loretta, she left me, couple weeks ago. We had a big argument, and it's important that you find her, so I can make it up to her." Two days in I discover that Loretta took out a third protective order against my client and is living in a women's shelter with two black eyes in mortal terror of my prospective client. Bad business.

Sometimes it's perfectly innocent. "Me and my girlfriend were just right for each other in high school, thirty-eight years ago. Be great if I could find her, see?"

What's her name? Where did you attend school? Where did she live then?

"Lisa Wilson. I think she was a year older than me. Or maybe she was a year younger. Had a brother named Steve. They lived over near Monrovia, or maybe it was Baldwin Park."

This is usually the case with the client having lost contact with a person, whose identity they cannot perfectly recall. In a matter like this, the first hurdle is identification of Lisa Wilson, a rather common name, and a woman who may have married once, twice, or even more. These matters demand work.

Usually, the client is a lawyer, wanting a subject located and interviewed, or located and served with process. This is to a detective agency what the "lubricate, oil change, filter" service is at the Buick dealer. These matters, also, can turn complex.

"Our firm is probating the estate of a deceased husband and wife, immigrants from Japan. They've two children. One a son in his forties, whose location and status is known. The daughter is early forties, and we need to locate her to give notice in the proceedings."

Where was she last? Was she estranged from her family? What is her name, description, trade, marital status, and education?

"All we know is her name and an old address in Orange County."

Can I speak with the brother?

"No. For whatever reasons, he is hostile to the proceeding and has stated that his sister returned to Japan, with no information more specific than that."

It isn't unusual for siblings to resent each other, with an uncomfortable past coming into sharper focus after the death of parents.

Using Department of Motor Vehicles data, old civil records, and a database, I found the sister's identifying information and an address almost twenty years old in Orange County. It appeared they may very well have gone there, but in contrast to what was reported by the law firm, she'd been born in the US rather than Japan.

Reaching out to past connections leftover from my days in Asia, I enlisted the aid of a respected private operation in Tokyo, run by a retired prefectural detective.

Some weeks later that detective reported to me. "Even though her name is somewhat common, we cannot find anyone with her name and date of birth in any prefecture. We expanded our investigation to include immigration records and marriage records, but no one comes up." Nothing. Could I rely on this report from Japan? It is my experience that Japan, like Korea, is a well-ordered civil society, where extensive records are kept at every level. The missing woman's parents were identifiable in Japanese records, with the father having been a chemical engineer.

I scoured various genealogical resources, trying to ascertain whether the missing sister had ever married in the US. Nothing. Nor were there any name variations. My next lead involved canvassing the apartment building where the sister had last been reported living. No one remembered her, and the building had changed hands twice since her record was current.

Making liaison with a source in Orange County law enforcement, I came to learn that the Orange County address was all that was left, and no one, ever, had reported the sister missing to any police or welfare agency.

When I reported these findings to the law firm, I learned a bit more of the brother. He'd been caring for his parents both, then just his mother after the father died, but ultimately a family friend had made a report of abusive neglect to Adult Protective Services, whereupon the mother had been removed to be cared for elsewhere, with the brother remaining in his parents' house.

Canvassing the neighborhood around the home where the brother still lived, I learned that he was sullen, surly, and hostile to virtually everyone in the cul-de-sac. The yard was overgrown with knee-high grass, and a pepper tree shaded a beaten Nissan pickup in the driveway. As the brother was lawyered up, there was no interviewing him. All that remained to be done was searching the home and probably digging up the yard for me to close this matter down. The affidavit I filed with the probate court speaks for itself.

Often, I am close to the party making the appointment with me. Not long ago, a woman came to me, distraught, her brother missing as of the Thanksgiving he'd failed to show up to. Two weeks had passed with no word.

When I searched his home with his sister, my sense was that he was dead. Nothing was right in his home, but his keys were gone, along with wallet and phone. His car was in the driveway. If he was in the house, I couldn't smell him. That has happened before.

Police had searched twice, and so did I. I kept my mouth shut with his sister about my sense of it all. Someone suggested he would be at another family property, out of state. In that state is an old, dear friend, Scott McMullin. He's a retired stock broker, and now a tree cutter, a father. He was also a reserve cop for several years with a good head about him. I told him my cause and the address.

"I approached the place. There was a dusty VW van in the driveway. I didn't need to open it to see there was no one aboard. It hasn't moved in six months. The house was dark but for a lone bulb in the kitchen. A radio was left playing—NPR, probably to deter a burglary. Food in the fridge was just a single beer and condiments. Nothing to suggest anyone was there. Neighbors haven't seen your missing man for eighteen months." A pro-job, Scott ran—thorough and low-key.

Days later he was found on the property where I had first searched, dead by his own hand. I can state his sister didn't have to see him as a deteriorated corpse, a shell of the good man he had been. It was enough that I saw him. His reasons were intimately his own, and I cannot say much more for this. A former girlfriend had received his suicide notice, by text message, but did not recognize this for its plain meaning. It was a communication of overwhelming despair.

When the coroner released his body for burial, it was a traditional Jewish affair, and somber. I was asked to be a pallbearer, and from within his box, I could finally smell the certainty of his death. Graveside, the rabbi instructed his friends to queue up, and each who were willing turned some earth on the box, then lowered him into the ground.

"Let this earth, this earth of God, be the last blanket our brother and son and friend is wrapped within. Let his sleep be eternal. Let him be at peace." There have been others, too many, like this.

Some are never found. One was an alcoholic, thirty or more years my senior as of 1993. Once a respected investment banker, he had lost job after job, and a couple of marriages, to the drink.

"My dad called me, drunk, on New Year's Eve, 1991. He was elated and babbling on something, and I couldn't take it. I was a new mother and had a baby to look after and he just couldn't stay out of the booze," said his thirty-year-old daughter.

Oh? Where was he?

"I think he was in New York City or New Jersey. He said something about getting a job. But he had said all that before. I knew he was drunk, and I couldn't take it. It hurt so much to hear from him like this. I did something I now wish I had not done."

What?

"I forbade him to ever call me. Not ever again." She was sobbing. She never heard from him. Nor had anyone else. Her father was an educated, garrulous man. For him to be out of touch for six months was unheard of, let alone two years. The sheriff had taken a report and said there was no record of the missing man in jails or hospitals.

The family had a particular need in this case, and I was enlisted. I spoke with old colleagues of the missing man, who all told a similar tale:

"He was a great guy. Smartest man I ever worked under. At (Japanese bank) he instituted investment of certain funds in Japanese banks. It was a big success on all sides. Then he'd drink, and his drinking got worse. We tried to cover for him, but he was trading on past glory." This is to paraphrase what was said by each colleague.

I tracked his last bank withdrawal to Newark, New Jersey, to a rough neighborhood. It was a day or two before his call to the sobbing daughter. The belief of the liquor merchant was that my missing man was camped at the waterfront. "I never seen him again. Great guy."

From a source in Glendale, California, I obtained old dental records. DNA wasn't as universally collected, then, and set about communicating the dental records to various medical examination agencies with jurisdiction in the port. In December 1994, I was even shown a series of *floaters*, corpses as yet unidentified, fished out of the water. None were my man. He shall be forever in the hands of God.

These cases are a perfect, divine punishment for any cop falling from favor. She will either reform, or retire, lest she die of a heartbreak that can even eclipse working homicide callouts.

CHAPTER

15

ORGANIZED CRIME

One might not think that a private detective would necessarily have to investigate OC, but the crimes they involve themselves in affect much of business, both California's and elsewhere. But these guys rival US steel for the scope of their criminal activities.

Metro Los Angeles has never been a haven for organized crime (OC), in the commonly understood sense, meaning Italian La Cosa Nostra. However, this just irrigated and fertilized local crooks like Mickey Cohen, Ed Nash, and La Eme (Mexican Mafia). La Cosa Nostra has a presence but doesn't control much of anything. The Italians in LA are derisively referred to as the Mickey Mouse Mafia by the bent-nose crowd in NY.

On the subject of Mickey Cohen, every half-baked news guy plying the trade would, at one time or another, intimate how well he knew Cohen—as if the diminutive hood was Mickey Mantle or something. I believed it the first few times but realized in my second year afield that this was like saying they'd sniffed Natalie Wood's ass at the Oscars party in 1966.

The Mexican Mafia is very well-established and uses the traditional method of recruiting from imprisoned street gang members, through a process of selection, requiring lifetime loyalty and violence. Their numbers are legion, and they have equity in the political cabal running California's government. This differs not at all from

Chicago, Cleveland, Boston, and New York City. Within our prisons, Mexican Mafia cross-pollinates with the Aryan Brotherhood, LCN, and, less often, Black Guerilla Family. They share resources as often as they kill each other over drug territories with and without the penal institutions. Mexican Mafia also enforces, mules, and distributes dope and guns for foreign narcotics cartels, mostly based in Mexico.

Nontraditional OC includes motorcycle clubs—some of them, or all of them. There are clubs which are strictly "civilian," some part-civilian and part-OC, and some of which are just OC. The bikers, new to prison, whether Latino or whiteboy, are recruited to the Aryan Brotherhood, or AB in prison vernacular.

The AB, like Mexican Mafia, is intensely disciplined, densely structured, ruthless, and violent. They make up for their smaller numbers with intensity and certainty of violence. What the AB and Mexican Mafia share is the death penalty for a whole variety of codified offenses: snitching, failure to obey an order to murder, snitching, stealing and/or diverting dope from the organization, snitching, and…snitching. Some might smugly proclaim, "We don't really have a death penalty in the California justice system." Bullshit. Men are executed every year.

These groups use women on the outside and prison staff on the inside to mule dope, money, phones, and weapons. Often their accomplices are corrections officers. Any sober analysis would conclude that these groups are a private, self-governing organ, operating independently of any official governance.

Most robberies of gun dealers in California are carried out by the AB and Mexican Mafia. Typical of their modus is to demand the wallet or purse of any customer or clerk in attendance, with the warning, "We know who you are and where you live. Don't testify." Sounds just as ominous in English as it does in Spanish.

This would be typical of OC interaction with civilians: rob, then intimidate. At the other end, city, county, and state government does its incompetent part, minimizing the punishments accorded to most OC defendants. Rarely will I meet an official who can acknowledge that incompetence and laziness are the most insidious forms of government corruption.

Ben "Bugsy" Siegel once told a contractor working on the Flamingo Hotel, "Relax. We only kill each other." Siegel was a legendary Jewish hood from the East Coast who had been in league with Meyer Lansky and Lucky Luciano. He met his end, a violent death, for perceived disobedience to a lending contract and construction costs of the first noteworthy casino in Las Vegas, the Flamingo. This code against killing civilians is loosely followed, lest clipping an innocent bring more negative attention or discredit OC in a way they'd consider unmanly.

For a risk management outfit based out of state, I was tasked to identify and build an airtight case in a series of cargo thefts and outright hijackings. There was a cargo terminal in Southern California suffering a steep increase in losses, and while public agencies had made a few arrests of thieves, including truck drivers and warehousemen, none had pinpointed who was putting the crimes together. The risk manager, a retired marine infantry officer, noticed a pattern.

The pattern was that the thieves always knew which loads, in sealed trailers, were of the most immediate value, and most easily disposed of through fencing. Fencing of stolen cargo is often done through a "gray market"—legit distributors of commercial goods who do not look too hard at the origins of what is being distributed: tobacco, liquor, and consumer electronics. Without fail at the terminal, no one had to cut the seals on one hundred trailers to identify which trailer was worth breaking into, hauling over a rundown fence, or hijacked at a stoplight at gunpoint.

This indicated that a man inside terminal dispatch was involved. Maybe more than one. My job was to sift through cases, records, conduct interviews and surveillance, then ID him. The local sheriff couldn't be bothered. There were twelve possible suspects: three women and nine men who had ready access to terminal records. In counterintelligence, like at Pinkerton, one always starts with first verifying the identity of each suspect, then combing through their past to identify moral turpitude and/or vulnerability to extortion.

A few of them had insignificant criminal records—drunk driving, domestic violence, petty theft. None of this was a pattern. A couple of the men had child support and tax garnishment orders scooping up a strong percentage of their pay. Neither appeared to live beyond his means. The rest were clean. Then I commenced interviewing each. Many volunteered information that they perceived as useful. None claimed to know who was involved. In conducting the interviews, I left my line of questioning open so as to bury my true purposes, beyond putting an end to the losses.

Then I went back over their backgrounds. Identification is key for any man's background: If I do not know *who* he actually is, I cannot effectively know *what* he is. This was an essential lesson in counterintelligence.

One of the dispatchers was mid-forties, of Hispanic or Levantine appearance, with an Anglo first name and Spanish surname. His job application stated that he was from Florida, had attended community college twenty years prior, and lived in an apartment in a large development comprised of four hundred units. He had no record of citations, lawsuits, tax liens, divorce. Nothing.

His credit information went back six years, then died. No prior credit of any kind, bad or good. He was a cypher. In my first interview of him, he spoke clear, unaccented English. His social security number had been issued exactly six years prior, with a sequence peculiar to New Jersey, when he was…thirty-nine. This made no sense. Unless…

Our second interview started like this: "Do you wish to remain in the program, or are you going to continue stealing?" This question had him looking out the windows for an answer.

After a minute he asked, "How did you find out? They was supposed to make me safe." He'd been in a version of the witness protection program, as administered by a state attorney general. In extended interview, he admitted this, but nothing else. He refused to give up his *crimee* or his true and correct identity. It was enough for the terminal to terminate him, but not enough to make a felony case. For the risk manager, this was enough of a win. I sent a copy of my report to the cargo theft task force administered by CHP, so that they were aware of the man.

Had I been given a broader imprimatur by the risk manager, I'd have put the subject under surveillance and made the felony case sufficient to properly identify him by prior record and identity, as well as his partners in cargo theft. But every time, these matters are limited by the budget, judgment, and the needs of my client.

How do civilians involve themselves with OC? They never have clean hands, and mobsters will advantage themselves in every way. This usually involves indebtedness to a bookie, shylock, or dope dealer (licensed or unlicensed). The most dangerous involvement civilians have with OC arises of solicitation of murder for hire.

Contrary to popular mythology driven by Hollywood, there is no vast, secret pool of hit men waiting to be hired by jealous housewives, greedy business partners, or embarrassed married sex partners. Murder for hire is a part of OC and always has been. In many organizations, it's how a vetted candidate establishes his bona fides (makes his bones). When a civilian attempts to hire a hit man, he typically goes to a criminal that he knows and makes the offer of seemingly easy money. Most criminals are shrewd enough to not involve themselves, or, if they're under indictment or trying to lever the freedom of a crime partner, they'll advantage themselves.

Such a suspect might take money for a hit that will never take place, then defy the civilian to do something about it (like Nick Barone), or maybe even extort them for more money. The criminal is more likely to go to his old enemy, the police, and trade the solicitation for a get-out-of-jail-free card. He will introduce the civilian to a detective duded up like a cartel bandito in cowboy boots, a white hat, gold chains, and a recording device. We've all seen it in the news.

Once, a restaurateur came at me with this: "My partner is in over his head. I caught him not just emptying our till, but he raided the safe also. I sat down with him. He's being extorted by a mob guy he met. If I call the cops, my liquor license is in the wind. You've got to help me."

My client had his whole net worth tied up in this. He could lose every single thing he owned, going in one direction or in the other. After I did a quick background of his partner and the partner's paramour, one of their waitresses, I sat the partner down in the office. Bill was a man in his early sixties, had been a military officer, and played college football. Bill was married and divorced, thrice, and had a self-acknowledged drinking problem. Around town he had a reputation as an affable, capable front man for the types of bars and restaurants businessmen like to inhabit. In Bill's favor, he wasn't much a gambler usually.

Bill's girl was a tall, buxom, forties cheerleader type with a brash mouth. Twice divorced, with a couple of teenage children, Glenda had no criminal record beyond a couple of drunk-driving cases and a nasty rep for hanging paper (bouncing checques). Glenda held a domestic violence order against her children's father. He was a man I knew by reputation, a "security consultant," and veteran of US Army Special Warfare. Don had slapped Glenda around, prompting Glenda to summon police. Upon their arrival, Glenda showed deputies where Don had some illegal weapons, probably machine guns. Nothing too dangerous. Don was serving years in prison, contemporaneous with my interview of Bill.

Over a cup of coffee, which Bill took with trembling, hungover hands, he set the stage for what had occurred. His partner wasn't aware of half of it. "It's like this, see. Glenda and me, we got together after Don got sent up. She divorced him and all. Anyway, Don likes to call the house from the joint and make threats. He calls collect, wanting to talk to the children. Glenda put me on the spot, wanted me to warn Don off…I'm her boyfriend now. Like that."

Like that. Don had offered to kill Glenda and Bill when he made parole. In Glenda's judgment, Don was capable of just this and more. To state that she was terrified of the man was an understatement.

Again, trembling, Bill mumbled, "Couple of months ago this big guy comes into the place, on a night when I'm up front and Glenda is working tables. He has a nice suit on, wears a diamond ring and an Omega watch, see? Anyway, he talks rather circumspect all about how he's connected, has a thick New York kind of accent. At the end of the night, he asks do Glenda and me want to go 'party' with him, further west, in Beverly Hills. I didn't really, but Glenda kind of has a nose for blow, cocaine you know. So, we go hang out with this guy. Everywhere we go, westside places, they all know him, call him Mr. Gambino.

"I asked him is he a real Gambino, like the famous gangster back east, and he asks me what I think. He walks the bill at two places, and the maître d' says nothing. Nothing at all. He has a big town car, and Glenda keeps giving me the elbow and shouts up my ear that I should ask him to take care of Don, you know?"

Glenda wanted Bill to settle her problematic ex. Bill asked Gambino if Gambino could reach behind prison walls, rough Don up, maybe have the air let out of him. "He says he has people, wanted to get all of Don's info, made Glenda write it down, see? So, he comes next Friday, we go out after closing time, and he gives Glenda some 'toot.' She snorts it, and he gets grabby with her. I told him, 'Be a gentleman,' and he says he will, then starts right up again.

"Next Friday, Gambino shows up just as we are shutting down and goes behind the bar and fucking empties the till! Like he owns the joint. I asked him what the fuck he's doing, and he says he's now a partner, that he done something for me, for Glenda. Next, he orders us 'get into the car,' makes me drive. And while I'm driving, he feeds Glenda his dick in the back seat. He tells me, 'shut up and drive.' We go to Dan Tana in West Hollywood. He runs up a big bill. He gets booze, food, whatever, and sticks me with the fucking bill. He's saying he'll be back on Friday, get his partner cut of the till, but that then only him and Glenda are going on the town."

He was frightened and wasn't accustomed to being in such a state. Bill was also shocked at the conduct of Glenda, who seemed to increasingly enjoy the malefactor's attention.

I took a retainer from the partners and the mobile number of "Gambino" and his description. The bartender at a westside place they'd attended knew him as "Gambino" and gave me the license plate of the town car. Was Gambino a straight-up hood from the east? Was he just an enterprising con man? Was he a hood and a con man? If the suspect was legit La Cosa Nostra, my clients could be in grave danger, having crossed a line of involvement wherein the suspect could, under the code of the Mafia, claim equity in their licensed establishment. If it turned out "Gambino" was a bold confidence man, neither partner had as much risk as he did outright embarrassment. The third question could also be a problem, with the connections and criminal bona fides being the deciding factors.

From the license plate, I made the name of a company that made stretch limousines in the San Fernando Valley. One of the partners was Gambino. I was able to make a home address on the man, his date of birth. From these I learned he had an extensive criminal record for robbery, drug dealing, attempted murder, and extortion—all on the East Coast. A retired NY police organized-crime squad detective categorized him as an associate of a different crime family different from the Gambino Crime Family, but known by name. Definitely LCN.

Under surveillance over a week, Gambino made stops at cigar lounges, liquor stores, body shops, and bars. Always short visits. Surveillance of this sort is strenuous, as many of these places had nighttime operations, and we slept little. We both used digital video cameras to capture as much discreet detail as we could. Moon and I had extensive photo and video footage of the man. Don being very organized cataloged all the video, and we collaborated on a detailed report, identifying each business "Gambino" was making short visits to, just as if we were conducting a short-term RICO investigation. In the middle of all this, Bill called to let me know that Don was still issuing threats from prison, that Gambino had just advantaged himself. This, too, was a crime.

My client was between the devil and the deep blue sea. If he involved police, he'd likely be exposed to a solicitation (attempted murder) charge. If he did nothing, his new friend would hose him dry. I could take direct action—something I am not philosophically opposed to. This would be waylaying Gambino and inflicting a fierce enough corporal punishment on the man that he fucked off, hopefully to the East Coast of his origins. He wouldn't know who I was, my cause, or employer. He'd have the ambiguity of the encounter hanging over his head, with the certainty that another encounter might mean his cruel death. Is this out of line? LAPD, under Chief Parker, used just this tactic to "take care of business" (TCOB) in the distant past. While I'm not opposed to such a thing, what militated against direct action was the certainty that "Gambino" was probably a law enforcement informant, or better still, under intermittent surveillance by one or more state or federal agency. And this was the key to solving our clients' problem.

Indirect action it would have to be. I met with a liaison in a law enforcement agency…the one he was most likely "on the pad" to, told them the story of the extortion, and shared with them my surveillance notes and photos. Our footage, notes, and report were so detailed that no law enforcement agency could draw a conclusion other than that Gambino was capering, involved in criminal extortion and/or drug dealing. Any such activity would be strictly proscribed for a man operating as an informant on a state or federal level. Within a week he'd returned to the East Coast, with Bill and Glenda having changed phone numbers. Problem over, perhaps forever.

CHAPTER

16

LAWYERS

It seems there was once a newly sworn lawyer, say a young man graduated from University of Southern California. This man eschewed going into a large firm, or even a boutique specialty partnership, opting instead to rent offices with his best fraternity buddy. The shingle hung and office furniture installed in Beverly Hills, his first prospective client, an elderly woman, ventured in and asked, "Does your firm handle divorce work?"

Inviting the older woman in, our young man bade her sit in front of his desk and answered that he did divorce work. Being a conscientious practitioner of jurisprudence, this lawyer warned her that he and his friend were new members of the bar, that she would be their very first client. "Maybe you'd need a more experienced lawyer to handle your case?" he asked, eyebrows arched in a pose of ethical concern for this woman.

"No. I don't want an older lawyer. My husband is a crook and a bandit. He knows every shit-heel, shyster lawyer in this county! A newer lawyer will do his homework and represent my interests." It turned out she was very wealthy, as was her forty-year spouse, and thinking quickly, the young lawyer quickly banged out a retainer agreement and signed his first client on the spot. Then, his mind turned, reflexively, to money.

"Can you leave me a checque today?" asked the eager esquire.

"I can go one better..." And from her purse, the woman produced a crisp bank note, a $1,000 bill. The lawyer had never seen one before. "These were last minted in 1969. My husband has a safe full of them, and I've liberated this one just to retain you." And out she went on the afternoon.

Sitting back in his oaken chair, the young lawyer lit a cigar and fumed up the office, marveling at his prospects, massaging and fondling the piece of currency. And then he realized, as often happens with crisp notes, there was a second $1,000 bill stuck to the first!

This was the very first ethical dilemma our young lawyer had to navigate: Should he tell his partner about the second bank note?

Lawyer jokes are easy to traffic in, as 98 percent of American lawyers give the remainder a poor reputation. But, if the public knew much about the bandits, grifters, grafters, and extortionate filth of my profession, they'd abandon lawyer jokes overnight.

In 2003 a Pasadena lawyer came to me, needing help with what he saw as a potential conflict of interest between a superior court judge and an opposing party in litigation over real estate in a family trust. "The judge has issued a series of rulings from the bench with little basis in law or fact. My client thinks the defendants have bribed her or something."

Anything else?

"Yes. She goes out of her way to be unpleasant and sarcastic. In the past I've not had issues with her," bleated the lawyer consulting with me.

I dove deep, looking at opposing party and judge. Investigating a judge is dicey, sensitive, and prone to explode. I checked for shared investments for limited companies of the opposing party and the judge. Both were early sixties, well-connected, and wealthy, but after a week of work, I couldn't ID anything other than coincidence.

Social registries, vanity pages of local media, club memberships, church, and temple. Everyone involved was middle class and Ashkenazi Jewish, other than the lawyer who'd brought me in. Going into filings and events of the State Bar of California, I found that the judge was speaking at a legal education seminar, mandatory training of a certain amount for attorneys. Her subject would be exactly the minutia of the body of law my client and the opposing party were battling over in litigation.

Then I saw that opposing counsel, the guy representing the opposing party, was also presenting. This stimulated a more personal look. He was just turning forty, a partner in a law firm, married, with children. By description, he was invisible, an Ichabod Crane. If he was any skinnier, he'd have a message taped to his ankle. The judge? Divorced a few years, and as ugly as a hatful of assholes. Could she be paid off? I had no proof.

Don Moon and I bought our way in to the conference, in a hotel space, dressed as lawyers (rumpled suit, sloppy necktie, half-buttoned shirt) with video cameras in briefcases. The morning session was a struggle to stay awake, with didactic prattle about highly esoteric parts of law. The judge and opposing counsel were seated at the dais and took turns putting Don and I to sleep. Glancing around the conference room, I could see the feeling was mutual.

Then came the rubber-chicken lunch. We studied the crowd and the two subjects for something, Anything. Then, Don went behind the dais while lunch was on, ostensibly to view notes on a whiteboard. He motioned for me, and we were standing behind the subjects, looking down. They were holding hands. When I returned with my camera, the judge lustily stroked the thigh of opposing counsel. Don and I each acted as if we were copying the whiteboard, but none were paying attention. With cameras, we captured a continuous image of the subjects' foreplay, then zooming out so they could be identified in the footage.

This was nitroglycerin, no matter how it was handled. I briefed my client and showed him the video. He croaked.

"Fuck me. How do I do this, Nils?" Had I created more of a problem than the one he'd hired me to solve? I told him, upon his next court date, to ask the judge if she and opposing counsel would allow him to address them in chambers.

"If she says no?" he asked, yanking at his collar as if he were choking. Usually, lawyers aren't nervous.

Tell her your client is distressed knowing of the personal relationship the court enjoys with opposing counsel. And say not else. Let her act. Don't accuse. Don't argue. After three attempts at the former, with the judge snarling at him to speak his mind, he detonated it in open court. "My client does *not* wish to proceed knowing you're secretly dating opposing counsel…"

She fled the bench, and Ichabod stumbled out to the hallway, eye-fucking me from across the hallway. He was plainly as mad as a burned bookie. After twenty minutes, a bailiff emerged from chambers, instructing my client that the case had been moved to another courtroom. Somehow, neither myself nor my client got any of this on our clothes or careers. He hasn't called me since. Maybe all the judges have reformed, but I remain skeptical.

Working at an office in Glendale, California, long ago, I had to report to Bob Souza and Curt Curtsinger, both great men, to whom I owe a debt of gratitude. A call came in from area code 312—Chicago. Ernie Rizzo, private eye, referred a Midwest divorce matter to us. Ernie died some years ago, but otherwise he was quite well-known in Chicago. True to the character of that city, Rizzo was a hard man with a reputation for closing impossible cases. He had helped me, and the inverse, several times.

At first this seemed to be strictly a fidelity matter. We were told Vito D. had been married for twenty-eight years, was successful in the trucking logistics business in the Midwest, and one day came home to announce to his wife, "I got coronary problems. The business is going under. I don't want to saddle you with my debts and problems, so I'm going to ask for a divorce." Their children were grown and off to college, and Vito had been generous enough to offer his wife full ownership of their suburban home and a retirement account with enough money in it to fund a modest middle-class life. That was two years before. On the eve of accepting Vito's proposed settlement, the wife's closest friend had suggested that Vito, who had moved to a blue-collar suburb of Los Angeles, be checked out, his tale of woe and heroic assumption of business debts verified. The wife asked her lawyer, and her lawyer asked Rizzo, who might be engaged in Los Angeles to ascertain Vito's status, disposition, and intent.

The immediate scope of the case involved ascertaining the income and lifestyle of Vito D. The address the wife had for her spouse was in El Segundo, mostly an industrial city, close to LAX. Her adult children had visited Vito, and when they visited, he'd been lodging in an inexpensive motel, close to the airport, which shared a parking lot with a titty bar called the Wild Goose. Apparently, he had moaned to his adult children about his health condition and acted as if he was making a great sacrifice for his estranged wife.

Using the information provided by the wife's attorney, whom I'll call Jacqueline, I determined that the address she had for Vito was not more than a private mail drop, the address of which could be written to look like an apartment. In fact, instead of using "Box #" for the return address, the envelopes addressed in Vito's hand read "Apt #," which was obfuscation. This was quite deliberate.

Department of Motor Vehicles had no cars registered to Vito D., and the address for his driver's license was of course the private mail drop. Our subject, Vito, was disciplined and deliberate in hiding where it was that he lived. He dressed in what is now called business casual—no necktie, usually jeans. He wore too many rings for an industrial guy, and his boots had zippers on the sides. This defines *densely structured* in terms of general business and personal profile. To an experienced hand, it sticks out like a dime up a billy goat's ass. Using well-trusted sources in various utility companies, I determined that there were no utilities connected in Vito's name, residential or business. The only Southern California addresses found in commercial databases for Vito were those well-known from his prior life in the Midwest and the mail drop. Nothing else.

With the secretaries of state for Illinois and California, respectively, we verified that Vito's trucking company was surrendered as a corporation, with no new corporation incorporated or chartered by Vito D. In official records, the name of the shuttered enterprise was VD Trucking & Logistics. Department of Transportation identically reported that Vito had surrendered all of his highway permits and that he had registrations prior to closing the business down for fifty-plus tractor trailer rigs. VD Trucking & Logistics was far larger a business than had been characterized in sworn pleadings.

The motel where Vito had visited with his daughter, a Northwestern University undergrad, reported that Vito had checked out the day after his daughter's departure. The address on the registration card was the mail drop, and the car he'd arrived in was a rental, taken out from an airport rental counter. I conferred with Jacqueline and sent her a detailed report, enumerating each lead covered in my work to establish Vito's status and lifestyle. In this case, it was a matter of negative definition, as I was reporting what I had not found, that should've been immediately identifiable. Our report troubled Jacqueline and piqued the curiosity of her client, and I was given permission to expand the scope of the investigation to locating Vito D., to obtain as much information as to his status as could be developed. This information would drive decisions of his estranged wife over what her life would be like after divorce. This may appear banal and trivial, but this is the core of the case, the needs of the client.

From Jacqueline, I knew that Vito had been a golfer, once a member of a golf course country club in the Midwest. From a pro shop, I obtained a nice set of golf clubs and a matching bag and boxed them up. I sealed the box with broad, red tape and shipped them to Vito at his mail drop, the return address a transit terminal in Montreal. I knew the box with the clubs would arrive at the mail drop on a Thursday and had a surveillance operative primed, staking out the lot in front of the place. He roasted in the sun all Thursday, the same on Friday. No sign of Vito coming for the box.

In those years, I had a pavement artist we had nicknamed the Fugitive, mostly because when he came into the job, he had a bunch of chicken-shit traffic warrants and other untidy matters to be attended to. The Fugitive could follow a man on a metro bus, discreetly film him whack off on the back seat, dismount one stop after the target, catch up in time to see the guy get in a car with a woman, then steal a car to stay with them, and abandon it later at the airport with the keys under the seat, with an empty tank. He could change his appearance in a minute and had learned from someone else an operating principle that I have always held to: We never run out of leads, just imagination. There are no dead ends as long as a client can bear the economic burden. As the Fugitive's fieldcraft was ace, he was worth the trouble. Don't ask me what I paid this man. It went to beer and titty dancers and motel rooms and the ponies.

The mail drop had truncated hours on Saturday, and the Fugitive kept his watch. Sunday, it was closed, and so we resumed on Monday. The sun climbed high, early, and it was again quite hot that day. And just before noon, Vito pulled up, circled the parking lot twice, and dismounted from a very expensive Mercedes Benz Coupe. The Fugitive photographed Vito, his car, and the license plate, then got more photos as our subject departed with the boxed golf clubs.

Pulling out of the lot, the Fugitive tailed Vito two miles, an easy drive, to an industrial park, adjacent to LAX. Vito parked, took the box with, and went into a suite where the door had a sign that announced LK & LOGISTICS. With the information developed that day, I identified the Benz as being virtually brand new...and registered to a woman I'll call Lisa Kazarian. Lisa was suburban hot, with big tits. Like some women so afflicted, LK took pains to make sure that she was dressed in a way that anyone with functional eyes could tell she had spent some money on tits. Nothing subtle about it. Gold jewelry and lots of hair. Big tits too. The secretary of state reported that LK was controlled by Lisa Kazarian, who was listed as president and agent for service, and had been incorporated in California two years before.

The US Department of Transportation had similar information about LK and added that this enterprise claimed fifty-plus tractor trailers operating in the Western US. As a surveillance team, the Fugitive and I tailed Vito, who drove with the very attractive younger woman we identified as Kazarian. They drove north on the San Diego Freeway, then west, arriving in a wealthy suburb of Los Angeles, in a gated community. That day, we dared not risk following them in and being identified by security officers to Vito.

Another report, quickly made to Jacqueline, expanded again the scope of our investigation. Now, it included status, identity, and assets of Kazarian. Were her assets and holdings funded by Vito? Were they commingled? I learned that Kazarian was also a realtor, and that the home Kazarian had purchased in the gated community, two years prior, was listed for sale. Kazarian owned no real estate prior to her purchase of the home, which appeared quite valuable and was on a golf course development.

In that era, the fanny pack was ubiquitous, and at a pet store I saw one with a mesh front…perfect for emplacing a camera. An older man I knew, retired from LAPD, held a real estate broker's license. He helped me dummy up fake bank statements, medical credentials, and a credit report in a cover name. It was a very plain name, one that would get a torrent of results should someone conduct basic diligence on a Michael Wilson, MD, originally of Toronto, Canada.

Appointment made to view the house with my "realtor," the surveillance team stayed on Vito, at his office, while I got a look inside the home. It was the legal opinion of Jacqueline that neither Vito nor Lisa had a reasonable expectation of privacy when their home was being shown for sale. This is the legal doctrine underpinning privacy rights, something we could not overlook. The camera in the fanny pack was modified with a ridiculous fish-eye lens to better capture interior detail. We were trying to establish assets and lifestyle, so the more detail it captured, the better. The distortion caused by these lenses can become an evidentiary issue, but this did not come up in working Vito under. In my earlier professional life, I'd been schooled and fielded using analog cameras, with high-speed film and fixed focal length lenses. In the middle of a clandestine matter, one could not be seen with a camera, so a Robot Star would be buried in a briefcase, or behind a belt buckle, or under a hat, with three hundred or some exposures, it could accomplish, approximately, the same thing. The MINOX, too, had a fixed focal length, with a chain fob of the correct length for photographing documents, if one were to conduct that type of New York search warrant or similar black-bag job.

What we discovered was that someone had spent a small fortune on a design interior, and this goes to lifestyle. It was palatial and furnished with designer sticks throughout. It could've been puffery, but the realtor representing Lisa Kazarian stated at least three times that the owner had done very well in business and was moving to the beach. She also revealed that the owner was male, twice, in casual conversation over the home for sale. After twenty minutes, we departed in the retired cop's Benz, cover intact.

As no offer was made on the home, there was no "impersonation," just cover for status and cover for action. The realtor was likely showing the place to three people a day, and in the course of the investigation, the house was sold—and at a profit.

My surveillance team now consisted of the Fugitive and a young navy veteran, who was in air force ROTC at a college. He had also just earned a second black belt in martial arts. I'll call him Jimmy. He, too, was a good man working the streets. Jimmy and the Fugitive made an odd pairing, but they were very effective, rarely missing our subject, and gaining more information about customers of LK.

In our fourth or fifth day of surveillance, Jimmy pointed out that when they followed Lisa Kazarian during the workday, she typically would depart the office, solo, late morning, then go to the Westchester post office and get the mail from a PO box. But when Vito made that run, he would check the same PO box, and then a second one. Vito, alone, would return in the late afternoon, look over both shoulders, key one box, then the other, again. This happened every single day. Vito awaited something.

We knew from the secretary of state and DOT that the first PO box was that of LK; we had no information on the second PO box at that time. This had to be figured out. After work, a long day watching Vito with Lisa, then following them home, we stopped for burgers in the San Fernando Valley. Jimmy mentioned that a young woman from the dojo where he did martial arts wanted to give detective work a try. The Fugitive then interjects: "Wait until you see her. She's hot…"

Let's called her Terry, this young woman. Over the weekend I met her and learned that Terry, also, was a black belt, in her late twenties, who had been working as a stripper three nights a week to pay for college. She seemed smart enough, could handle herself physically, obviously, and was very attractive. Some cut and paste, a fake resume, and a new mobile phone created Lisa Wilson, originally from Bakersfield, who wanted to be a flight attendant when she finished college. She just needed a part-time secretarial job, hopefully close to the airport.

Come Monday, the surveillance team picked up Lisa and Vito in Lisa's Benz. They stopped at Starbucks with the team waiting. Meanwhile, I had Terry, and we hung close to the airport in Westchester. I briefed Terry on what could be done, per the lawyer Jacqueline. She could not read Vito's mail, or copy his documents, or toss his briefcase. But anything going in the garbage was fair game—same for overheard utterances and any details of the business that Vito didn't own that he might share with Terry, should she be hired as secretary. As far as we could tell, the only employees in the offices of LK were Lisa Kazarian and our subject, Vito.

As always, the surveillance team trailed Vito driving the Benz. This morning, however, Lisa looked disheveled…something was awry, and the Fugitive called me to meet them alone, with Terry waiting in my car. "Man, you won't believe what happened," Jimmy gushed as soon as I rallied with the team. Vito, in the middle of morning commute, had pulled the Benz over on the shoulder of the San Diego Freeway and had punched Lisa Kazarian all over the interior of the car.

"Did you get footage of this?" Yes, the woman was beaten, and if we weren't operating sub rosa, any of us would have called the highway patrol. Jimmy had captured footage of the beating. This was a troubling development. Once returned to my auto, we briefed Terry on what Jimmy and the Fugitive had witnessed, telling her, "No one will blame you if you decide to take a pass on this assignment."

Dressed like a professional woman, made up modestly, Terry looked the all-American girl next door. Like a soldier, in she went, right after Lisa departed to pick up the mail. Later, at the end of our day, Terry told us, "He hired me on the spot, hardly looked my resume over."

I asked Terry if there were any complications, and she replied, "He leers at me and Lisa is pissed he hired me, threw a fit." In her first trove of documents was a checque stub, the bottom half of an instrument payable to Vito, personally, and addressed to him at the second PO box. The maker of the checque was a payday lender and checque cashing company we'd never heard of before, based in Fresno, California. I conferred with Jacqueline, who stated it was an unknown player in the schedule of assets and liabilities and that Vito had no known ties to Fresno. Liaison with the secretary of state got us a make on the owner of the payday lender, who turned out to be an associate of Vito, who had also relocated to California.

In the subsequent days, there was money every single business day, sometimes two, amounting to thousands of dollars. From the envelopes thrown away, we knew where Vito kept bank accounts, same for LK. Terry witnessed Lisa Kazarian signing checques under direction of Vito, and in ten days of working at LK, had a fair idea of every single customer and vendor of LK.

"Whenever Lisa is out, Vito is on me like an octopus…" Terry stated. I asked her if she could handle the situation, and she replied, "I could smash him like a bug."

Our final day of surveillance came, and the surveillance team documented a second beating Lisa Kazarian took, again on the shoulder of the freeway. Vito was brazen. It was as if he was accustomed to doing whatever he wanted, without a concern for the consequences. Our final report to Jacqueline included a schedule of banking relationships; the address of the next home, now in Malibu, that Lisa Kazarian was sole owner of; a list of customers of LK & Logistics; and video footage of what the team had seen. The invoice was promptly paid, and other cases came in. Terry continued, as did Jimmy and the Fugitive, picking up cases from my practice as well as a few other practitioners.

After nine months, Jacqueline called us and stated she needed us to make a presentation before the court, in the Midwest. We flew out there, Souza and I. The day before the trial was a mandatory settlement conference, very proforma, instituted to reduce court time in complex divorce proceedings.

There was a mediator, and Jacqueline informed me that while she had expressed the belief in communications with Vito's lawyers that he was working was the defacto owner of LK, they continued with the fiction of him being broke, disabled, and advising his "friend" Lisa Kazarian on how to run her business.

I was a surprise introduction to opposing counsel, and in front of the mediator I was asked by Jacqueline to enumerate the assets and activities that I had uncovered in the investigation. Vito was solo, Lisa Kazarian wasn't present, and the slugger was doing his best to look old, used up, and pitiful, his pompadour smoothed down.

After Vito's lawyers made their presentation, arguing again that LK belonged to Lisa Kazarian, as did the houses and Mercedes Benz. The mediator was an older woman, slow talking and elegant, who then asked Jacqueline if she had rebuttal evidence. This was when we put on the video footage of Vito battering the Kazarian woman around the interior of the Benz, on the shoulder of the freeway, the car noticeably rocking for Vito's exertions as traffic sped past, not a care in the world. Vito looked ashen, and the mediator told Vito's lawyers, "Are you sure you want to take this case to trial?" He settled with his wife for over $10 million, on the strength of our investigation. Conferring with Jacqueline on my way to the Palmer House, an old hotel in Chicago, I said, "I imagine your client saw a bit of that too."

Jacqueline departed with, "You don't want to know." Some men are garbage. Every lawyer with a client has to maintain an arm's length relationship, lest she or he get knocked over emotionally. *Vito. Vito D. V.D. What a guy. Some men survive for the simple fact that it's forbidden by law to shoot them outright.*

Sometimes I am engaged on a matter undertaken just to satisfy the litigation needs of a lawyer, or even a group of them, with divided, competing interests, focused on an objective that benefits the clients they represent. In 1994, I was brought in by a high-power firm, which already had a PI on the case. "We represent creditors of a film production company in bankruptcy. They owe our clients one hundred plus million dollars, and while we are in discovery, with forensic accountants combing their books, they claim to have 'lost' two years of financial records, crucial to ascertaining their status and assets."

The other PI was doing the basics competently enough. This included studying the subject company's garbage, until…"They put a lock on the dumpster, so we can't go in no more." This is standard. Once something is in the garbage, it is open to inspection. Whether or not this was true if it was under lock and key was a matter of debate. A lawyer is a chameleon, capable of arguing both ends of a fact until it is rendered moot, untrue, and becomes fiction. Attorneys possess doctoral degrees in this, and it is at the very heart of their being.

I ran it up to a third-year associate lawyer, who wanted to make partner in the group of lawyers. She said, "If the lock is on the dumpster to protect (subject company) privacy, you may not go into the dumpster."

That night, I had a pretext conversation with the janitor of the building where the dumpster was—in an alley parallelling the boulevard. "We put a lock on the fuckin' thing to keep the fuckin' derelicts outta the fuckin' thing. They scatter trash all over the fuckin' alley lookin' for fuckin' aluminum cans I get sick of fuckin' cleanin' up the fuckin' alley. That's why it's a lock on our fuckin' dumpster."

The trash hauler had a key, and maintenance guy had a key. I picked the lock, three early mornings, and made study, and progress. Driving past a locksmith on Sawtelle, I ventured in and had him make me an identical lock with no pins in the tumbler. This is much faster, and the keys of the janitor and garbage driver still worked. If any of the skells diving the dumpster for aluminum ever figured it out, I do not know.

Two weeks further and from this dumpster I secured a Colorado backup tape. This was a primitive (now) computer drive, used to preserve company records. The handling of evidence like this is sensitive. A computer-forensics type would term this drive an *electronic crime scene*. I did not plug it into my computer, as to do so would alter it from its original state and render it, arguably, compromised. It went to the lawyers. There were records of payments from accounts of a series of sub-corporations, which the bankrupt company claimed they had no ownership of to the officers of the bankrupt company both in advance of and during the bankruptcy. This was a home run. The case was looking as if the men operating the bankrupt company hadn't just committed loan fraud, but also bankruptcy fraud and obstruction of justice.

The company had assigned royalties to companies formed on an island nation called Tuvalu, in the Pacific, to disguise ownership of the rights and evade creditors. To get clarification of this, I called an old friend who was once attorney general of the Marshall Islands. "Tuvalu, yeah. I have been there, and it is amazing. Once a week they clear the kids from the soccer field so a plane can land. Every week there is a fresh series of incorporations, handled by an Englishman with a purple nose. The whole island thrives on fraud. It is their GDP."

Tuvalu is now famous for another scam, with western "scientists" claiming that global warming is about to swallow the island up. I first read this waiting to have a tooth drilled in 1999, and the island is still there. I often wonder if the scientists are as corrupt as the government running the place. Eventually, the lawyer advising the partners in this proceeding had to flee the US, in quite a bit of trouble.

On the subject of garbage and evidence, getting holographic evidence from a dumpster is quite common. The IRS, CIA, FBI, and the like do this on the regular. Sometimes they hire mecs like me to do the actual dive, lest they get their striped pants soiled.

"We have a case, in discovery. We represent a third-party distributor of cosmetics. Our client is being sued under the civil RICO (racketeer influenced corrupt organizations) law in US district court." The lawyers came to me for help.

The case was a ridiculous abuse of process, as the distributor had no contractual obligation to the maker of the cosmetics. They were buying unsold goods from retailers at a steep discount and flogging them in stores all over North America. At the heart of the complaint was the certainty that this was embarrassing to the luxury brand that plaintiffs thought they owned.

Lead counsel briefed me: "In discovery, opposing counsel has provided us a customer list, but there are only about seventy-six customers listed. We think it is much more. We need you to figure out their actual customer list." The law firm was huge, and they'd been referred by another PI who was retiring. Knowing this, I developed a plan to closely guard my operation and assured them that I operate within the law, but that my methods are secret. One of the lawyers was skeptical and demanded that I divulge my approach.

I work secretly. If you cannot stand it, find someone else, or stay the hell off the sidewalk. They were on the eve of pretrial motions and needed quick action. The plaintiff company had a big warehouse in another city. I rented a motel room and took advantage of their dumpster. While I was doing this, Robert Ferris in San Jose was contacting former employees of plaintiff company. They uniformly reported it was a miserable employer and filled in what blanks they could.

My nightly forays into the dumpster were richly illustrative, as I found a spreadsheet with nine hundred and more customers—all retail places, with points of contact, sales numbers…nothing too serious. This covered all the US and Canada. Richer, still, were the angry letters and faxes from various customers, thrown away, containing a litany of problems with the marketing, quality, and abusive nature of the contracts they held customers to.

To protect this source, I cited an informant in my billings and reports. A large law firm is porous, with lawyers and staff coming and going, and too much shared information. I had no idea if I would be called to do more in this vein, so I gave the dumpster the codename "Michael" in reports and invoices.

Months later, astride the witness stand, counsel for the plaintiff company tried to make me divulge my source for the letters, faxes, and customer list. The lawyers I was employed by had a sustained objection. They won their case, perhaps for the evidence I found, but more likely for being persistent and having facts and statutes on their side.

"Remember that RICO case we brought you in on?" I did. How could I forget? The lawyer who'd been skeptic at the outset was calling me. "They got ahold of your reports. It isn't a problem, really, but I wanted you to know they fired seven of their employees, all named Michael." I probably did them a favor. Every time I would see a TV advertisement for the products sold by the plaintiff in this action, he himself was "acting" in the commercials. Smug, insufferable, and obnoxious. If I had needed to take another approach, I would identify former employees and likely get exactly the same evidentiary result for my client.

Some of the attorneys I have gone afield for have been a cut above. In these matters I have learned more of the law, the nation, and the world. Los Angeles has been graced with many interesting people who could have done anything they cared to, and they chose law.

Maxwell Keith, Esq, was an odd bird. Max was intensely cerebral, with a vast vocabulary in English, Latin, and Greek. He once represented Charles Manson in one of the cult leader's many trials. Max was a criminal lawyer, who could create an argument of double meaning, get the DA to an agreement, lose the trial, then use the Trojan horse he had baked into the record on appeal. Some might call this dishonest.

"I represent the US Constitution. If they want to keep up, they might should do their homework and learn to read. I do mine," was Max's summation of this. He was one of the few defense lawyers I enjoyed working for, because I always learned more of men and law. Max had me appointed by the superior court on two gang homicides.

The ultimate conclusion to each was a determinate sentence, meaning his clients knew when they would get out in ten years or thirty. I once ventured to ask Mr. Keith how he managed to stay awake and concentrate while pretending to sleep in court.

"Just out of college, I went in the navy during the war. They made me fly long patrols over the Northern Pacific, for Jap submarines. Some of our patrols were eighteen, twenty hours of staring at hypnotic, blue ocean. I'd recite Homer, Herodotus, Josephus while the rest of the crew took turns yawning." He also admitted that he was sometimes asleep.

In a humorous aside, Max once asked me, "Did you ever hear how I got kicked out of the Valley Hunt Club, forever?" Valley Hunt is as private, elite, old money, and button-down as Los Angeles gets, and it is the seat of all holy power in Pasadena.

No, Max. How did it happen?

"It was when I was representing Manson, Charles Manson, in one of his murder trials after the big trial, the one where Charlie was convicted. I wanted to warm up a witness, get her talking because she was a little bit nuts. We went to the Valley Hunt, and I had a few cocktails for my afternoon. So did she. And while I was potted, she stripped down and skinny-dipped in the pool. They banned me. Can you imagine?" He was sporting a lopsided grin.

Who was the girl?

"Squeaky Fromme." He wasn't joking. Later, Fromme went up for an attempt to assassinate President Ford.

Shortly thereafter, I got a letter from Judge Pounders, dismissing me from any further appointments, as I had not been approved by the panel for this. He administered the panel, which has always appeared to be soft, oily corruption. The PIs listed on the panel were a noxious mix of bleeding hearts and slow-moving, barely conscious, retired cops who went through the motions for a second paycheck at taxpayer expense. There were, and are, very few competent defense investigators.

The clerks handling the paystubs for this were supercilious martinets, with whom one had to form an oily, close relationship to get anything paid. I may as well have been working pro bono. The work was never about facts or justice, always about paper, forms, and middling asshole welfare for anyone making this their client base.

This work involves interviewing witnesses, developing leads, reviewing records, and serving subpoenas—all with the goal of helping defense counsel explain, refute, or mitigate whatever crimes her client is accused of by the state.

The very last time I worked a criminal defense case, I interviewed witnesses, recorded statements, and reviewed records. The cause at hand was a man in his forties, an acknowledged gang member, who was identified on a cold DNA hit for a rape that had occurred ten to twenty years before, in the course of a takeover drug robbery. He answered the description of the rapist. His DNA was found in three orifices of the victim, a woman whose husband was a cannabis dealer in a neighboring county. He was identified by her in a lineup more than ten years after the assault.

The lawyer took in my report and invoice and responded, "Now, go find evidence that they had consensual sex, and I will pay your bill." He had been a client of Don Moon, otherwise I would not have taken his case at all. In another conversation, this lawyer extolled the virtues of a very prominent defense lawyer who had once told me, "If you would just wiretap people for me, like Pellicano does for his clients, I could send you a lot of business."

Never, ever again. Not ever. If I wound up on charges, I know whom I would have represent me. He is able, devoted, and traditional. Jim Gallo is nothing of this ilk, nor was Maxwell Keith. A lawyer who believes in the death penalty is more likely to have a true sense of justice. This is because death itself is often the correct punishment for murder. I do not want a lawyer who has blinded themself with an agenda that excludes justice.

Homicide merely denotes man killing man; *murder* is classically defined as "the unlawful taking of the life of another, with an abandoned, and malignant, heart."

CHAPTER

17

THIEVES

Some people will never steal; others steal sometimes. But our research shows that most theft is perpetrated by three percent of the population. They are occasionally caught, and rarely prosecuted.

—Security Pacific Bank Internal Risk Unit, 1971

Los Angeles, as a metropolitan area, attracts quite a bit of thievery of every description: Men who steal from their employers, or those who steal from…employees. There are guys who steal honestly—backing a truck up in someone's driveway, loading every bit of their victim's property aboard, and driving off with it.

There are women and men who establish incorporated, chartered enterprises, and steal using a smile, a handshake, a sharp pen, and a bend or two in the law. Such people brought the United States to its economic knees in 2008. Their political allies then legalized the theft, after the fact, and papered it over with a whole new set of economic, banking, accounting, and real estate laws. What was the effect? Maybe it was just painting a bright new color of ring around each smokestack of the *RMS Titanic*, so it might look fresh and all better, on its way to the bottom.

We have thieves of every stripe and style, men that steal with both hands. Can the police keep up? They cannot, and in many cases, the politicos elected by their victims do all in their power to thwart effective law enforcement. But that's a philosophical discussion, and I'm hardly Socrates.

I was once asked by the inventory manager of a warehouse company to interview their controller, meaning the person in charge of disbursing payments to vendors, overseeing accounts payable. The company had offices and operations in several counties of California, was very successful and established, with their corporate HQ in Los Angeles. There were more than five hundred employees, and the inventory manager had been tasked by a VP to oversee investigation of money going out. In reviewing payments to vendors, it appeared that the controller had issued payments to purported vendors of his own creation as well as slipping his own mobile phone bill and credit card bill in, to be discreetly paid from company accounts. These, among other thefts.

For this case, I was working with one of the greats. Detective 3 Robert Souza, retired from Robbery-Homicide Division, LAPD. He was a good man to work with, as he was detail-oriented and knew psychopathy inside and out. Neither he nor I was especially a financial crimes man, but as the framework of the crime was already known, our job was to elicit, in a friendly interview, a few admissions, and potentially a confession from the controller.

Being interviewed by private detectives is easy, right? Nothing to it. If a suspected embezzler doesn't wish to sit for a friendly interview, it makes him look a thief. Same if he demands a lawyer, something he has no right to in that context. He might comfort himself with the certainty that it's just private detectives, not the FBI, or the district attorney getting up him.

At the plant there was a windowless conference room with a table and chairs and a water cooler. It was the perfect setting for a friendly interview. To warm the case up, I had already seated three other employees, one at a time, and asked them a laundry list of questions, some of which I already had answers to, but never accusing anyone of embezzlement. From the questions I was asking, none could've sussed out the depth of the crimes, nor what had already been ascertained about their structure.

I'd already done background on the controller, a CPA in his early fifties, who was divorced for a third time, with a tax lien and two priors for drunk driving. Souza took it in and said, "This guy will be as nervous as a virgin at the prison rodeo." We agreed to start with easy questions and then build him into a corner, with one of us (me) turning it confrontational. This was quite purposeful, as Souza was large, avuncular, and bearded…like a big, friendly Kodiak bear. The controller could get warmth and emotional sustenance from Souza, while I bore down on him.

This style of interrogation is called good cop/bad cop by your mother, your high school dean, whatever. Detectives call it *Mutt and Jeff*, named for a forgotten cartoon strip. Our controller was shown in by the inventory manager, and I bade him to sit. Before he did so, the controller, whom I'll call Tim, insisted on shaking our hands. His hand was slick with perspiration and as flaccid as Mitt Romney. Souza and I traded looks.

Tim was between five foot five and five foot seven. It was impossible to tell, as he was wearing platform shoes. To add some more height, Tim had on a toupee, teased up into a pompadour rivalling John Travolta. How did I make it as a toupee? It was of an entirely different color and consistency than his own hair. A bead of sweat was running down Tim's temple already. I clicked on the tape recorder, a large, black one, and started, "Nils Grevillius, on the record this date, assisted by Robert Souza, we are interviewing Tim…"

"Uh, I didn't agree to *that*. Can you please, uh, turn it off?" Tim licked his lips, and I switched the machine off.

"It's a formality, to protect you, Tim. Each of the other interviews was recorded, and I was about to ask your agreement," I explained, then smiled.

"Well." Tim grabbed his collar, to loosen it.

"Unless maybe you got shit to hide from us, Tim. You don't have to sit for an interview." Souza smiled at him, closing his own notebook.

"Uh, I don't have to do this?" Tim asked, searching us visually for a clue.

"That's right." Souza stood and looked out the window that didn't exist, his back to Tim, then turned around to add, "You don't need a job, right? You're a CPA, can get a job just about anywhere."

Souza sat again, and Tim motioned for me to turn the machine on. "I got nothing to hide, I'm just the controller. I work hard around here to keep this place going. Just wasn't sure what all this is about," he nervously explained.

Souza smiled affably and said, "These interviews are easy, Tim. A truthful man doesn't have to remember much." (Higbie). "How long have you been with the company? Where did you take your professional education? Do you have a CPA license? How about in other states? Who reports to you in the company structure? Can anyone beside yourself sign company checques? What are the procedures for this?" were the questions I was asking. These establish rapport, potentially, and get the subject in the mode of answering questions.

Within this, I am listening to how he communicates and asking a few questions I already have correct answers to, looking for variations, for distortion, for an expression of ignorance to a line he should know. Now, years later, I cannot recall if it happened after the third question or the thirteenth question, but Souza interrupted to state and ask the subject, "You know, Tim, that's a nice hairpiece, man."

"Oh, thanks," the controller answered, shifting in his chair. His eyes were getting bigger behind his glasses. I asked another question, and Souza interjected again. "You must've paid a lot of money for a toupee like that, Tim. At least fifty, sixty dollars." I was looking at the controller, and Souza was studying Tim's hair, which now glistened with perspiration.

Eyes flashing, the subject barked, "Is this interview about my hair or company procedures?" he erupted, empurpled.

"Oh, yeah. Sorry." Souza went back to his notepad, and I proceeded. Souza was eye-fucking Tim, and I didn't want blood on my shirt.

"Did you authorize payment of a credit card bill for a Visa account drawn on…" I didn't get to finish my question. "You know, Tim, I could hardly tell that was a toupee when you came in here," Souza continued, smiling in a most unfriendly way at the much smaller man.

"I don't have to put up with this shit!" the subject croaked, close to tears.

"You do if you want to keep your job," Souza smiled.

I then went back to the line of questioning. "Why did your Visa bill get included with the company bill?" I showed him a copy of the bill.

"I just don't know." He gulped.

"Okay, now, Timmy, I told you not to lie. Let's start over here, with you only lying to us about the shit where we don't know you're lying?" Souza was now unfriendly and menacing in his line of intervention as well as body language and the context of badgering the diminutive controller over his ill-fit wig. Within forty minutes, Tim gave a tearful confession, with the tape recorder going. To back it up, I had him initial several documents and render a written confession as to how, when, and how much money he could recall having stolen using his position as the controller to do so.

One of the questions I asked, and Souza followed up on, was, "Tim, who else in the company is stealing?"

"Is anyone aware of how you've done this and helped you?" We suspected a clerical employee, whom the controller had "lent" a sum of money, something we knew from having vetted each of the accounting unit employees. I obtained a second confession, wherein Tim the controller implicated his lover, whom he had lent the money, hissing that she had extorted these funds from him in exchange for her silence. Money that wasn't his to "lend."

Tim's confession looked rather at odds with the statement we had taken from her, earlier in the week. After we'd walked Tim over to the office of corporate counsel, to be sat upon by another colleague, lest he warn the woman what was coming, we invited her back for a clarifying interview.

Her second interview started out friendly, again, just to relax her enough to speak with us. Sheila, we shall call her, was fifteen years younger than Tim, quite attractive and married. Married to a sales manager for the company. After she was seated, the machine on and pleasantries disposed of, Souza started, "We think you were less than honest with us the other day, and this is your chance to keep your job, Sheila. Tell us what you left out of your prior statement."

And when she was done, Sheila implicated her husband in a larger, more damaging, kick-back-and-embezzlement scheme that involved a vendor, another salesman, and a competitor. All this resulted in jail time for Tim, for Sheila, for Sheila's husband, and a partial recovery of money stolen from the company that had engaged us. I wish every such case worked out this way. When we took signed, recorded confessions to the police agency having jurisdiction, arrests followed quickly.

We could have arrested Tim and Sheila, ourselves, but to do so as a private detective is potentially fraught with peril. The way California tort law works, in the event they beat the charges, I could expose myself to a claim for false arrest. But, based upon prior experience, I had the sense that the police would involve themselves in a positive way. That the victim was a major employer in that city certainly carried a bit of weight. No watch commander or lieutenant in charge of a detective bureau within the department would want to ignore a series of serious crimes within this company.

In another case, I was contacted by the bookkeeper for a professional investor, in Mid-Wilshire, who'd bought a storage lot for boats and recreational vehicles in Riverside County. The idea when he bought the place was that it would generate money, with rent being collected for storage. The bookkeeper explained that they employed a resident manager, who lived part-time in a trailer on the premises, with 120 parking spaces, for which each space was supposed to pay rent on a monthly basis. The bookkeeper became suspicious because the money sent in was always less than what it should have been for the number of spaces rented.

On a trip to Palm Springs, the bookkeeper had diverted herself from the freeway on a weekend, trying to get an idea of how many vacancies actually existed at the lot and was surprised to see that it was completely full. On the next business day, the bookkeeper, whom I'll call Ginny, called the resident manager, Jennifer, and asked her why the rent was being underpaid. Jennifer told Ginny, "We got a lot of spaces where they not paying no rent."

Ginny told Jennifer to use the lien sale process to get rid of the boats and trailers for which no rent was paid and instituted an application form, wherein every renter had to identify himself, what was being stored, and for how long.

With another quarter of underpaid rent, Ginny drove by again and saw the lot in the same condition. She called the police department in the city where the lot was and stated she believed Jennifer, the manager, was embezzling. After a series of telephone calls, Ginny was told, "Sounds like a civil problem to us, lady. Good luck." And the police washed their hands of it. Her next call was to my office.

I borrowed a derelict RV from a guy and drove out to Riverside. The place looked full, but Jennifer told me, "I can make room for you." Emplacing the RV, I counted the number of spots for parked storage and saw that someone had painted different lines in the asphalt, totaling 144, twenty-two more spaces than Ginny believed.

"Are you paying cash or checque?" Jennifer asked me. I told her I'd pay by checque, monthly, and she had me fill out the form, an exemplar of which I'd already seen. Jennifer never asked for my identification, and if she'd noticed that the RV registration was five years gone, she didn't say anything. As I'd noticed from the smell of cooking that there were people actually living in the lot, I asked Jennifer, "If my brother-in-law needs to stay in the RV a while, what's the rent?"

"That's one hundred and twenty dollars, weekly, but we can only take cash on that. Zoning ordinances and all, like that." Jennifer winked at me. It took a week for my checque to be deposited, and I issued my first report to Ginny, that someone had repainted the lines, making for tighter parking, and an extra twenty-two spaces, and that for $120 cash, weekly, I could move an operative in.

Ginny related at that point: "Jennifer has lived and worked there for eighteen years. She has a separate place she owns, somewhere in the foothills, goes home on weekends." Using two other operatives, we did more "buys," wherein space was rented, these times for cash. Instead of filling out the bookkeeper's form, which Ginny had created, Jennifer instead had each fill out a three-inch-by-five-inch index card, which went in a blue plastic box, which then went into—under surveillance—the pickup truck Jennifer was driving.

Upon the third cash buy, wearing a wire, my colleague Donald Moon and I arrested Jennifer, and from the office called 9-1-1, explaining to the police dispatcher that we'd made an arrest on probable cause for grand theft and embezzlement. I asked dispatch to send a female officer and a patrol supervisor. Jennifer was gobsmacked and explained to me that I'd made a mistake, that she'd never stolen anything from her employer. I asked her, because I could not find the blue box, "May I search your car?"

Jennifer responded, "Do whatever you like. It ain't my car, though." It took forty minutes, and the police arrived. When I explained the charges, the patrol supervisor, a uniformed sergeant, asked me to write a paper report before they could transport Jennifer to jail. Using a computer in the office, from notes, I described and detailed each buy, by cash, comparing it to the one done by checque and attaching an exemplar of the form to my report, which I signed and dated.

The vehicle that Jennifer was operating was locked, and her keys were gone with Jennifer. I called a locksmith, and relying on Jennifer's consent to search, had the truck opened, whereupon I found the blue box that contained the duplicate books, detailing the level of thievery Jennifer had engaged in. When Ginny arrived to take custody and stock of the company, I gave her the books, explaining that this was the evidence of grand theft, to make copies of it all, and commence to account for it so as to enumerate damages.

In searching the office, I found escrow paperwork, predating Jennifer's arrest by five years, wherein Jennifer provided ersatz evidence of an income quadruple what she was being paid by her employers, including bank deposits of cash. As close as Ginny could get to accurately fixing the damages, she estimated Jennifer had embezzled $1.5 million within the eighteen years preceding her arrest. And here is when things became problematic. A week in, a Detective Garza called from the police department, stating he needed the recording of my buys and interview with Jennifer. I had backups of all of them, except the tape wherein Jennifer said, "Do whatever you want. It isn't my car." When I asked for consent to search. These were given to the police, and the DA filed felony grand theft charges. Because of the changes in ownership of the lot, Jennifer's status had changed back and forth between 1099 independent contractor and W2 employee, with the DA reluctant to file felony embezzlement charges against Jennifer.

Jennifer's lawyer started in on a plea bargain, tentatively agreeing to plead her to a single felony charge of grand theft. That's when the tape I'd given Detective Garza, with consent to search recorded, was produced, and Jennifer withdrew her plea. And it only got better. That week, I was contacted by a second detective from that department, who said, "The grand theft matter involving Jennifer is in the works, but I'm working on something else. The owner of the truck has made a burglary charge against you. You broke in without consent and damaged his truck."

I wished the detective luck with his "burglary" case and concluded the call. Someone had tried to fix the case. To identify who owned the truck, I ran the license plate, whereupon I discovered that Jennifer's brother, Rod, was the owner. I dug deeper. In conversation with Rod's former girlfriend, a bank teller, I learned Rod was once a police officer, who'd been fired from the city department adjacent to the town with which I was dealing. He'd been a reservist, then full-time sworn, but ultimately fired from his police job for poor performance.

The Riverside County sheriff's office revealed that Rod had attended police academy with Detective Garza. I put all this into a formal report and forwarded it to the DA prosecuting Jennifer, then to the chief of police supervising Garza. Had I not arrested Jennifer for her crimes, the police would never have investigated or taken action of any kind in this matter. My move against her was risky, but it served the needs of my client and was a risk I was willing to take.

Jennifer took the plea to grand theft but was only ordered to pay back a fraction of what she had stolen. It is rare for me to encounter such blatant corruption in a California police agency, the more common corruption being indifference and incompetence. Of these I won't complain so much, as this marks job security for me. At the very moment that police agencies become perfect in their work, I'll be on a freeway offramp, selling vegetables.

Sherman Block—the ossified, arrogant former sheriff of Los Angeles County—once told me in a snide aside, "No one made you take that job you have, you volunteered for it." Once a respected law enforcement official, Block had become what he'd campaigned against: smug, insular, and completely detached from the hazards citizens in his county had to contend with. I told him he could eat a bag of it. I'll take my chances with the rank-and-file deputies, officers, agents, and detectives.

Let us also consider this: Government as a whole is much more tolerable with a certain level of predictable, static incompetence, and a slick veneer of pissant corruption, otherwise by dint of perfect efficiency, we'd live in a top-down tyranny. One must always be grateful for mercy.

CHAPTER 18

INFIDELITY CASES

In his noteworthy encomium to our profession, *Gumshoe: Reflections in a Private Eye*, Josiah "Tink" Thompson wrote how he'd meet a civilian at a civic event, a cocktail party, a lynching…whatever, and upon answering that he was a private detective to the question as to his line of work, their eyes would get big, and couple it to the standard response, "Oh! How interesting!"

Then, titillated, the next several questions involved catching philandering husbands, wives, or the like. It is what many think of and associate with the profession, and to be fair, it was once a mainstay for many detective agencies.

In the days before no-fault divorce, a husband or wife had to build a case for divorce, separation, or annulment with infidelity being a solid cause of action. I beg off the question, as I rarely take any such work. I'm not opposed to it, generally, but dealing with the expectations of infuriated neurotics is no great joy. Often, having built a perfect case, the final bill doesn't get paid, as the client has been given some remarkably bad news, with explicit photos to punctuate their disappointment.

There are, also, some clients who believe they should go along with the investigator, for the magic moment of confrontation. No investigator of sound mind ever does this, not least for the mindless, clingy mien of the client. To do this is a textbook perfect recipe for manslaughter…or womanslaughter, should you wish to put too fine a point on it. What makes for cringe television could crash a detective agency, and even get an investigator, or client, or subject killed.

Early on, I was referred a case by a white-shoe law firm in Brentwood, strictly the carriage trade. Oddly enough, the lawyer involved was unconcerned with attorney-client privilege and bade me, "You deal with this, and we will get your report from him (the client) if he elects to proceed."

Close to lunch, a man knocked on the door, and I brought him in and sat him before my desk. He was twenty or more years my senior, coat and tie, and searched my office with his eyes. "Is anything I say to you in here confidential?"

Yes.

"How do I know that?" He looked at me quizzically.

I am not a hairdresser, mister. This is what I do for a living. What do you do? He was a successful dentist. I knew he was a successful dentist because he added that part. He was a dentist in his fifties with a younger wife of five or six years, no children.

"I happen to know she is stepping out on me. She gets off work between three and three fifteen every day, and she doesn't come immediately home, and I am very sure she is seeing a man." He had rehearsed these things, it seemed.

What time does she get home?

"She doesn't get home until almost six, most nights." He was fumbling with a manila envelope.

Oh. Does she ever come home late?

"That. That is late, but once she was home a couple of weeks ago just before nine and couldn't explain where the hell she'd been. I just want you to install a tracking device on her car, so I know where she is at."

I can't do that. Your lawyer said you needed me to investigate, but it seems you've made up your mind.

"All you guys do the same thing. You'll just take my money and send me a few photos of her shopping, give me a big bill for nothing." He was quite angry. From the manila envelope he'd produced a photo of his younger wife, a brunette with freckles. She was quite attractive. In my mind I weighed the words of his lawyer, what he was saying about his wife's suspected infidelity, and I made a decision to discharge him into the streets, lest I take the case as an opportunity to beat him out of more money and fuck her myself.

Unethical. Oh, it would be, and I did not do it. But there are sins worse than theft, and adultery, and fornication. Among them, pride. By ridding myself of him and his words and low opinion of the wife he clearly didn't deserve, I'd be able to take a clear look at myself in a mirror the next morning, or even the day after that.

To satisfy the needs of long-term client law firms, I'll still find myself embroiled in these. To quell the lurid winking of the guy who thinks I'm one step above an opportunistic voyeur, I'll offer to sell him candid nudes of his wife. What's he going to do? Kick my ass or something?

Once referred to me by a lawyer, a woman executive came in, sat before me, and explained, "I'm in a marriage, for nineteen years, with my second husband. We are both getting close to retirement. I'm not sure if I want to spend my golden years with him, so I'd like to place him under watch for two weeks, see if he has something going on." There was no prior infidelity, nor was there violence or other abuse within their marriage she would admit to. It was just about making a decision whether to stay with him or not.

She was going out of state, with her executive team, for ten days, and from the moment they went to the airport, she wished for her husband to be under watch an hour before rise, and an hour after he went to bed. Money was no object, and she left detailed photos, car, and office details, and a sizeable retainer. Come the early morning departure from a metropolitan suburb, it was as if there was a convoy: his car carrying her, my auto, and that of Don Moon, and yet another car—a battered Toyota with one headlight out. As we were departing in hours of darkness, this unknown operator stuck out like a fly on a bride's lip.

We hung back, and the Toyota was on his six all the way to the airport drop-off and then to the health club my client and the subject were members of. In the meantime, I got an infuriated call from the client, convinced the bum in the Toyota was something I'd put in the case. By then, I'd already run a make on his car and had a fair idea who he was, just not his purpose.

The client was having none of it, instructed me to suspend all investigation, and she'd collect a refund upon returning to town. Two weeks later she came in on her broom, and I gave her a full refund and a report as to the identity of the unknown party who'd made a convoy of what I was trying to run as a discreet surveillance. She was so convinced she was being given the gears that she dropped it in my waste can and stalked out the door. Had she bothered to read the report, she'd know that the banana in the beater Toyota was a field operative for an investigative outfit that specialized in embezzlement cases out of Orange County—the area where her husband's office was. I'd done what I could and washed my hands of it. By her behavior and attitude, I'll guess the pair deserved each other.

This isn't always the case.

In 2001, right after I met Don Moon, I had a referral from a Santa Monica law firm, specializing in representing medical practices, rather a specialty. Don was there for the consultation, and as his entire experience prior was disability claims investigation for some jackass in Anaheim, I asked him to sit in when the client came, so he could see the process, know what questions to ask. The client was a medical doctor, married to a research scientist. He was in his mid-sixties and arrived in tennis whites, with his Porsche 911 parked in the alley next to the building. I know this because he later sent me the parking ticket, believing I'd pay it.

The doctor explained his belief that his wife was seeing a man she'd met at a private club, connected to California Institute of Technology. He, too, was at a crossroads, with their children off to university, and wasn't sure whether he might stay married to her. He described her as sullen, aloof, and hostile. He produced recent photos, her schedule, a description of her auto, and a key card so we could get into the tennis courts of the private club. The doctor had a McDonald's bag full of US currency and left us with a hefty retainer and instructions to call him in a week. Come the next scheduled tennis date, we surveilled the wife, who was lovely, vivacious, and connected to a group of women from their mid-thirties to their mid-sixties. They enjoyed a tennis match, and then she went shopping, then home. We took video footage, still photos, and identified as many of the women she interacted with as we could.

The next week was identical, unremarkable and without change, and I left a message on the doctor's exchange. He did not return my call. On the third week, the wife did not arrive to the tennis courts, and we spied her car at their house in San Marino. I left the doctor a third message. Five more days passed, and my calls were returned, by the wife. "Hello. You've left a few messages for my husband on his exchange. I'm calling to let you know he has died, somewhat unexpected, a heart attack."

Ironic, as he was a cardiologist.

Before doing anything else, I verified with the county that a death certificate had been issued for the client. Then, next day, I returned the subject's call. "I have a good idea why he hired you. He has done this a few times. Has affairs and feels guilty, wants to see if he can prove to our friends I'm not a good wife," she murmured over the lines.

I bade her come collect the unearned portion of the retainer, without stating under what purpose we'd been hired. Even in death, I owed this ridiculous man my discretion. She came up, and Don showed her in. She sat before us, and I gave her the McDonald's bag. From it she plucked a hundred-dollar bank note, smiled, and said, "You boys seem like nice men. Enjoy his money." She left the McD's bag of currency on my desk and found the elevator.

The currency I handed to Moon with the instruction, "Pay the motherfucker's parking ticket and cut the remainder in half with me." Once an infantry officer in our marine corps, Don was a good man and knew a solid thing when he saw it.

When I'd met Don, it was him coming into my offices, unannounced, in a suit and tie, with a resume. There'd been others over the years, and I am polite enough to take their temperature, give their resume a read, and find out why they'd chosen my chambers to debut their ambitions. There is a secondary purpose, an ulterior one, that isn't always so obvious. At least once I have had a party drop in, unannounced, with pretenses of seeking work in the field, when in reality they're trying to learn something of my practice, of me, or of a client. In short, they're investigating me.

Moon was doing disability insurance surveillance for an outfit I'd never heard of before. He was college educated, with ten years of service in the Marine Corps, and obviously a man of some ability. His employer was paying him a pittance for fairly grueling work, and Don wanted to broaden his horizons. When I interviewed him, he spoke of being a platoon leader in the Gulf War and had seen combat in Desert Storm. Recently divorced from a flight attendant whom he'd met when he was a military officer, Donald Moon had a haunted, resigned quality about him.

That evening, at home with my wife, I said to her, "A man came by the office today with a great resume." She asked if I was going to hire him, and I told her, "I don't know. There is something about him, like he has one foot in the grave."

CHAPTER

19

PSYCHOPATHS

What is a Psychopath? This was once perfectly understood…at least in psychiatry, criminal investigation, and penal institutions. Over the years, by dint of dilution through popular culture, denoting someone as a Psychopath seems to have lost its original meaning. A Psychopath is someone who is bereft of conscience—feels no remorse for having done illegal, immoral, perverse, and or selfish acts, inclusive of murder.

Characteristics of the Psychopath can include:

- pathological egocentricity
- utter lack of remorse for grotesquely antisocial acts
- the amazing ability to evade punishment
- inculcating sympathy and protection from dupes, within and without institutions
- pursuing a parasitic lifestyle
- no capacity to identify with the pain their acts cause in others
- the ability to shift blame and externalize their acts to such an extent that many Psychopaths can confuse a veteran polygraph operator
- a smug, arrogant certainty that they're entitled to behave as they please, that their victims deserve whatever has befallen them for the inferiority, status, or vulnerability of the victim
- abuse of alcohol and other drugs, perhaps out of compulsion, but also to blot out what might remain of his conscience

- inability to be treated beyond containment or death, as the Psychopath derives training, gratification, and refinement in psychiatric treatment, therapy, and rehabilitation, making them more skilled in stealing, lying, and killing

There are many other facets that could be added here, but not all Psychopaths are uniform in their presentation or level of offense. It is my opinion, however, that for a true Psychopath, there is no proscribed offense or transgression that's off the table…they're capable of anything under the right circumstances.

I've seen mindlessly stupid writing in magazines, blogs, websites, introducing us to a business executive who calls himself, or herself, a Psychopath. The author is usually titillated, thrilled they could get an executive in a publicly traded company to "come clean," confess to hating people, and counting the sins of capital. These articles might include a chickenshit checklist, so the more neurotic consumers of this bilge can vapidly compare their boss to the guy in the article. In what way is the subject of the article a Psychopath? He doesn't care that he laid off seventy-one workers from a plant, that he outsmarted other executives to obtain his lofty corporate posting, or that he cheats at golf.

Just as often, the article is the pablum of chick magazines, wherein the author is bemoaning her latest failed relationship with all the emotive strokes of dating a narcissistic narcissist. "Like, oh my *God*! He exhibits every sign of being a serial killer!" Again, with the banal and obvious checklist: "Is your boyfriend a Psychopath?"

At the most basic level, these authors take the sociopathic ennui of someone beyond their control and conflate drunk driving, philandering, campaign literature, stock price manipulation, and indebtedness with psychopathy.

Early in my career, I was engaged by a company that had received a bum checque from a man whom the client identified as a "bank officer." His name was Brian Harrington, and he was living with his wife in the cottages that surround the grounds of what was once the Huntington Hotel in Pasadena.

Upon contacting Harrington, I learned that he wasn't particularly concerned about the checque drawn on insufficient funds, and he treated the matter as if it were a joke. Delving deeper, I discovered Harrington had other problems, which include domestic violence charges, wherein he was indicted for beating up his wife. The only way the victim company could get the money Brian Harrington owed them was by threatening criminal prosecution. Harrington reluctantly paid it off, as if he was doing the firm a favor.

Harrington drove a nice, imported automobile, wore expensive clothing, and comported himself as if he was a celebrity of some acclaim. Perhaps a year after this, I encountered a perturbed lawyer, who was irritated that he'd paid an "advance commission" to a young banking officer to arrange a business loan for the lawyer's firm. The loan never materialized, and the bank employing Brian Harrington had him prosecuted for graft.

Not long after, Brian Harrington set himself up as a "mortgage broker," operating out of Plaza Las Fuentes and the Commons. He was seen in all the best places around town, often in the company of an attractive woman, twenty years his senior. Harrington once boasted, to me, that he had the highest rate of jumbo mortgage defaults in the Pasadena Area. As if it were a joke. Casual perusal of the civil indices revealed lots of small claims cases filed against Harrington for rent, for unpaid tailor's bills. He made a hobby of stiffing anyone he could and behaving as if it were a joke.

While still living with the older woman, Brian Harrington made a show of romancing an attractive cocktail waitress at Monty's on South Fair Oaks. One Friday night, incensed by his behavior, the waitress threw a heavy glass ashtray through the windshield of Brian Harrington's Jaguar. Naturally, he evaded paying the man who replaced the wind screen.

In casual conversation around the various bars, restaurants, and upholstered dives of Los Angeles, Brian would intimate to strangers and acquaintances purported ties to organized crime. In another conversation, Harrington informed me that his father, Bill Harrington, had been in navy special warfare and was once on the protective detail of Henry Cabot Lodge. Later investigation proved that Bill Harrington, perhaps a navy veteran, sold Oldsmobiles in Santa Clara, California, and once took custody of a troubled teenaged son.

To round up his offenses, and offend further, Brian Harrington was arrested and prosecuted and convicted a few times for drunk driving. Again, he never seemed to do any jail time. The older girlfriend stood by him, despite her complaints of having been beaten. Brian Harrington inculcated the sympathy and partnership of a real estate broker, a necessary element of his business. As a convicted felon, there was no way Harrington could officially transact business. Yet here he was, forcing loans through every mortgage institution in the Pasadena area.

The broker, Raymond Madison, was also a reserve police officer. I thought it awfully odd, jarring, that a respected businessman would want to ooze around in the criminal mud with Brian, and one day I braced Raymond, telling him "That man, Harrington, is a felon, convicted of loan fraud. Do you really think you should be doing business with him?"

"Fuck off. I know what I'm doing" was Madison's answer for this.

Things started to happen fairly quickly after that. Starting in the autumn of 2008, men and women who practiced the mortgage and real estate rackets as Raymond and Brian did became a plurality of the home-lending market, and that started to topple, with foreclosures atop defaults, tied up with more of the same, coast to coast. In 2007, Harrington had taken up with a newly divorced socialite in Pasadena, a woman with school-age children. To make himself sound heroic and noble and honest, Harrington told this woman he was a Navy SEAL and former elite police officer. He even paid a couple of men to rent navy uniforms and pick him up from her San Marino Home in a black SUV.

This woman didn't live with Harrington. He still shared a home, vested to a straw man to avoid creditors, with his real girlfriend, whom he told the socialite was "like a retarded older sister." With the mortgage business crashing, Brian reinvented himself as a loan modification specialist, taking in tens of thousands of dollars in advance fees from people desperate to save properties underwater. As of this writing, I haven't found a single customer of this whose mortgage was modified into anything other than a default, followed by a foreclosure.

The socialite's ex-husband, and her brother, were both alarmed about her relationship with a known cad like Brian Harrington. Together, they showed his criminal records to the woman. When she asked Brian Harrington about the extensive criminal record, including several drunk driving tickets, the lack of a driving license, fraud, and domestic violence, Brian explained to her that he was "investigating banks and shady operators for mortgage fraud. This is part of my cover with the FBI."

Harrington convinced the socialite woman, a single mother, that she should no longer pay her mortgage, that he'd renegotiate her loan. Brian also began forging checques on her account, laundering the proceeds through the coffers of Madison Financial, the company operated by Raymond Madison. Brian Harrington moved hundreds of thousands of dollars in stolen money this way; Raymond Madison knowingly allowed this and took a cut as it occurred. When the socialite discovered she'd been cleaned out, there began a series of confrontations, then a breakup between her and Harrington. Wanting to believe there was a way to get her money back from Brian, our socialite agreed to go to dinner with him to discuss. When the drink flowed and it was apparent he was providing more excuses, she asked to be taken home.

What occurred next is the woman fleeing Harrington, locking herself in her rooms, with him breaking down the door to assault her over the evening. In the morning, after he'd sobered and departed, his victim reported having been assaulted, the door broken in. Harrington later admitted to breaking down the door, attributing it to booze and ardor, characterizing the rape as "consensual." The San Marino police had extensive files on Harrington, took a report, and promptly arrested Brian Harrington for PC264, Rape, in addition to other charges. Raymond Madison immediately bailed Harrington out of jail. It was at this time that a detective from San Marino police called me, saying, "I understand you've extensive case files on this suspect."

The other thing stated by the detective, who'd called other agencies studying the man being prosecuted, was that Brian Harrington was responsible for "$30 million in mortgage fraud over these past few years." It seems like a lot of scratch, but on the scale of Pasadena, San Marino, it really wasn't—just to victims like the socialite. The San Marino police elected to file a probation violation against Harrington and bring him in as a threat to the community on a no-bail warrant. But he was nowhere to be found. It was then that the police called me again, with more conversations. I could only describe Brian Harrington as a Psychopath who'd been not more than a one-man crime wave in Pasadena. The comments from San Marino police as to the conduct of Raymond Madison, I'll keep to myself.

The police asked me to help locate Harrington for arrest. I barely knew his latest victim, and I had no real client in this matter. I had the choice to let it go, allow the police to handle it all, or to take action. Brian Harrington had wowed Pasadena, evading punishment for two decades. He was a real problem, so I signed on.

Myself and a San Marino detective took Harrington at gunpoint at a house in Pasadena. The door kicked in, after five minutes of us pounding upon the door, Harrington emerged from a bedroom in shorts and grubby T-shirt. The San Marino Detective had Brian in the glare of the lights mounted to his sidearm, and I frisked our man. Looking up, Brian asked the detective, "Henry, is that you?"

Henry Todd answered, grinning, "Yeah, it's me, Brian."

As I put my cuffs on Brian, he turned his head and asked, "Who's this behind me?"

As I closed the second cuff with a ratcheting series of clicks, right up on Brian's ear, I gently announced, "It's Detective Nils, Brian." Henry grinned wider, holding his piece on the felon. This was the culmination of almost twenty years of work. The man was a low-life crime wave.

Initially cocky, Harrington howled. I have a nice photo of the man wearing my handcuffs, sitting on the curb. His next move was to fake a heart attack, hoping to get favorable consideration at the Pasadena city jail. Instead, he was dispatched from the ER and directly sent to Inmate Reception Center, Los Angeles County.

And that was just the beginning. The night after arresting Harrington, I sat down with this woman and with a trusted associate Joe Cornet, who knew the socialite and her family for decades. We briefed her on every single thing known of Brian Harrington. It was eye-opening for her, and she realized how badly she and her children had been victimized. More charges were filed, for grand theft, as additional victims came forward. A few weeks after his arrest, locked away in Los Angeles County Jail, Brian started causing more trouble for the woman and her children.

Another inmate, a former member of the Mexican Mafia, notified the jail staff that Harrington had tried to hire him to kill his victim and her children. For evidence, the informant provided thirty or more pages of instructions, stating where the socialite lived, the car she drove, her parents' address, where her children attended school. Harrington expressed to this man the ability to pay him tens of thousands of dollars and arrange for a new luxury SUV in payment for murdering them. The police notified me immediately. San Marino Police Department is a small agency, and their ability to protect a citizen was rather limited. In terms of threat, Brian Harrington's greatest asset as a criminal was his ability to convince other men of his willingness and wealth to reward them for acting on his behalf. He posed, in this sense, an almost unlimited threat.

I extended myself into protecting this woman, as did her former husband, and her brothers, moving her to a more secure location. To her credit, she started making herself a little more aware and something of a GI Jane. The socialite took the threat seriously. In order to mitigate the threat, I established an intelligence network, keeping eyes on various people who might act locally on behalf of Harrington, evaluating each visitor Harrington had at the Los Angeles County Jail, including his mother, a brother, the older woman who still believed Brian Harrington was her boyfriend, and a criminal lawyer I knew named Anthony Brooklier.

I enlisted the aid of Larry "Kit" O'Brien, who wanted to apprentice toward his private detective's license. Kit had been closely checked out and was an authentic asset in protecting this woman as well as her children. Kit had been a trust and estates man with a bank for more than twenty years, knowing real estate inside and out. Methodical and tough, he'd been trained as a Court Clerk, having been a yeoman in the US Navy. We conducted a clandestine operation, which included background investigations, surveillance, threat assessment, and regular liaison with police agencies.

In executing our protection operation, we knew who Harrington had hired to interview defense witnesses: a retired Pasadena police detective who was friends with Brian's mother. We regularly monitored Brian's movement in the jail system and derived predictive amusement from Brian boasting to the sheriff's deputies that he was a former police officer. He wasn't, and they knew this, using his mindless bonhomie as a chance to elicit his continued criminal intent toward the victim.

While the former gang member did testify at Harrington's felony probable cause hearing, he refused to testify at trial. The jury gave Harrington benefit of the doubt, and he beat the murder-for-hire charges. Convicted of rape, grand theft, and other charges, Brian Harrington was sentenced to seventeen years in prison, and lifelong registration as a sex offender. Whether Harrington ever paid Brooklier for the first-class defense the man delivered in court is a matter of conjecture.

The socialite, having put Harrington away, sued Raymond Madison for fraud, for living off the money she had counted on to keep house with her children. This resulted in a substantial judgment against a man who should have known better.

If you were to sit Brian Harrington down, and, as if by magic, make him honest for the space of a minute, he would tell us that he stole the money from his victims—all of them, fair and square. When he assaults a woman, she'd best enjoy it. It's all she's entitled to, and she should be grateful. That's the essence of the Psychopath. Trying to hire the Mexican Mafia to murder a woman and her children is a necessary business decision. Who knew that so fearsome, violent, and connected an organized crime group as La Eme, the Mex Mafia, were more cognizant, more ethical, more principled, more refined than a greased up, has been, junk-juggling mortgage broker from Pasadena?

Sometimes I think that I've seen it all. I have experienced pretty much everything a man could see in a single lifetime. Then someone comes along and schools me right. A man has to keep his wits, his eyes open, and pay attention. In recounting Mark F. Weddle, a man of similar bent to that of Brian Harrington, keep in mind the characteristics of the Psychopath.

Weddle came to me from a retail jewelry company for which I'd done theft investigations. Their internal procedures were very good. Their management—pros, in every way. The sales and technical staff were not just versed in precious metals, gemstones, sales, and credit, but also loss prevention. In a city like Los Angeles, sharp thieves can pick apart a loose company in quick time.

The vice president of the client company, I'll call him Frank. He'd taken a statement from each salesperson who'd handled Weddle and was at least satisfied this was not an inside job.

"Mark Weddle came in three times, once by himself, twice with his fiancée, a realtor named Kathy. They're both attractive, upper middle-class people. Mark used to be a police officer in Texas and has been establishing himself as a mortgage broker here in Los Angeles. He drives a forest green Jaguar Sedan."

He and Kathy picked out a platinum engagement ring, with a two-karat princess-cut diamond. Retail on it was just over $12,000. Expensive, but not a purchase out of line for a professional couple in LA. We verified funds available on his checque and took it in. Nine days later, the instrument bounced, being returned stamped "NSF." "We have called him, repeatedly, and he doesn't answer" was the VP's summation of the matter. He wanted me to make contact with Weddle and determine what the situation was, extract from Weddle his intentions, and either recover the ring or the funds.

It didn't strike the VP as particularly odd. Los Angeles has a godly number of flakey people, vogue on the outside and vague on the inside, who wish always to be evaluated for their stated intentions rather than the irresponsibility of their actions. The retail jewelry operation wanted to have the benefit of a sale, without the hassle of collection action. There is nothing outrageous in this, and I went to work on it.

One of Weddle's phones, his landline, was disco (disconnected!), while the voicemail for his mobile was larded full and could take no further messages. There were no text messages then. Calls I made to informants in the State Department of Real Estate as well as the Corporations Department revealed Weddle possessed no real estate or mortgage banking bona fides, of any kind. A call to the notaries public desk at secretary of state also came up bust. My purpose was identifying an employer, or colleague, with the potential of putting the irresponsible man on the spot.

I repeated these steps with Mark Weddle's fiancée, Kathy, whose identification was contained in the retail sales record. This also came up with nothing. The lack of a record in vetting is actually a positive. It instructs me that these people are not what and/or who they claimed to be. There is nothing ambiguous about a negative record. With the State of Texas, I repeated each of these steps, and lacking informants in that state, made for almost a day of work.

Kathy's address was a private mail drop in the San Fernando Valley, and Mark Weddle's was a condominium complex in Simi Valley, Ventura County. I knew this from consulting a reverse telephone directory, called a *Criss Cross*, which listed addresses in sequence in the front of the directory, and phone numbers in sequence in the back half. This analog tool of investigation is gone forever, done in by the internet. At the end of a hot afternoon, I motored over to Simi Valley, to the condo where Weddle purported to live. I'd already checked ownership and discovered the condo was owned by a management company, for which it was just a rental.

There was no mail in Weddle's box, and no answer at his door. The condo was a two-story arrangement, of new construction, and L-shaped. I went around to the garage, which was made a part of the unit, so the owner could enter his home from within the wide garage. The garage door could also be seen from the second story. I was studying the garage door, which had no padlock on it, when I thought I saw the curtain in the second-floor window move. It could also have been late afternoon glare. I did not have my gun on me, and I got a queasy feeling. My temptation was to force the door enough to reveal whether the green Jag was docked in it. I resisted the temptation and stood down for the evening.

Next day, I changed gears and rang a security colleague in the bank whose negotiable instrument had been bounced. "This one has a lot of these, and if you ask me, Nils, it appears he may be 'kiting' checks." This was the nub of our discussion. My colleague identified two other banks, one in Texas and another in Nevada, where Mark Weddle kept his accounts. In the days before instantaneous checque clearing, a mec of some enterprise could kite his checques, meaning write checques from Banks A and C, for deposit to Bank B, then from Bank B to Bank A, and from C to A, so as the amount on deposit was artificially inflated long enough to justify a loan, or keep a job, or even purchase a diamond and platinum engagement ring.

The time between states for paper clearance, then, was around two to three days, for an out-of-state checque. The routing and account numbers on the bottom of any such item are printed in a typeface called OCR, which stands for optical character reader. Swiping a checque through an optical character reader initiates the clearing process. It was a problem when funds were not replaced, or when it was done for the purposes of theft. If you look 'round the boardroom of any business populated by older women and men, you'll see people who've had to do this and replace funds in order to close a deal, obtain funding, and other legal purposes. Legal? Not by the fine print issued by your bank, but who cares?

Under our California penal code, when it was still enforced, to do so with mens rea, or criminal intent, was a matter of grand theft and also of forgery. Did Weddle fake the signature of another? He did not. But to deposit worthless instruments knowingly *is* forgery, in context. Any longer, Los Angeles Police Department has a four-year backlog on financial crimes, sometimes causing death of a case by statutes of limitation. These matters are prioritized according to losses and the relative outrage arising of a particular financial crime.

At this stage, I knew that Weddle was committing crimes. But why would a man styling himself a mortgage broker, engaged to a realtor, take risks such as these? I combed through the sales record anew and found a phone number for Kathy's employers. There was no name for the company, and based upon the statements made to the jewelers, I was supposed to believe it to be a real estate company. There was a record of the number in the back pages of the *Criss Cross Directory*, and of course it was a titty bar, in the San Fernando Valley.

Two phone calls and a reconnaissance of the cabaret in question later, I learned Kathy was a stripper, in an on-and-off thing with a bouncer, named Mark Weddle. The management of the titty bar had not seen either for three days, and I was told there might be drugs coinciding with their absence.

My visit at Kathy's apartment found no one there, so I started the process necessary to file a felony case against Mark Weddle and, possibly, Kathy. The VP of the jewelry company gave me a limited imprimatur to do this in pursuit of a recovery, and to deter any such action at their stores. This took me to the Van Nuys station, Los Angeles Police Department. I'd written a probable cause affidavit, enumerating and delineating the crimes, fully identifying Mark Weddle and Kathy the hot Realtor. The desk sergeant looked my work over, made a call, and sent me up to the detective bureau.

Detective 3 Mike Pavelka of LAPD, Valley Financial Crimes, was at his desk, with a look on his face like someone had fed him a dog-turd hoagie. "A private detective? What do you want?" I laid out my case and afforded Pavelka the affidavit, for which he replied, "So what? Happens all the time. They'll never file on this guy. Don't waste my time."

I went back to the front desk, spoke with the sergeant, then a captain, and I told him, "Look, this is a serious crime. My clients own several stores around Los Angeles, and this is a hell of an attitude to take about theft and forgery." The captain agreed, suggested I get some lunch, and return in the afternoon. Next contact was with

Detectives Sheldon Kaminsky and Wayne DuFord, both of whom read my affidavit, with Wayne telling me, "If this is as you say, it's a felony case we can file. Shel and I have to go over your leads, verify what you've taken in."

A few days passed, and I got a call from Kaminsky. "Nils, not only was all your work right on, every single lead, but when we tossed Weddle's pad in Simi, we came up with guns, lots of ammo. You wanna watch yourself with this guy." Turns out on the hot afternoon, unarmed, I was going to check Weddle's garage for the presence of the Jaguar, he'd had a Colt automatic rifle at his shoulder, weighing whether or not he could shoot me for having a look. Weddle was booked for grand theft, worthless instruments, and related charges, and then bailed out.

DuFord and Kaminsky were very thorough, and a pawn ticket came up, showing that Weddle had pawned a platinum and diamond ring at a San Fernando Valley pawnbroker. LAPD seized the ring as evidence, and my clients put in the necessary claim for it.

Kaminsky shared with me some background he'd elicited in running my leads with the banks. From a banker in Texas, Shel determined that Mark Weddle had been a reserve deputy sheriff in Galveston, Texas, and had been discharged for unknown reasons. Further, Weddle had a mother, an aunt, and a grandmother, who'd bail him out of any situation or trouble and were convinced he'd either make it in California as a mortgage broker movie star, or would have to rescue him from stupid choices. It was my opinion, like those of DuFord and Kaminsky, that Weddle was way beyond stupid choices. His crimes showed a fair amount of criminal sophistication, deliberation, intent, and effort to evade detection. In his thirties, Mark Weddle had crossed over from sociopathic behavior to Psychopath—a permanent state.

There are various theories about what makes a man into a Psychopath, and the one that makes the most sense to me is random reward for negative acts. In youth, if a man or woman is rewarded but not predictably for negative, harmful, gratifying, or abusive acts, the random reward remakes the pathways and chemistry of the human brain, rather like the compulsive gambler yanking the lever of a slot machine, never certain when the wheels might line up for the jackpot. But they're always willing to try again. This state of being cannot be changed by therapy, by punishment, by reward, by education. It can be mitigated for society by penal containment, penal supervision, and to some extent, psychotropic medications. The offender always remains a menace.

Weeks later, I appeared and testified at the felony preliminary hearing, or probable cause hearing. Weddle sat next to a private lawyer, presumably engaged and paid by his family, smirking at myself, DuFord, and the district attorney. Held to answer for multiple felony counts, Weddle immediately jumped bail and fled California. With so many cases burdening the criminal courts, it was unlikely Los Angeles County would extradite Mark Weddle. The pawnbroker took a beating on the deal, as he'd lent Weddle half the value of the ring. But that's the breaks when a man runs little more than a legalized fencing operation.

I consulted the bail schedule and discovered that Mark was only out on $50,000 in bail. I could've taken a percentage from the bonding company if they commissioned me to arrest him, but the percentage wouldn't be much. Hardly worth it for me to go to Texas, clap him in irons, and bring him before the California courts.

Working other matters, time got away from me, until I got a call from Detective Kaminsky. "You want to hear an update on your boy Mark Weddle?" It was a good one. In 2000, Mark Weddle cased a Galveston bank for robbery. Because his sister worked at the branch and institution Mark elected to rob at gunpoint, he waited for his sister's regular day off. Masked, Weddle invaded the bank with a gun and held the place up. His sister had been called in to work, replacing a sick teller, and instantly recognized his voice.

To her credit, she called him out, identifying the gunman as her brother. Weddle locked himself in the men's room and ate his gun, dead of suicide. Was this the act of a contrite conscience? Or is it the act of a Psychopath who can't do time? I vote for the latter. Men like

Mark Weddle are too good to share a berth, breakfast, and chapel with honest criminals.

Another Psychopath that stands out, among many others, in my professional case count is John Meehan, made famous—and infamous, postmortem—as "Dirty John." Antemortem, I handled a few matters with Meehan as the subject well before Chris Goffard wrote his outstanding series of articles in *The Los Angeles Times*.

The first matter involving Meehan came as the referral of an attractive, successful entertainment executive, who had questions about her fiancé, a man she believed was a nurse anesthetist to whom she had lent a good amount of money. Her approach was rational, as one would expect of a business exec.

Sandra wanted me to verify Meehan's identity and professional bona fides. He claimed to her, just before she took him on holiday to Europe, that he was employed by a prestigious hospital in west Los Angeles and lived in Palm Springs. He was divorced from a wife who was cruelly withholding two daughters from him.

Sandra described how John Meehan would weep and always had photos of his teenaged daughters with him. He was devoted, by all appearances, to these daughters. When I asked how Sandra had met her fiancé, she stated they were introduced online through a dating and singles service. "In his ad, I at first thought he was a surgeon, but I guess a RN is just as important." The client reported that John Meehan was often in scrubs or hospital togs, as one might expect of a doctor or nurse. He kept odd hours and was usually unavailable.

"He needed a bit of money, in advance of the sale of his house in the Midwest, so I lent him thirty-five thousand. I don't know him as well as I should have, and he hasn't paid me back yet" was her explanation. She was embarrassed at the idea that she needed the help of a private detective to sort the situation out with a man she believed in and cared for. With a fair amount of work, I verified John Meehan's identity, then his prison record in the Midwest. John Meehan had been arrested, prosecuted, and imprisoned for stealing narcotics, and had lost his nursing license as the direct result.

"Sandra, your fiancé is a junkie, a thief, and a liar." Clients often can't be told the truth in such plain terms, otherwise the emotional experience of learning makes them pull back, even to their own detriment. "Sandra, using discreet methods and proven sources, I've learned that your fiancé has a prison record in Michigan for theft, specifically theft of narcotics. As the result of this, his license was pulled in several jurisdictions. He has no license to practice, of any kind." This is how I told her.

"I always knew he was a liar. We were in France. He told me he had been before, but he was lost. John knew nothing of Europe. He told me his father was in the Mafia, suggested, without actually stating so, that his father was a hitman. I didn't believe it," was Sandra's retrospection of Meehan.

I interviewed Meehan's ex-wife, who spoke of his thoroughgoing, unstinting dishonesty, how he had abandoned any notions of fatherhood and left her to fend for herself with two children. His pathology included narcotics addiction; theft; and compulsive, continuous manipulation of women for sex, narcotics, and sympathy. Meehan idolized and idealized a father who rewarded his aggressive and untoward behaviors. The former wife knew the stories of John Meehan's father, but there was never any evidence of the father doing anything other than petty criminality, alcoholism, and womanizing.

From his fraternity brothers, John Meehan derived even more reward for his aggressive abuse of women. Meehan's ex-wife described how they were drunk and disorderly at her wedding to John and openly joked about his history of bedding and leaving women. Something that struck this woman as odd was the fact that not a single member of her husband's family was in attendance at this wedding. For Sandra's purposes, this was enough. She knew that Meehan would never repay the money she had lent him, that he wasn't employed other than as a handyman, and that he was likely still using narcotics. This was never a question in my mind. Sandra ended her relationship with Meehan, and he changed gears as if she never existed.

Shortly after my case was concluded, Sandra put me in touch with another woman who had more extensive knowledge of John Meehan. Sarah was a healthcare professional who had briefly dated Meehan, and when she identified continuous, multiple profiles he maintained on dating sites, she had ended her relationship with John. Sarah had posted a warning on an informational website, identifying John Meehan as a manipulative abuser who was out for money, drugs, and was insincere in everything in his profile. Sarah deserves credit for fully documenting these things and for engaging with John Meehan in the online forum in which she outed him. It occurred to me, contemporaneous with this, that there were so many women he had played, or attempted to play, in online personals that he wasn't sure which of his past connections was outing him.

Sarah was the woman who had John Meehan figured out, and she showed me his various dating profiles. For Dirty John Meehan, playing the personals was like yanking the lever of a slot machine, never exactly sure what he might get, but certain to play again. This is what creates a Psychopath: random reward. He also learned how to tailor his approach, through the online profile, to make himself more appealing: Be a medical professional—sometimes a surgeon, other times an anesthesiologist, then back to surgical nurse. He was divorced from a cruel wife, who denied him visitation with his daughters.

By the number of responses, or by the lack, he sharpened and honed the profiles to bring in more potential victims. The play was as gratifying as the reward for John Meehan. From the website where Sarah had posted, yet another victim was identified, whose story went like this:

"I was out of a twenty-five-year marriage and took a job in retail. A friend convinced me to try online personals, and that is how I found myself connected to John Meehan. In his profile, he called himself a military trauma surgeon, divorced, about eight years younger than me. He posted pictures of himself in scrubs and with his daughters when they were young. We corresponded by email, and he explained to me that he was in Afghanistan, working with special forces for a few more months, but otherwise lived in San Diego. He was very romantic, and we seemingly had in common difficult former spouses and children. My children were already adults. I fell in love with John but had never met him. He always knew what to say and communicated in romantic and emotional terms. He seemed to miss his daughters but was dedicated to the men he served with. John would describe where he was staying, the operations the special forces went on, and how he would treat the wounded, sometimes even going out into the field to treat civilian Afghanis. After we declared our love for each other, we engaged in online sex—nude photos I sent him, and some of it was pretty explicit.

"About six weeks into this, John would email late at night, which I attributed to our time difference. He told me he was coming to San Diego for a couple of days, to get trauma supplies. I was very excited and hoped to see him, at last. John asked me to book a hotel room, and he would repay me, which I did. He showed up late to dinner, but I was so excited that I didn't care. For some reason he was wearing scrubs. I'd hoped he'd wear his military uniform. We talked, and John seemed…off, or maybe on some medication. He explained he had jet lag. I'd had a few glasses of wine, and we went up to the room. I wasn't prepared for sex, and I probably shouldn't have. All my alarm bells were going off, but I ignored them because I had feelings for the man I'd corresponded with. John Meehan was like an imitation of that man. As soon as we got in the hotel room, John assaulted me…held me down and sodomized me. I was very upset, and crying. He said 'Go ahead, dummy. Call the police. Think they'd believe you? Give it a try. I'm a military doctor, and you're a clerk at a grocery store. Make trouble for me, and I'll show the world what you look like with your clothes off, including your kids, bitch.'"

That's John Meehan, Psychopath. In 2016, John Meehan was killed by the young adult daughter of his final victim. He attacked her with a knife (anything is on the menu with a Psychopath), and in self-defense, the daughter gained control of the knife and planted it in Meehan's eye socket. In each of my personal interactions with John Meehan, he was glib, dishonest, and fearful of being exposed.

He denied every single thing he had done, for which I had almost perfect knowledge and evidence of. John Meehan is remarkable for his calculated, predatory pathology—his use of technology to identify and select victims. Ultimately, his end is poetically Old Testament.

In the past, Psychopaths have written autobiographies in which they alibi their predation, drench themselves in self-pity for the reaction of society. Among neurotics, who often are like the dupes who protect Psychopaths, these works of hedged self-confession have their fans. Some are even heralded as genius authors. If one absolutely has to experience works such as these, I can recommend a few as richly illustrative. Cell 2455 Death Row, by convicted and executed serial rapist Caryl Chessman. The thesis of this book is "I didn't do it, and if I did, you can't prove it. You have no business executing me, even though I have been tried and convicted."

British traitor Kim Philby excused his own treachery, espionage against the West, and aid to the monstrous Soviet regimes in his postdefection, solipsistic hagiography *My Silent War*. To call this man a narcissist is a gross understatement. His thesis is "I did it, damn you all. I'm an elite, born to privilege, and when I betray my nation and its allies, I do so to make the world a better place, no matter how many millions my Leninist masters have slaughtered."

Norman Mailer, often celebrated as a great writer and public intellectual, read the prison book *In the Belly of the Beast*, an ersatz philosophical examination of Western society and criminal justice, authored by Jack Henry Abbot. A lifelong skell, Abbot had learned to write what can only be described as grievance literature while parked in a fetid jail cell.

Abbott had opened a correspondence with Norman Mailer while Mailer was in the throes of his man-crush on Utah murderer Gary Gilmore. Gilmore died by firing squad, and Mailer mourned, documenting his disappointment and melancholy fury in *The Executioner's Song*, a forgettable work, not nearly as expositive as the works of Abbott (or Philby and Chessman for that matter).

So pronounced and prolonged was Mailer's ardor for Jack Henry Abbott, that Mailer championed his early release from prison in

1981. Norman Mailer lauded the convicted killer, forger, and robber Abbott was as a sensitive, praiseworthy poet who was a product of societal cruelty, in all ways a misunderstood wunderkind intellectual. Six weeks after being paroled, Jack Henry Abbott let the life out of a working man in a New York City alley, a waiter who had dared offend Abbott's genius, we may presume.

If Abbott's thesis differed from the theses of Philby and Chessman it would only be for his turgid, fake introspection and perfectly enunciated venom for civil society. In 2002, Abbott took his own life in a prison cell. Some may lament his passing, still considering Jack a "victim." I suspect the Psychopath Jack Henry Abbott was too egotistical to die on God's terms. Any allocution he may have penned would have read like his book: "You made me do this, so fuck you. Now let me out. I'm not done killing."

Within my trove of documents, mementos, and artifacts exists a letter from arsonist thrill killer, John Orr. Imprisoned for multiple acts of arson and murder, Orr was a fire captain and arson investigator with MDSO pathology that included erotic excitement from watching fires, then officially involving himself in the ensuing investigation. One can wonder which was foreplay and which was consummation. Just at the Ole's Home Center in South Pasadena, Orr murdered four people on an October evening in 1984, then made himself available to investigate this fire…first thought to have an electrical cause. Pathology.

What is the thesis of Orr's letter? That he is a police officer, wrongfully convicted of murder. He also states that many officers believe he is innocent. He has no money to pursue an appeal (despite his assertion that police officers believe he is innocent) yet wants me to work on his cause for freedom. I don't do this sort of work, nor did I solicit Orr's unpaid business. It isn't so much a "letter" as it is an exhibit.

As with many cases, I have been approached in odd ways, by prospective clients. In 1988, while a Pinkerton, I was approached by a man I had known even before I was in the army. His daughter was missing, for four years by then.

"My daughter was fifteen, ran away from home. We haven't heard from her since. My wife is quite concerned." They had other children and had moved from Pasadena area to San Bernardino County sometime before 1984 when his daughter went missing. "Can you check around, see if there is any kind of record of her?" As I was a Pinkerton, this would be off the books. Using my own sources, I checked, finding nothing, not a trace. This I reported.

In 1995, established in my own practice, this father came to me anew. "It's been more than ten years, the cops don't seem to be much interested. My wife wanted me talk to you, see what you can find out about her." He had almost no budget. As I'd known him a long time, I did what I could. Nothing. Zero. No trace of her in DMV, in credit, or banking. The sheriff of San Bernardino had a thin file, with her father having told them that she'd run away.

I reported my findings. And I shared with the father, "I suspect she is either dead or established a new identity." He casually agreed and took my report. Then, fifteen years passed, and I heard that the father had died. Curious, I looked up his widow and called her, wondering if her daughter was ever found.

"No. Never. It was so strange how she ran away and all." The mother was always a bit off, and I could never decide if she was lacking intelligence or autistic. I asked her why her daughter might have run away.

"Probably because she didn't wanna testify" came the mother from the other end of the phone line.

Testify?

"Yeah, she was going to testify at the trial of Eddie ______ that next day, and we always thought it was too much for her. Eddie was being tried for molesting his stepdaughter. They were best friends, my daughter an' that girl."

Often, what people omit is the roadmap. Her father had omitted all mention of his daughter's pending testimony. I knew who Eddie was—a drunken, low-life beast. But the father had very carefully omitted all mention of this. I tried to get the detective and the deputy DA who had prosecuted Eddie to speak with me. The DA is now a superior court judge. He is as silent as a Macy's mannequin.

Recently, Mark Lillienfeld, who was long for sheriff's homicide was employed by the agency that had arrested Eddie for molestation and rape. I still hold out hope that this can be resolved. I suspect she was killed by her father, lest she, in cross-examination, reveal that she, too, was molested. I can think of no other reason for her father to not tell me of his daughter's status in Eddie's case.

When I interviewed Eddie's victim, by then a mother herself, she said to me, "I have always believed that _____ saved my life."

CHAPTER

20

WORKING DOPE

In the late 1990s, I was paired with David M., a retired detective of Los Angeles County Sheriff's Office, and LAPD, with stints in both as a "narc," or narcotics detective. Our cause was identifying a "fence," or a criminal who buys and sells stolen property for other criminals—in this case, junkies, street argot for narcotics addicts.

By the time a junkie hits the streets, having disposed of job, family, and civilian friends, she or he is awash with need. Thievery and prostitution or both are how they acquire their next spoon of smack.

David and I were prowling, during daylight hours, an industrial belt of the San Gabriel Valley, looking for a junkie. We didn't have to discuss the particulars of this, as a female addict would be prostituting herself and may know the fence we were looking for, but she could just as easily not and be desperate enough to make up a story to lead us astray for the price of a spoon.

"Do you hear that?" David asked me.

Hear what?

"Do you hear the wind rushing through the holes in that hype's elbows in that phone booth?" He was pointing at a phone setup a block away. His ability to ID a junkie was uncanny.

The addict was a skinny man, in purple corduroy pants and sandals, wearing a long-sleeve shirt with the cuffs unbuttoned, who kept sweeping his sweaty locks of dark hair from his eyes as he scanned the urban horizon for a fix and pretended to use the phone so no one else could.

His clothes were oversized in the same way his hair was overgrown, a shattered wreck. I hauled him from the phone booth, to which he surrendered. He gave us a lead, and two days later, David and I identified the fence we sought, trafficking in stolen cargo.

Most theft is attributable to addicts. Two percent of the urban population commit ninety percent of theft crimes. They, their families, are public charges, with all of us paying the freight on these wrecked lives.

I didn't have David's company on another caper, apprehending a cocaine dealer, whose scene was a series of bars and night clubs, in Long Beach and Orange County. He was out on bail, and his bail was forfeit. Two other operators had already attempted to snag him.

"My main guy took a beating trying to grab MoeMoe in a bar in Anaheim. I guess he is their connection. The last guy pinpointed where he lives, Long Beach, but it's a big apartment complex, with about seven ways out and in. It's in the shitty part of Long Beach, up by Compton, and whenever someone comes around, there is a safety signal. Everyone scatters."

The photo of the dealer showed a skinny lizard of a guy with priors for domestic violence, possession, receiving, and a bunch of other crimes. Drug dealers, even some of the cute hippies, arm themselves, lest they get taken down by other dealers, or starchy customers. The MO is typically low-key charisma and flashy clothes so that their prospects can find them. He had no car and was using a series of autos belonging to female addicts in exchange for drugs.

"Most nights he is on the town between 10:00 p.m. and 3:00 a.m., making hand-to-hand sales" was the observation of the Orange County bondsman.

Does he live alone?

"I don't know. My other guy didn't ID anyone like a girlfriend or a *crimee*."

My reconnaissance of the apartment building confirmed what the other operator had seen. It was Ali Baba and the four hundred thieves, an open dope bazaar, with a payphone in the courtyard that was constantly manned by a lookout. The only time action died down was early morning hours, just before sunrise.

I parked my short (my "beater" vehicle) a block and a half away, under lights, at a market, and approached the building on foot. It was almost 4:00 a.m., and I was in a public utility uniform, including vest, helmet, and toolbelt. MoeMoe's apartment was on the first floor, close to a service hallway, with the locks sprung on the exit doors so skells could come, go, breed, and bleed as they pleased.

There was no light on in MoeMoe's unit, and no sound. The man on the payphone napped in a folding picnic chair. I picked the locks—first the bolt, then the doorknob. Both keyways were identical, and I oiled them so they'd open easier, careful to wipe off the excess oil, lest it leave a telltale stain on the door. And I was in.

Once my eyes adjusted to the darkness, I stealthily cleared each room. I was alone. With a penlight, I checked every crevasse, corner, and closet for a bootleg entry. Some years before I'd worked with a mec who never was seen entering or exiting his mother's apartment. He had burrowed a way through a storage closet ceiling, into his mother's rented apartment. This is the rat brain of a dope man. That apartment had bootleg electric and cable, with water being the only legit utility connection, and that account was in the name of a dead man.

In complete darkness, I waited. The unit was uninhabitable, infested with roaches and ants. His bedroom floor was littered with fast food wrappers, so most of the pest activity was in there. I waited, and the sun came up.

The normal people who had to suffer the criminals of that building exfiltrated, stepping over the mess, and went to work and school. Rap music blared throughout the complex from various sources. Addicts came and went. I could see out, but none could see in, and I waited.

Just before lunchtime, I heard a deep voice, in casual conversation with a woman, outside the door, then a key in the bolt, threw that lock, then the doorknob. I waited by the bathroom to hear the sound of the door being secured, lest someone ride to MoeMoe's rescue from the Boogie Man. I figured after motoring north, MoeMoe would need to take a leak. I looked, and he was four feet away, with his back to me. A man's center of gravity is his waist, so I aimed my tackle for his belt and took MoeMoe off his feet. I outweighed the lizard by fifty pounds, but he was wiry, grunting and calling for help. I tried to wrest his hands, get them behind his back, but he was quite strong, and I had two broken fingers for my trouble, with MoeMoe trying to push himself off the stained carpet. I drew my 1911 and pistol whipped him, one, two three blows to the head. Blood mixed with hair grease, and Moe whimpered. No one I have ever pistol whipped has ever just fallen to the floor like in the movies. They always cry and bleed.

MoeMoe cuffed, I straightened out my broken fingers. In the course of my job, I have broken every digit at least once. I am not a hairdresser, so this goes with the job. Had I drawn down on MoeMoe, it could easily have been a gun battle, endangering civilians and skells in neighboring apartments.

From MoeMoe's clothes, I took a Kool cigarettes pack, with seven bindles of what later passed the cocaine test, a .380 automatic pistol, and a small notebook with what narcs call pay/owes. This is the bookkeeping of a dope man.

MoeMoe rolled half over, no longer crying, eyed me, and said, "Ain't this some shit, getting robbed by the gas man?"

He found out later when I bundled him out, late the next night to avoid his friends, and rode him to jail. The booking deputy in Santa Ana asked, "He got any property?" I responded by bagging the gun and dope, and a fetid wad of bills equal to $1,000.

Searching for missing persons, runaways, and absconders who are addicts often just involves staking out their dealer's operation. No need to pick the locks, and I can wait in the comfort of my car.

Heroin and crack, and now fentanyl, are a low, *low*, common denominator. In the early 2000s, a familiar bondsman asked me to scoop up a man whose trust fund would run dry, so he didn't have enough scratch to feed his habit. He was a thirty-nine-year-old divorced father from a nice suburb, whose father was a race car driver and had left him enough to live without working, but dope gets expensive, and why work?

I took him down on the boulevard, dressed in wig and skirts, prostituting himself for dope. Last time I checked on him, he was dead, and his children were without a father. Fentanyl was introduced to the heroin supply by Mexican cartels, increasing their profits, and wiping out a generation of hypes in four years. For whatever reason there are always replacements. Men and women and teens, and housewives, and veterans who think they'll be the exception, that they can use industrial-grade smack without being felled to their knees, stripped over their dignity, then their lives. Their families suffer, mourning them before they die, with the death being a sad, seemingly inevitable denouement.

Families sometimes take action when the police are overburdened. Recently, in a blue-collar city close to LAX, I ran a defensive source operation, having enlisted the trust of a woman running a cafe.

"If you see Mr. X, discreetly learn his license plate number." The subject is a foreign national distributing fentanyl pressed into counterfeit Xanax pills. He has killed at least two people, one of them the fifteen-year-old son of my clients. Five months later, she saw him and texted me immediately. I got my surveillance team on him and visited her. She and her husband are elderly, maybe can't retire yet. They made me a whole red snapper with plantains and rice.

My surveillance guys are the very best. They are invisible, and as of this writing, I have figured where this dope man lives, whom the last legit owner (dead addict) of his car is.

Speaking of shorts, your short is your car. Back in the late '80s, early '90s, I was always tight for money.

There was a general type of car my dad would call a flyver. Some call it a beater, meaning a minimally reliable car, cheap to operate, that you don't mind losing in a wreck, a theft, or to mechanical failure.

An operable Datsun B210, with stick shift, could be had for $200 to $500. I never bothered registering or insuring them. Wasn't worth it. And there were so many around LA that they were invisible even in an odd color. The keyway was so weak it could be started with a popsicle stick. This is part of being indigestible. No one eats indigestible men.

I had a series of cars like that, used for surveillance, hauling men to jail (cuffed in front with the seat moved as far forward as possible and interior handle removed). An Englishman I worked with once "borrowed" my Datsun while I was laundering my tonsils in a dive bar. In pursuit of a mec in Hollywood, Roger popped the clutch, causing the U-joint to break and drive shaft to dig into a pothole. It wrecked the whole rear end of the auto.

He rang me at the bar. "Don't worry on it," I said. "Just pay me half the value," and he left it at the scene.

It was replaced in four hours by an identical bucket of bolts. This B210 was modified to include an "eye bolt" mounted to the passenger side floorboards, so I could lock my charge's cuffed hands low. Once maneuvering toward Riverside on the Pomona Freeway, a problematic mec pulled the eye bolt from the rusted floor, still chained. He then proceeded to assault me at 75 miles per hour, in traffic, and had the door half open. I got the Datsun over to the right shoulder on the quick, pinning his door closed against the cement barrier wall. I quelled this addict's suit with mace, reducing cabin pressure enough that I could get him to the lockup in Rubidoux without doing him permanent violence. All the way there, my window down, with me snarfing fresh air against the residual tear gas. Upon arriving at the jail, I had to haul my man over the shifter, in handcuffs and all, as the passenger door was banged shut. The booking officer made a salty remark about the odor of tear gas, and my bloody head and shirt. Next day, I had Harry Marmarian fix the door at his body shop, and remove the door handle from the passenger side. No more freeway flyers. In my country I am the King. Never doubt it.

A decade ago, right after I moved to a Los Angeles suburb, there was an OD death of a fifteen-year-old. His friend had a "cool mom." He never had heroin before and died as soon as she injected the boy. "Cool mom" was just out of an elite rehab, and was "fixed" with suboxone, a "harm reduction" narcotic. Were this boy one of mine, I'd have taken her head. It is the only thing I fear.

Dope has eased into, oozed into, pop culture. Cannabis is now widely believed to be harmless. For some people it is. As always, though, I get to see the worst of it. Legalization of cannabis has legitimized long-established organized crime rings. Every few months I get a new case involving a naive civilian who believes they can make a tidy profit from investing in legal cannabis. Often, they get hosed hard and hosed fast.

"I took my divorce settlement and bought all the equipment to cultivate in my garage. I worked really hard and put a lot into it and grew an amazing crop of high-grade cannabis. I have this 'consultant' who showed me how to do most of it, then he was going to connect me with a cool buyer, and I would commission him eighteen percent, a very fair deal."

What happened?

"When we went to deliver, in Sylmar, we got robbed at gunpoint! It was terrifying!"

Turns out her consultant got a 100 percent commission, because he was the party staging the robbery. Does the city, county, or state care? Only if there is a dead body. What was supposed to be a tax windfall has been a boondoggle, as the gangsters know all the profit is in bootleg pot. Why pay taxes when you already have a long-standing distribution network set up, organized, protected, and rewarded?

Humboldt County, California, ground zero for cannabis cultivation, also accounts for a majority of the unsolved missing-persons cases in this state. It is directly attributable to the dope trade.

The other half of this problem is the public cost. Cannabis dealers compete to deliver the highest-grade THC-laden product possible. In states where cannabis is legal, there has been an explosive growth in cases of paranoid schizophrenia and schizoaffective disorder arising of cannabis use. Men and women with no prior history of schizophrenia are becoming so affected in middle age.

Two years ago, I was hired by a European family to locate a daughter who was a grad student at a prestigious college. She went missing suddenly, with no known reason and had been missing for five days. Ultimately, she was found hospitalized in another county as a Jane Doe. Afflicted with cannabis psychosis, she had abandoned her car and was wandering around in traffic.

These cases strike hard and devastate families. In July 2024, Evan Wright, author of *Generation Kill*, took his own life in what I believe to be the throes of cannabis psychosis. He had a new manuscript for sale, three small children, and a wife. Cannabis is a scourge.

CHAPTER

21

THE LIFE NOIR— FICTION AND FACT

On a day that could be any day, I was in search of a man wanted for bank fraud, a Chinese national named Gwai-Lo Mao. I went to his last habitation, a large house in San Marino, the front lawn overgrown with weeds. As I got closer, I saw that it looked like a shitty, early '70s plagiarism of a Frank Lloyd Wright design: terraced with pebbled paths and large slabs of textured concrete demarcating steps up to doors standing sixteen feet high that were flanked by stained glass windows with abstract shapes like amoeba, colored like aged piss and green Jell-O.

The door was ajar, yet chained, as if someone with a key attempted entry, only to find that the chain was on. Through the opening I could see that someone had hastily packed, and left devices on the scrap of shag rug next to a broad but plain fireplace. The hearth was filled with Sino take-out cartons, which was a possible (though not the only possibility) source of a cloud of flies in the living room. Through the right window, next to the door, I could see a business desk, with files strewn about. Like a Wright creation, there was a view all the way through to the back to an unattended azure pool, and beyond, to a cabana made as a miniature of the house.

A missing man, an abandoned mansion, scattered files, a cloud of flies buzzing above what might be a corpse.

It looked like the movie set of a crime drama—but then it's hardly surprising that reality would mirror art in Los Angeles, the hall of mirrors where reality mirrors the fiction that mirrored reality. To be a detective in this city is to walk in the footsteps of the private eye personified by Bogart, Mitchum, Ladd—an outsider, part hunter, part white knight, equally canny about the criminals he pursues and the clients he serves…at home with neither.

A civilian friend asked me whom I'd most wish to depict me on the big screen, or on television. I'm vain enough to have devoted some thought to this very idea, and it's like this: Orson Welles is dead, Peter North is too busy, Jon Hamm is the wrong sort of handsome, and Danny DeVito is too svelte. It will have to be Kevin Dillon.

Among my favorite aspects of cinema have been detective stories: cops, private eyes—it matters not at all as long as the story is good. Often, when people the world over think of these films and TV productions, they think of "noir." I'll confess to being a lifelong fan.

Erle Stanley Gardner was a master of small screen noir, with his creation *Perry Mason*. Perry was a crack defense attorney who always delivered a crucial witness, argument, or fact to thwart an unjust prosecution. Mason employed a dapper, low-key private man named Paul Drake in many of his episodes. The pulp novels are as good as the flickering TV shows. Now nearly forgotten was a racier series of novels, starring a pair of detectives named Donald Lam and Bertha Cool, emblematic of this series being the novel *The Bigger They Come*, published in 1939 under the pen name A.A. Fair. In my ill-spent youth, I enjoyed each one in the series. Every one of them was tense, taut, violent, and vulgar, without being pornographic.

In my father's long, slow decline when I was a teenager, he and I took rooms in boarding houses and traveled a bit. It was during this era that I was introduced to his taste for pulp novels and television shows that often featured private detectives. Often, we'd also take crime dramas. *Cannon*, *Barnaby Jones*, *The Rockford Files*—these were all entertaining, but especially the latter. The opening credits of *Rockford* included a ringing phone, followed by an answering machine, then a snappy score of harmonica music.

Jim Rockford, private investigator, was played by a dapper, charismatic James Garner. He solved every matter in an hour of network television, enduring fistfights, disarming men with guns and knives, and always charming an attractive woman. He wore a sport coat and open collar. Nothing ever seemed to bother the man, other than maybe an unpaid bill, or whatever schemes his ex-con friend Angel Martin had going on. This was great fiction, and one summer night, in our rooms at a place close to MacArthur Park, I asked my dad what it would be like to be a private eye. "That'd be something," came Norman's reply, wholly unconscious of what might unfold before us. It is a warm, sepia-tinted memory, my father.

In late 1982, I came to meet James Garner. He was filming a picture at Fort Benning, and our brigade area was the backdrop. An enlisted veteran of the Korean War, Garner ate in our mess halls and was convivial with the troops. Each day he was attired in battle dress uniform, and the title of the production was *Tank*. Garner always seemed to enjoy being around the troops, though we all kept a respectful tone for the man. Years later, I met him again.

One night I was on a protective case, at an event staged by the Playboy Mansion. The event was well-attended, and I was in a sport coat and chinos, trying to blend in. The husband of the couple I was assigned to was another outgoing actor, and he was friends with James Garner, who was in attendance and dressed as if he was still Jim Rockford. The husband made a show of introducing me to Garner, who asked, "And you are…?" Not sure of my status or association with his friend.

"I'm just a Pinkerton agent. Just working tonight." I was polite.

"Oh. I've been a private eye," Garner quipped past his famous grin. As no one was really paying attention, I risked a transgression outside Pinkerton's orders and said to Garner, "We've met before."

"I meet a lot of guys around this town. Remind me, Nils," Garner asked.

"We met a few years back, at Fort Benning," I answered the man, and he brightened right up, switching on the thousand-watt grin.

"Oh? You must've been one of the men in the 197th Infantry Brigade! I had a terrific time making that picture." He was the real deal, James Garner. We met a few times, even after this, and Garner always remembered me, as a veteran and a private detective. I couldn't help but think of my dad, who'd have enjoyed every minute of this. Years have passed since his death. Thinking on this, I posted a letter to Stuart Margolin, the actor who portrayed so effectively Angel Martin. Recounting meeting Garner, I thanked Margolin for the years of solid entertainment. My hope is that they both had a wonderful time acting these stories out.

A child of five or six in Terre Haute, I was transfixed by the noir cover of a crime novel my mother was reading. It featured a man, lying across an unmade bed, his head in a pool of blood and his mouth open. In the shadow of a doorway stood the figure of a woman, clutching a knife. Even I was curious in childhood, and I asked of my mother, "What is this book about?"

"It's a detective story," she said, and to my query about what a detective is, Enid said, "A detective is someone who finds missing people, with only 'trace' evidence, who solves crimes secretly, by discerning things that others have overlooked." This in words that her young son could understand, though.

Dashiell Hammett was not only a Pinkerton agent, in Barbary Coast San Francisco, and a member of US Army Intelligence, he also authored a series of detective fiction stories. These included such titles as *The Glass Key*, *The Continental Op*, *Nightmare Town*, and Hammett's most well-known, *The Maltese Falcon*. These stories were always hypnotic to me, with hidden detail. Like all true noir, they're sentimental, yet never maudlin; violent, but never without purpose, depicting corruption, the wages of crime, and human betrayal. Hammett's works captured the imagination of Josiah "Tink" Thompson, a philosophy professor at Haverford, to such an extent that he chucked his tenured, staid position to become an hourly operative of the Pinkerton Agency in San Francisco. He graduated from field work—surveillance, interviews, background investigations, to his own practice. Tink's encomium to the profession is *Gumshoe: Reflections in a Private Eye*.

For private detectives, the San Francisco canon has many worthy, august names: Thompson, Hal Lipset of Watergate renown, David Fechheimer, Mike Zanoni, Sandra Sutherland, and Jack Palladino. Part of what made these detectives stand out was their intellectual rigor, with doctorate-level degrees for several. Los Angeles and San Francisco are as different as night from day. Otash, Danny Stewart, and a few other fired cops comprise the Los Angeles cohort. Stewart was dismissed from LAPD after the notorious Hollywood audit of 1972—a debacle of public corruption.

My esteemed, longtime colleague Robert Ferris apprenticed under Zanoni, and has worked with Fecheimer, and that man's son. Ferris is also a studio musician who never wore a uniform. No one could safely define Robert as a "civilian."

Was Stewart corrupt? While marijuana was certainly found in his locker at Hollywood Station, this always seemed a bit too pat and obvious. Chances are just as good that Danny Stewart was the patsy for other detectives who were accused of extorting money from burglars and fences for the favor of dismissing felony cases. This was complicated by the certainty that some of the criminals being extorted were long-term informants to LAPD.

We can also look to Gene Ingram, accused of many things, including running his own prostitution operation while employed as a vice detective in LAPD. This only got better when Ingram was represented by lawyers from the Church of Scientology at various hearings and proceedings.

Within the halls of power in Los Angeles, Scientology embodies a role analogous to that of the Borgia popes in the era of the Medicis. The church employs a lot of private detectives, but I'm not one of them. Among other hard-and-fast rules I have is to never do business with the Church of Scientology, its lawyers, or the various operatives they employ in suppressing dissent. Los Angeles is a "company town," reminiscent of a Johnny Cash song, about being surrounded, monitored, beholden to, and wary of the dominant enterprise of the city. In this case, this means Hollywood. Am I part of this apparatus? I'm not Swiss, in any way. I'm strictly Hessian—for hire. Sometimes I go up against entrenched powers, and other days I am protecting the assets, personnel, investments, and prestige of these same enterprises.

How may we separate fact from fiction in a place that churns out fiction like poop from a flock of garden geese? Detectives in Los Angeles—public or private—mimic the artists who mimic them. Within fiction, it seems the Los Angeles style was set in stone by a few writers, among them Ken Millar, writing under the name Ross Macdonald; Erle Stanley Gardner; Raymond Chandler; and, later, Joseph Wambaugh. More recently, sclerotic, jumbled tomes were written by James Ellroy, whose fiction chews the shrubbery. Ellroy's true-to-life work, *My Dark Places: An L.A. Crime Memoir*, is so good, accidentally, that it's required reading in the Grevillius Detective Service.

Russell Poole, now gone, also a homicide detective of our sheriff's office, was the subject of a work titled *Labyrinth*, by Randall Sullivan, which is a Rosetta Stone for deciphering Los Angeles's present miasma of corruption. *Labyrinth* is about the murders of Tupac Shakur and Biggie Smalls. It also delineates the relationships of a few police officers mobbed up with Death Row Records. Art and life… life and art.

When Millar was in town, he'd show up at a bar in Pasadena, styled an English pub by its owner, the John Bull. It was in the shell of the Hotel Carver, cum-Onyx. He and my father would drink beer, fling darts, socialize, and philosophize. Sometimes they were joined by Richard Feynman and an artist named Jirayr Zorthian. It was at this bar that I met Millar in the tenth grade. He gifted me a work of his titled *Meet Me at the Morgue*. From cover to cover, I read this, and it included a passage where his protagonist brings a pair of half-pints of whiskey to tempt the obsessive mind and unsettled soul of an alcoholic witness, so as to coax information from a reluctant mouth.

Wambaugh's fictive works, like *The New Centurions,* broke fresh ground, but this mostly dealt with the uniformed patrolman. Wambaugh is honest to a fault, and his depictions of the souls and lives of cops can be melancholy. *The New Centurions* is as heartbreaking as *The Onion Field.* Hollywood could never quite do justice to a Wambaugh Treatment, but the performances of Stacy Keach and George C. Scott in the movie cannot be turned away from.

And Chandler. This man, often described as an alcoholic (as Hammett assuredly was), so perfectly threads every needle in a noir story: desperation, impossible love, aching loss, fear of the unknown. His characters are bad people at their very best and good, decent Americans at their level worst. Written in the 1930s to 1950s, the argot and pacing are vintage, yet so timeless that a modern reader can relate to every line, every situation, every paragraph. Chandler's chapters are dipped in stolen whiskey, banged out on a typewriter missing two keys, in the small hours, in the upper story of an SRO hotel next to the slaughter pens, by a man awaiting a woman. He doesn't know if she will arrive to make love, to kill him, or to hump him then kill him. She departs in a taxi, driven by a snake charmer, to meet a train that never arrives.

The very best, and most evocative and haunting of Chandler's works, is *The Lady in the Lake.* It is timeless, tense, and riven with the most effective characterizations of bad and good people, starting out with the initial consultation Chandler's protagonist detective, Philip Marlowe, undertakes with the designer husband of a missing woman. That this work has never been made into a good piece of cinema astounds me, as every element is there. Had Robert Towne or Joe Eszterhas or myself been commissioned with writing the screenplay, it would be as romanced, spoken of, marveled over, and studied as *Double Indemnity* is now. Billy Friedkin could bang this story like a screen door in a hurricane.

Long ago I attended to Robert Towne, the auteur of *Chinatown*, who revealed a few unknowns to me. Towne stated, to my inquiry, that of course his subject matter expert in the world of private detective craft was Fred Otash. He also revealed that Jerry Goldsmith executed the score for *Chinatown* in six or seven days. Otash is also reputed to have lent color and texture to Ellroy's *L.A. Confidential*, which, as a novel, defies casual reading. Hats off to Curtis Hanson and Brian Helgeland for making that story mesh with *Chinatown*, as if *Confidential* was the sequel to *Chinatown*.

When I met Otash, he was much older and introduced to me as an expert in detecting camera traps and wires connected to analog phone systems in the late 1980s. Russ Mancini, my boss at Pinkerton knew Fred well, though he never told me the all of Otash. That was left for my discovery.

Completely divorced from noir there was a police detective TV show that near every police detective I have ever known considers the best depiction, and most realistic, of the workaday toils of a city detective. It ran from the late 1970s to the early 1980s and was filmed in a single room. The network billed it as a comedy, and while *Barney Miller* delivers some comedy, it is Shakespearian and gritty. Hal Linden, Jack Soo, Ron Glass, Steve Landesburg, and the great Abe Vigoda populated the squad room. In nearly every episode, there was a thirty-second running gag of Fish, Vigoda's character, grabbing a newspaper and making for the "terlet."

I was once fixed up on a date with a girl whose mother turned out to look so much like Abe Vigoda, that her mom could've been the actor's stunt double. I ran like hell and didn't look back.

CHAPTER

22

GYPSIES

Gypsy males are less creative in the crimes they perpetrate, usually involving driveway and roof repair, or the mending of an automobile fender. Without their women they'd starve to death, here or anywhere else. This means they are not so different from the rest of us.

—Detective Greg Ovanesian, San Francisco Police Department, Bunco Squad

When police officers are trained in gypsy crimes, they're now taught to use the nomenclature *nontraditional organized crime transient criminal groups*, lest they, their agency, or their class be accused of racial bias. At least one Western city had to pay out a hefty settlement for correctly identifying a group of car thieves as Romanes gypsies. Amazing, eh?

I've freed myself of any such burdens or pretenses and will call them what they are: Romanes-speaking gypsies. These people are an East Indian group, originally from the Punjab. They even have a caste system, which gypsies call *vitse*. Why are gypsies of interest? Because a plurality of them are engaged in crime, from simple fraud involving driveway and roof repair scams, the financial abuse of the elderly, and the sorts of con games common to fortune telling.

Within the archives of *The New Yorker* are two lushly brilliant, sober, expositive essays, written by Joseph Mitchell. Nearly every observation Mitchell had of gypsies in the essays, dating to the 1930s and 1950s, is true today. Most gypsies are, by choice, illiterate, and there is a purpose in this. An oral tradition language is less susceptible to assimilation than a written language. With their language reduced to a common dictionary, the Romanes speakers would be quickly absorbed and subsumed into whichever culture they might exist, from the Black Sea to the Gulf of Alaska.

In decades of investigating gypsy crimes, I have never met a *gadjo* or *gadje* (nongypsy man or woman) who knew more than a few words or phrases of Romanes. Every gypsy I've ever known—whether a crime victim, criminal, witness, or accessory—kept their true name a secret, and presented a gadjo name to the gadjo world, a name that can be laundered, altered, abandoned, or even adopted and adapted by another gypsy. Until fairly recently, with the rise of live-scan fingerprinting DNA sampling with a felony case, gypsies were able to cross borders quickly, present new documents for welfare, take the welfare documents to Social Security, and change identity in a matter of weeks or even days.

I've seen a nine-person gypsy family pack up and abscond within ninety minutes, with me following them from Hollywood to Phoenix. In Hollywood I may have known the *hrom barro* (group patriarch) to be Nick Yonko, but upon arriving in Phoenix, he's Steve Mitchell and is facile about it. Most gypsy crime is small-time, though there have been high-dollar exceptions. Because of this, not many people or institutions are going to engage my services to make a recovery, to identify a swindler, to disambiguate a relationship between two groups of Romanes gypsies. I've had a number of gypsy crime cases and learned quite a bit from each one.

In working these cases, I've developed gypsy informants, which is often the only way of solving these crimes. A typical *bahjour* (crime of confidence perpetrated by a gypsy woman) goes something like this: An elderly widow drives by the palm-reader shop (mitt joint or *offisa*) and sees the sign that suggests the palm reader can see into the future. She goes in and is asked a series of questions by the palm reader, who is taking the temperature of the widow. What is the gypsy woman looking for? Insecurity, loneliness, separation from family and wealth.

Having secured the trust of the vulnerable widow, the gypsy woman asks her to take a simple chicken or goose egg home, sewn up in a silken pouch, to sleep with the pouch overnight or for a few days…it matters not with the bahjour.

Upon returning to the parlor of the gypsy woman, our lonesome widow hands over the egg, sewn within the purse, and when it is cracked open and contents dumped on a plate, a piece of gristly meat is dropped from the palm of the palm reader into the yolk and effluvia. "Oh my god, lady!"

"What's wrong?" asks the widow.

"You got a bad curse! Maybe your husband done some'ting bad, very bad," declares the gypsy woman with great drama. Her children, and mother, too, might gaze upon the bad omen planted in the egg on the plate.

Of course, the cure for the curse is an old-world, gypsy incantation and prayer, and instructions on how much money has to be "blessed" to lift the curse. It might be something like "You get from that bank cash money, a stack of a hundred-dollar bills. Don't bring it nowheres but here. We protect you fix this money." The next day, or later on the afternoon, her victim shows up with the currency as directed, and with great ceremony and more incantations in Romanes, the stack of thousands gets sewn up into the silken purse, prayed over, and returned to the lonesome, unprotected, vulnerable widow. Only, not. A switch takes place on or under the table, and the victim gets back an identical silk purse, stuffed with newspaper, cut to size to match the weight and cut of the currency.

"You take this home, say prayers, sleep with it until the full moon, next Saturday. Then it's safe, you could open it" is the instruction, completing the bahjour. And off she goes, our relieved old woman. And while she is sleeping, the gypsies are packing, moving, and handing the palm parlor over to another Romanes gypsy family who can express complete denial, should the police ever happen by to investigate. "We don't know them people. Maybe they moved to St. Louis, something." If the elderly victim ever bothered to call the police. Many are too embarrassed and fear their distant relatives overtaking their affairs to protect them from the bahjour.

It was precisely this state of affairs that prompted an elderly dentist, a long-term resident of the San Gabriel Valley, to call me. He had a new wife and was a bit concerned for something a friend had told him. "I was married, last month, and an old friend said to me he thinks my wife is a gypsy. Can you imagine such a thing?" he said over the phone.

He had been retired, for more than twenty years, and was five years widowed, living alone. In line at the bank, Dr. Solomon encountered a woman who said, "Aren't youse the Dr. Solomon used to be our family dentist long time ago?" Dr. Solomon wasn't sure that he remembered her, but she was kind, solicitous, and for twenty-six, very attractive. "To be frank, and with all candor, I suspect my friend is a bit jealous I have married a younger woman," observed the doctor. It sounded funny to me, so I quoted him a fee, and told him that I'd find out what his wife's background and status were and discreetly report back.

Her name was Christina Mitchell. She was indeed twenty-six, according to the driver's license that had been presented for their Las Vegas wedding. Christina and her brother, Bobby Mitchell, had driven Dr. Solomon to Nevada to be married. Christina didn't actually live with Dr. Solomon, having extended family to care for, and I knew enough to not inflame my elderly client by asking how the consummation went. Christina had one prior address and no credit. Her prior address was a mail drop. The car she was driving was registered to Bobby Yonko.

Romanes gypsy family names have been adapted in North America, to those of the prevailing Anglo-Saxon culture. In Argentina and Mexico, they're Spanish names, and instead of being called gypsies, they're called *gitanos y gitanas*. In those parts of Old Europe that are Orthodox, the gypsies are faithful Orthodox, and in the Catholic nations, rosary-praying Roman Catholic. Bulgaria, the Balkans have Islamic zones, where their gypsies are Muslim. They adapt, overcome, and survive, all while assuming just enough cultural DNA to blend, to move, to conduct the bahjour, then move on.

In North America, I have encountered Romanes gypsies with the Family Names Stevens, Nicholas, Costello, Ristic, Gonzalez, Yonko, Uwanawich, Steves, Adams, Kaslov, Gainer, and Bimbo. There are others, and new ones invented weekly.

With Dr. Solomon, I knew that the old guy had fallen prey to the Sweetheart Swindle, just a variation on the bahjour. Christina Mitchell had no romantic interest in Dr. Solomon. She intended to clean him out and would do so with her victim's assent, so pie-eyed was this elderly gentleman. I prepared a report containing everything I'd learned and made an appointment with the doctor. It did not go well, and he departed my office, with his "wife" waiting at the curb in the expensive European auto Dr. Solomon had purchased her as a wedding present. In the back seat was Bobby, her brother.

My next move was to call Adult Protective Services of Los Angeles County. From that afternoon, to this one, that agency never responded or helped in any way. The Sweetheart Swindle comes with its own insulation: forever, or for just a while, the victim is in on the robbery. Having identified distant relatives of Dr. Solomon, I finally got in touch with a cardiologist and distant cousin, whom I'll call Ben Solomon.

When I shared my concerns with Ben, he acted immediately, really stepped in to protect his protesting cousin. The ensuing case involved death threats against Ben Solomon, pursuit of elements of the Mitchell family, and identifying prior victims of Christina and Bobby Mitchell. As it turned out, Christina and Bobby Mitchell were also Christina and Bobby Yonko...and Uwanawich. They may be operating under another series of names by now. I contacted a family in Sacramento, wherein Christina had convinced an elderly widower to mortgage the equity from his home and turn it over to her. First for an operation for her "niece," then for a series of commercial sewing machines and a delivery van for a purported business. Christina told the Sacramento victim that she was opening a business to sew drapes for Las Vegas casinos. There was no such business, and this rationale was a well-worn device within the Romanes gypsy crime community.

A detective in Sacramento County confirmed what I believed: That Bobby was Christina's husband, but they were not married under our civil system, only in the eyes of the Romanes vitse. They have their own government, courts, kings and queens, all within our borders. Are they American? Of course they are, but the Romanes gypsies never assimilate more than is necessary.

One might ask if gypsies are an ethnic group of Psychopaths, who feel no shame or remorse for the crimes they perpetrate. While there are Psychopaths in the realm of the Romanes gypsy, they are not Psychopaths as a group. To the best of their ability, they care for their children, keep homes, and maintain family ties. They watch sports, hunt, and fish. They have cautious, tentative friendships outside of their vitse, with *gadjo* and *gadje*, but remain secretive and cloistered.

Many of them are adroit bullshit artists who have an amazing collection of colored, colorful yarns about their own cultural origins. Said a member of the Gainer Clan, who operates a scam whereby he comes in with measuring tapes, swatches, tile samples, and paint books, then pretends to remodel suburban kitchens at and advantageous price, "Detective Nils, I tell you once, once an' for all, where the gypsy he comes from."

Judging from Gainer's accent, I was going to guess New Jersey. "My people was in the baggage trains of Alexander the Great, the Greek Guy, who took all of India, but had to leave. My people was chased outta India for being his allies, Alexander the Great, and we had to leave India. We went all over."

Including New Jersey, we may all presume.

Sometimes, on the fly, a gypsy family will shoplift. Joe Cornet's Father, Joe Sr., told me a story when I was a Pinkerton that went like this: "Must have been about 1970 or so, in the Bakersfield store, a great hoard of gypsy girls entered the store, then the men. In the front, up close to the registers, these two girls started yelling to beat the band at each other. This became what appeared a catfight, and within moments both girls were stripped to the waist, tits everywhere, and fighting. This, by design, attracted every man in the store, and the rest of 'em picked us clean."

Like many Bronze Age cultures, the Romanes gypsy affixes no sexual connotation to female breasts, yet they know them to be an object of titillation for the gadjo, and envy for the gadje, hence the distraction. Gypsy men will have dalliances with gadje with no particular shame attaching to his infidelity unless his wife can catch him and beat him with a pan. But no Romanes gypsy woman, of any vitse, will consummate with a gadjo. To do so will render her forever *marime*, which means unclean.

Within the folklore of Eastern Europe, the Balkans, the West and North America, are tales of heartsick gypsy women stealing gadjo children and raising them as gypsies. Over a Chinese meal at Hop Louie in Chinatown, Gainer's wife, Dolly, told me, "We was growing up, in the East. My grandmother warned us we was beautiful, we was smart. Gadje womens wit' no baby would steal us for their own, to be careful."

When Dr. Solomon could finally be convinced by prior booking photos, and reports, and surveillance, and the statement of the Sacramento detective, Ben Solomon hired him a divorce attorney. No prosecution, beyond the divorce, ever took place, with the Los Angeles County district attorney declining any criminal charges for Bobby and Christina Mitchell. They got away, with a sum of money under the quickest of divorces, but it wasn't as bad as it could've been.

One of the scenarios I ran to ground, including a trip to Rawlins, Wyoming, involved the possible belladonna poisoning of another elderly man. This could never be proven but seemed a distinct possibility. Romanes gypsies, in their outlook on the crimes they perpetrate, have taken up the justification that it is what they must do to survive. They use the internal rationale that men at war use when they kill each other: If I do not, he will get me.

Because of their reticence to mix too much with gadje and gadjo, the prospect of jail and prison is vexing and weighty to the Romanes gypsy. She would rather make full restitution than risk being thought unclean. They pay the money back, change identity, and move seven cities away and do it all over again.

Sometimes, like other citizens, gypsies need help. On a hot spring day, I returned from too much a lunch to her message on my answering machine: "My daughter, she was kidnapped an' I need your help, urgent-like."

I dialed her number, a pager, and entered the office line.

Three minutes passed, then a knock on my door, and she was there, as if she'd been waiting close by for my return.

"My daughter was kidnapped and I need you to get her back for me." She was late thirties, slender with obsidian-black cascades of hair, that could only have been tinted. She wore cheap, goggle-like designer sunglasses, black dress, black shoes, black purse, black gloves. For effect she wept, sending mascara down sucked in, rouged cheeks. Between heaving sobs, I could see she had the silver fillings and dental crowns once common to Latin America and Asia.

How old is you daughter? Where was she taken from? Is this a custody situation?

"It's complex, this. She got kidnapped by another family and I need to get her back." Now the shades came off. My office was dim, like me, and her eyes couldn't adjust to the lack of light sufficient for her to study me. Her eyes, first green, then yellow, were quick as she took my measure and that of my office.

How old is you daughter? Where was she taken from? Is this a custody situation? I reloaded my questions, still unanswered.

Her daughter was fifteen, taken from her Glendale Apartment. Daughter, Sabina, was kidnapped by her seventeen-year-old boyfriend and his family.

Is her father in the picture? Where do you think they've taken Sabina?

"I can't involve my husband and no kind of police. They'll *kill* her." This last part I knew was concomitant to the situation.

Where have they gone? They'd taken the girl to a big city in the Northern Midwest.

"It's complex, and I need to get her back." This was already said and understood.

What's your name? Her name was Debra Ricoletti. "I'm from Argentina."

Her accent? Pure Newark, New Jersey. She had all the makings of an attractive woman—poise, posture, physique, hair, clothes—but remained decidedly unattractive.

I explained that a kidnapping investigation, with no police involved, was a costly matter. As if by magic, her purse opened and money was atop my desk to be counted. This came with no questions about amounts or prospects for success. She was ready, like "when I get back from lunch" ready.

I didn't touch the currency on my desk. It was Canadian by appearance, these bank notes. As a matter of course I've no specific objection to Canadian currency, in the right amounts. It was the state of play that had me weighing and measuring. An "Argentinian" woman, from Glendale, with a New Jersey accent, who doesn't want police involved, retaining me with Canadian scratch.

In this office we work on American dollars, Ms. Ricoletti.

"I got a couple of valuable watches to secure it. Collateral, okay?" she told me. Out came two suspect-looking Rolex watches. I didn't bother to handle or examine them, as their value was obvious, and equal to my lunch tab.

No. Not interested.

She returned the next day, knocking on the office door, not ten minutes after my arrival. Same outfit and smelled of tobacco. The US currency that spilled from her purse also stank of tobacco. I counted the retainer while Debra feigned reading the retainer agreement. When I was done, she scrawled a mark on the last page, and I burned her a copy, which went in the purse.

"You sure you don't want one of these Rolex. They expensive watches?" I was sure.

She had a photo of Sabina, who looked a younger version of Debra. Also, the boyfriend, Nicky Yonko, with his family, on a snow-covered road, next to a rusted Cadillac.

I showed her out while she made another try to sell me a watch.

A series of phone calls, to trusted sources familiar with gypsy crime, identified which Yonko family, among so many Roma, were involved. Debra was quickly identified as Naomi Costello, wife of Steve Costello…all common Roma names.

Speaking with an old touch in Ontario, Canada, I got a solid lead to a "mitt joint," fortune teller place, opposite Windsor, Ontario, on the Detroit River. It was run by Nicky's mother.

Before buying a ticket to Detroit, I paged Debra. Ten minutes passed, and the phone rang. "Who's this paged me?" Different voice.

I'm sorry. I must have dialed the wrong pager. I was trying to reach Debra Ricoletti.

"Hang on sorry." Hasty answer.

Then she was on. I explained that her daughter, Sabina, was out of state, likely, and that I'd travel only if she authorized it.

"Go an' get her!" was the response.

I found the Yonko fortune-teller parlor. It was lit up like a Christmas tree, with more signs than a gas station "know the future." In the driveway next to the place was the Cadillac. It had endured so many salted roads that the rocker panels had the cancer of rust. It was a warm, sticky, late afternoon, and I went in. Out came a woman in her forties, who could've been Debra, alias Naomi, but for a few years and a shock of gray hair up the middle of her scalp. "Whadda youse want?"

Just then, from behind a beaded curtain, emerged a younger woman, decidedly pregnant. Sabina.

I'm visiting from California, to tell you your fortune.

"You a cop, *gadjo*?" A more-sour look than before creased her face, and Sabina darted back through the beaded curtain.

You're not that lucky. Is Mr. Yonko around?

As if on cue, a hunched, graying Roma man emerged with Mrs. Yonko hollering at him in Romanes.

"What are you here for?" he asked me with a cigarette being processed by the other side of his mouth.

Are you the hrom barro?

He extended his hand. "Mike Yonko."

I'm a private eye, asked to locate Sabina, for her mother.

"There's a Chinese place, two blocks down the street. We could talk there." I agreed, knowing that they could all pack and leave and be gone, maybe to Canada, with another series of names, or a blend, in less than an hour.

I'll see you there.

"You going a get dinner?" asked Yonko, unloading himself opposite me, his back to the door. I ordered and so did he.

"Need to get some dinner to go. This is a pretty good place." It appeared the Cantonese knew Yonko, knew what to order for his family.

Tell me about this with Sabina and your boy.

"It's like this. They made a marriage deal, their family and the Yonko. Naomi's husband, he's my cousin. Me and him are good. Gypsy good." He started in on some chow mein.

Over dinner I learned that, like all Indian cultures, a dowry had been paid to the Yonko family. "Now she tryin' a get the money she paid back, took me a while figure it out why."

Why is that?

"The money she paid was counterfeit. She don't want to go to jail."

Canadian currency?

"Yeah. How you know that? You pretty good for a gadjo..." He smiled.

Paying the dowry in counterfeit would be a good trick, if it worked. But it left Naomi Costello wide open to extortion within her own vitse, or tribe. Her husband was likely out trying to swindle up enough cash to extinguish the fire created of greed. Gypsy family practices mimic all antiquity: the men would starve in the streets without their women, and all else is barter.

Mike Yonko departed in his Cadillac, with two sacks of Hong Kong–style to go. Debra Ricoletti paid the bill. Returned to California, I paged Naomi, alias Debra. She arrived, dressed the same, in a cloud of tobacco smoke and heisted Chanel perfumes.

I handed her a slip of paper with the address of the mitt joint on the Detroit River.

"What's this?"

It's where your pregnant daughter is, Naomi. Get the money together, pay off the Yonkos, and make peace.

"Shit! You can gimme back th' retainder right now! I paid you to get her back!" She was purple.

You paid me to find her, Naomi. All bets are off when you lie. If you could read, you'd have seen that in the "retainder" agreement. She's found, case closed.

"I'm going put the eye of the Evil One on you!" she said as the office door slammed. Between airfare, hours of work, auto rental, and Chinese for six, the "retainder" was spent. A day passed, then a few more. I returned from court, unhitched my necktie, and pressed the fun button on the answering machine. "You sure you don' wanna buy a Rolex watch they very high quality...."

CHAPTER

23

SUNSET

"I am sure you have seen many amazing things!" said a young Danish father as his wife and children slept in our train compartment. They were on holiday, to Innsbruck, Austria, and we were tracing the Rhine River in Germany, having boarded at the main station in Copenhagen. I was not in Europe for a holiday, but for work. My case involved tracking two prostitutes, who'd witnessed what was reported as a kidnapping in Hollywood. The case took me to Denmark, Sweden, Poland, and now Germany, and nothing was as it had been reported to LAPD, nor the FBI. Another PI had lost his life in this case, in a single-car accident in Georgia. Murder? Only to the extent that he murdered himself. To the young father I turned and said, "There is still some knowledge that is not worth having." His family slept.

On a June day in 2024, I'd to make a missing-persons report of my sister Louise. Figuratively she'd been missing since she fell into narcotics. But by that date, it was more than a year since anyone had heard from her.

"What does Louise do for a living?" asked the deputy taking the report.

She is a drug addict and does what drug addicts do. Louise is the brightest of our father's children and was once the best looking. She has had a variety of short-run jobs when living under probation: cleaning houses, phlebotomist, retail. Louise is multilingual and makes friends, then loses them fast. My youngest sister has had her heart broken a thousand times, at least twice by me.

"My sister traffics heroin." He had already found her rap sheet, and some hairy booking photos. An older, more experienced hand with a Basque surname, the deputy probed further. "Does she have any enemies?"

Only Louise. Louise is her worst enemy. She is my feminine analog.

"None that are on my radar." I walked out with a report number.

Seven months later, she resurfaced, alive and resentful. She can change, but it remains unlikely. Louise was our father's favorite, and he died asking me to find her, bring her to him in his last weeks on this earth. At twenty-two, she was already on the run from the law and hiding out in Central America.

Louise discovered his death when she stiffed a call in on Thanksgiving, the next day, and it was as if we had concealed it from her. But she was already bent. And so on from there. Norman's death was the dividing line in my life, and it directly led to my second wind—the life I have enjoyed ever since as a detective and father. Not everyone makes it, but all can. Another page turned was that with Don Moon.

Don was everything I could never be. He was disciplined, dedicated, faithful to God, from a traditional Catholic family. He had a beautiful fiancée, had been an officer in the marines. But it was as if he was haunted by something he could never properly define.

In March of 2010, Don took his own life. I will not call it suicide, this. He had Gulf War syndrome and had lost the sensation in his feet and hands. Over a few weeks before, he expressed concerns to me that I could not properly understand, which are too personal for this writing. He shot himself, in a ditch, next to the Angeles Crest Highway. Don is a casualty of war.

This event changed me, and I do not think I will ever have another professional relationship like that. Don cannot be replaced, and I don't think I have it in me to trust another mec on that level again. I did not see this coming, and curse myself for failing to know, failing to help the man.

A few have walked in my door, wanting to apprentice as a PI. They come in with credentials of some sort, sometimes having attended one of the hokey trade schools. Anyone of them could have the drive and talent of the Fugitive, or Moon; most do not. When Kit was finishing his apprenticeship, I got a call from a company, referred by a lawyer, with an embezzlement problem. The company business manager, Ed Brancieri, had already figured out the structure of the embezzlement. He had a lot of experience supporting an acting career by working in bookkeeping and business valuations. He seemed bright.

"I'd like to sit in the interviews, okay?" he asked. There were a few suspects. Kit was there to proctor and participated in the interviews. I took confessions, with consensual recording, from two of the employees, who eventually made restitution in the thousands of dollars to their employer.

The situation done and file closed, I got a call from Brancieri, asking to have coffee. Seated in my office, he was direct. "I don't want to do what I do anymore. When I saw you break those guys down in interrogation, I was amazed. What can I do to be in your line of work?"

There is no school, course, or university. Not all of us start as soldiers, or cops, or whatever. Pinkerton was a school teacher. He was the "amateur" who showed everyone how terrifyingly corrupt and incompetent the "professionals" were at almost every police agency in North America. And, while doing so, he ran what eventually became the US Secret Service and was a model for the development of the FBI. In fact, it may just be better to come in from the cold *without* any such background. A trusted colleague in Ohio, Suzie Daniels, characterizes herself as a Midwest housewife. Elizabeth Farkas in New York City got her start in the arts. They are both consummate professionals. Never doubt it.

Robert Ferris did a lot of criminal and insurance work, learning the basics under Mike Zanoni. Among other things, Ferris has been a forensic diver, retrieving ditched weapons, searching for bodies and other evidence flung from bridges into various bays, sloughs, canals, and barge tracks in the greater Bay Area.

A lot of cops fail at this for a few reasons, starting with being risk averse. Without the protection of sovereign immunity, they are overtimid in private cases. Also, they are too suspicious of their clients to understand the gravity of what must be done. Within my operational network are former high-level cops, hackers, soldiers, a few ex-cons, but all have the secret sauce.

A person could be well-educated, rational, analytical and intellectual and fail at detective work, lacking the secret part. It took me a while, but I put together an approach to assess an aspirant. Call it a series of tests, assignments, and homework, which I shall never fully reveal. Of Brancieri, I asked, "What have you done, professionally?"

He was an actor and a model, from the northeast. Never in the military, Ed held a series of waiter and management jobs while trying to get traction in Hollywood. "Anything else? This isn't so much, Ed."

"I used to be a racecar driver. Bondurant, all that. I did some stunt driving in TV commercials." This piqued my interest. "What can you do in a car, Brancieri?"

"I can take a passenger sedan at 120 mph in a banked turn and not shit my pants," he said. Not sure if he was being an assclown, I made him show me in my XK8 Jaguar on the Foothill Freeway, 135 mph in afternoon traffic, no sweat. This what I was looking for. The rarest human emotional quality in the world is the ability to deal with ambiguity under stress. This is the unknown element US Navy Special Warfare identifies in Basic Underwater Demolition School. Any healthy guy can be made into a physical specimen, but emotional toughness cannot be created where it does not exist. Brancieri completed and went on to do very secretive undercover and surveillance work.

My next candidate was a Frenchman, Gregoire Lavollay, raised in Paris by an American mother and French father—both classic academics. Greg was a schoolteacher, a boxer, and a martial arts practitioner. He moved to the US, already speaking English, and earned a law degree. He is among the best in the world at surveillance and evaluating men and women for what threat they might pose. Again, the mastery of martial arts coupled to cerebral pursuit of law and art, makes for an indigestible man. Kit O'Brien is also cut from that stuff.

Within my association, if needed, I can have a woman under surveillance in Dublin, a bank staked out in Istanbul, a criminal record disambiguated in Sydney—all with a short series of calls. I, too, am expected to climb in the saddle and execute for a fellow operator. Of late, we have had to be more circumspect, with nations like Iran and Communist China using American PIs to conduct surveillance of dissidents. Sometimes there is an anodyne middleman, disguising the origins of the case. In all matters we must be cognizant of whom we are engaged by. We owe even marginal people a duty of care.

Impersonation, wiretap, and obstruction can end our licensure. This is certain. But also some clients can, if we get drawn in, destroy us. I am not immune, having fallen for a woman introduced as a client. Men, or women, prone to vice and temptation, can fall hard and long in this line of work. To paraphrase Souza: "This is the kind of job where you can make money, get laid, take advantage of the naive, and there is hardly anyone around to stop you."

One might think that we are immune, that we have seen it all. Maybe it is this approach that renders us all the more susceptible to rank stupidity. The artist friend, Joe Ferris (no kin to Robert), once told me, "If you love anything enough, it will surrender every secret to you." Loving this calling and having a safe, beautiful hearth and home are the best insulation from falling down the heated, greased sloped-iron stairs to Hell itself.

And me. In my vanity, I sometimes entertain the absurdist fantasy that I am a self-made man. Everyone I learned from has shaped me. My family, the army, Pinkerton, the Repetti Bonding Agency, the various retired cops I ran with, a few special lawyers. Sometimes the negative experiences were the more valuable and resonant. But on honest reflection I am a God-made man, forever in His hands. I pray that I am always worthy of his grace.

SUGGESTED READING

Gumshoe: Reflections in a Private Eye by Josiah Thompson
The Good Detective: True Cases from the Confidential Files of Hal Lipset, America's Real-Life Sam Spade by Hal Lipsett
The Century of the Detective by Jürgen Thorwald
The Molly Maguires and the Detectives by Allan Pinkerton
You Can't Win by Jack Black
Dirty John and Other True Stories of Outlaws and Outsiders by Christopher Goffard
The Mullendore Murder Case by Jonathan Kwitny
The Green Berets and *The French Connection* by Robin Moore
Inside Delta Force by Eric L. Haney
Stalking the Viet Cong: Inside Operation Phoenix by Stuart A. Herrington
Generation Kill by Evan Wright
The Onion Field by Joseph Wambaugh
Special Tasks by Pavel Sudoplatov
A Man Called Intrepid: The Incredible True Story of the Master Spy Who Helped Win World War II by William Stevenson
The Looming Tower: Al Qaeda and the Road to 9/11 by Lawrence Wright
The Spanish Civil War by Antony Beevor
Homicide Special: A Year with the LAPD's Elite Detective Unit by Miles Corwin
The Venona Secrets: Exposing Soviet Espionage and America's Traitors by Eric Breindel and Herbert Romerstein
Big Trouble by J. Anthony Lukas
A Cowboy Detective: A True Story of Twenty-two Years with a World-Famous Detective Agency by Charles A. Siringo

The Happy Hooker: My Own Story by Xaviera Hollander, coauthored by Robin Moore and Yvonne Dunleavy

Malice in Wonderland: The Inside Story of the Police Investigation of The Laurel Canyon Murders by Tom Lange and Robert Souza

The Big Con: The Story of the Confidence Man by David W. Maurer

Norfleet: The Actual Experiences of a Texas Rancher's 30,000-mile Transcontinental Chase after Five Confidence Men by J. Frank Norfleet and William Franlin White

Stealing from the Rich: The Story of the Swindle of the Century by David McClintick

Rise and Kill First: The Secret History of Israel's Targeted Assassinations by Ronen Bergman

The Lady in the Lake by Raymond Chandler

Night Soldiers by Alan Furst

Tinker, Tailor, Soldier, Spy: A George Smiley Novel by John le Carré

The Day of the Jackal by Frederick Forsyth

The Talented Mr. Ripley by Patricia Highsmith

The New Centurions by Joseph Wambaugh

ABOUT THE AUTHOR

Born to ruling class progressives, Nils Grevillius couldn't dash his parents' hopes fast enough. Ejected from school, enlisted in the military at seventeen, Grevillius went from scout to counterintelligence operative to the Pinkerton Service in Metropolitan Los Angeles. Having failed at every single thing, he finally found his way, founding his own detective and clandestine service in 1992. Kidnappings, Romani Gypsies forgotten murders, and conflicts of interest from domestic to all over the world, Nils Grevillius has executed jobs on every continent. Keeping a network of colleagues, contacts, informants, and operators, Grevillius has been able to bring cases in when every public agency gave up, or was too conflicted to act. From hunting down witnesses to a Hollywood kidnapping, absconded to Europe, or secreting a family with their last remaining assets from a hostile nation in Africa, Nils Grevillius has made the cases others could not.